COCHRANE IN THE PACIFIC

COCHRANE IN THE PACIFIC

Fortune and Freedom in Spanish America

Brian Vale

I.B. TAURIS

LONDON · NEW YORK

Published in 2008 by I.B.Tauris & Co Ltd
6 Salem Road, London W2 4BU
175 Fifth Avenue, New York NY 10010
www.ibtauris.com

In the United States of America and Canada distributed by Palgrave Macmillan
a division of St Martin's Press 175 Fifth Avenue, New York NY 10010

ISBN: 978 1 84511 446 6

A full CIP record for this book is available from the British Library
A full CIP record is available from the Library of Congress
Library of Congress Catalog Card Number: available
Printed and bound in Great Britain by TJ International Ltd, Padstow, Cornwall
From camera-ready copy typeset by Oxford Publishing Services, Oxford

CONTENTS

LIST OF MAPS AND ILLUSTRATIONS

PREFACE

In 1818, the revolutionary government of Chile was poised to move north against Peru, the last bastion of Spanish power on the continent. The liberation of South America had up to then been dominated by land campaigns. But the need to move the army of General José de San Martin up the coast and support it there made it necessary to seize control of the Pacific from the Spanish. The new Chilean Government therefore turned its energies into creating a navy. Short of indigenous naval manpower, Chile recruited officers and men overseas and within a year had signed on over 2000 sailors, large numbers of which were North American or British. And, as the new navy's commander-in-chief, the Chileans recruited that wayward genius, Thomas, Lord Cochrane.

In 1819, Cochrane blockaded and attacked Callao, the Spanish naval base in Peru. In February 1820, he captured Valdivia, the last Spanish stronghold on the Chilean coast. In August, having effectively swept the Spanish from the seas and seized dozens of British and American merchant ships, he escorted the great seaborne invasion force to Peru. Then, while San Martin's army slowly advanced on Lima, Cochrane blockaded Callao, cutting out the frigate *Esmeralda* in a dramatic night attack. Six months later, Peru became independent and Cochrane sailed north in pursuit of the Spanish Navy's two surviving frigates, but was frustrated when they surrendered to the Peruvians. He then returned triumphantly to Chile before resigning his commission to lead the Brazilian war of independence.

The history of the naval war in the Pacific is an exciting one. But when Cochrane came to tell the story in his 1859 epic, *Narrative of Services in the Liberation of Chile, Peru and Brazil*, he introduced a less agreeable, almost paranoid, element by claiming that his victories had been won in spite of plots and disloyalty by his subordinates and jealousy and obstruction by his superiors. This version was first retailed in the memoirs of three South American residents which were published in the middle 1820s – William Bennet Stevenson, Maria Graham and John Miers. It has been claimed that these books provide corroborative evidence of the truth of Cochrane's allegations. In fact this is not so. All three writers were intimates of Cochrane during his time in Chile and Peru, and each repeated the admiral's own bitter version of events – indeed, they were primed to do so. The result of all this, is that for 150 years it is the Cochrane interpretation of the history that has been accepted as the truth and repeated without challenge in innumerable biographies.

The aim of this book is to describe what really happened during the war in the Pacific. It is also to reassess Lord Cochrane's behaviour in a campaign where dramatic opportunities for action and administrative worries – both real and imaginary – brought out the best and the worst of him. It does not repeat yet again the version of events put forward by Cochrane and those who today would be called cronies and spin doctors, but tells the true story as it emerges from original documents, letters, dispatches, diaries and newspapers of the time. Ironically, the task has been made easier by Lord Cochrane's reluctance to throw away any piece of correspondence that went across his desk. The mountain of unedited and uncensored personal and official papers he left behind him provide a major source of information. They can be found in original, duplicate or microfilm form in numerous locations, principally the National Archives of Scotland and the respective naval archives of Chile and Peru. For the convenience of readers, when these documents are cited, it is their location in the National Archives of Scotland that is given rather than the place where they may have been actually consulted. Thanks to the work of David J. Cubitt, these papers are now more easily penetrable. Likewise, where documents have been published – and South Americans are very good at doing that – it is that source that is quoted as being the most accessible.

I would like to express my thanks to the directors and staffs of all these archival collections, together with those of the National Maritime Museum Greenwich, the National Archives in Kew, Canning House in London, the Essex County Archives, the University of Liverpool Special Collections, the Club Naval in Valparaiso and the Archivo General de la Marina, Madrid, for help and assistance over many years.

Brian Vale
Greenwich
2007

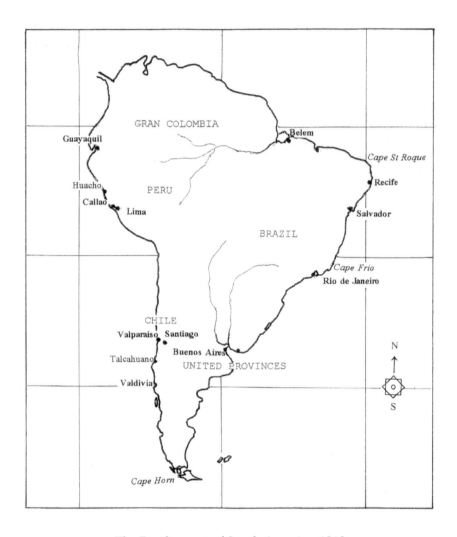

GRAN COLOMBIA

Guayaquil

Belem

Cape St Roque

Huacho

PERU

Recife

Callao

Lima

Salvador

BRAZIL

Cape Frio

Rio de Janeiro

CHILE

Valparaiso Santiago

Buenos Aires

Talcahuano

UNITED PROVINCES

Valdivia

N

S

Cape Horn

The Pacific coast of South America, 1818

Chapter 1
THE ANDES AND THE SEA

On 18 January 1817, the Argentine General José de San Martin, wearing the blue uniform of the Mounted Grenadier regiment he had founded, a thick fur-lined pelisse and jackboots with golden spurs, ordered his army forward on one of the epic marches of South American history. His intention was to cross the icy peaks of the Andes from the east, launch a surprise attack on the royalists in Chile, and ultimately threaten Peru, the last bastion of Spanish power in the Pacific. With only 5000 men, San Martin's Army of the Andes was tiny compared with the hosts that had fought their way across Napoleonic Europe – but it was enough. Marching out of the Argentine town of Mendoza accompanied by 10,600 mules and 1600 horses, and driving 700 head of cattle before it, the army headed in two columns westwards towards the towering wall of the Andes. San Martin and the main body then took the more direct route of Los Patos. For three weeks, they climbed into the mountains, snaking up precipitous defiles and crossing rushing torrents by improvised rope bridges while animals and equipment were swayed across by block and tackle. They scrambled up the shale-littered valley between the peaks and glaciers of the Aconcagua and Tupungata mountains, then over the natural rock bridge of the Puente de Inca, before climbing the high pass which crosses the Andes at 12,000 feet and descending at last into Chile. Meanwhile, a second column under General Juan Gregorio Las Heras, made up of the remaining troops and the artillery took the quicker, but no less rugged, Uspallata route, filing up the gorges of the Mendoza river between towering icy peaks before crossing the bleak wilderness of the Paso de la Cumbre at 12,600 feet, and clambering down the broken ravines on the other side.

San Martin had planned the crossing with all the skill and care for which he was famous. Each line of march was secretly surveyed in advance by an able 37-year-old major of artillery, called José Antonio Alvarez. Detailed time-tables were drawn up, emergency supplies and special equipment prepared, and diversionary forces sent north and south to deceive the enemy. No amount of planning could, however, control the elements, and exhaustion, freezing temperatures and lack of oxygen took their toll. Most of the troops got through, but only half the mules and one-third of the horses survived the journey. Nevertheless, the crossing went like clockwork. After three weeks, on 11 February, San Martin's army emerged from the narrow defiles of the mountains, regrouped, and deployed itself on a long ridge overlooking the Spanish position at Chacabuco. Next morning, it descended the slopes and fell on an astonished and unprepared royalist army. After a battle of move, countermove and improvisation, the Spaniards were decisively defeated. Next day, the victors entered Santiago and triumphantly proclaimed the independence of Chile.

The events that led up to this victory had been set in train ten years earlier when the Emperor Napoleon had kidnapped the King of Spain, put his brother Joseph on the throne and occupied the country. From the highest to the lowest, the Spanish people rose in rebellion while Juntas were established at home and abroad to rule in the name of

General José de San Martin, Liberator of Chile and Peru,
Canning House, London

the absent King. The arrangement was supposed to be temporary – but of course it was not. The locally born creoles in the Spanish colonies in the New World seized their chance. For centuries they had been kept in a state of subordination – ruled by autocratic Viceroys and peninsular born officials, and restricted by monopolies that made the merchants of Old Spain rich. Now they took control of the Juntas, acquired a taste for running their own

3

affairs and began to talk of self-government. Back in the mother country, the provisional authorities were dismayed. Though politically liberal, the idea of compromising the enormous economic benefits that Spain derived from its South America possession was out of the question. Tensions mounted and were made worse by the behaviour of some local officials who continued to operate in their usual high-handed style. Indeed, in Peru, the Viceroy refused to have any truck with Juntas at all and insisted in ruling alone in the name of absent King Ferdinand.

Peru remained a centre of royalist power: but elsewhere on the continent from Caracas in the north to Buenos Aires in the south, radical politicians and military strongmen took over the local juntas, overcame royalist opposition and began to push for full independence. In the north, Simon Bolivar was the dominating figure, establishing the Republic of New Granada in 1814. In the south, the radical Junta in Buenos Aires took the lead. Basking in the prestige of its defeat of the British invasion in 1806–7, it masterminded an armed rebellion that ejected the last Spanish Viceroys from Buenos Aires and Montevideo. In 1813, the United Provinces of the River Plate was established as the republican predecessor of the modern Argentina, and immediately began to send liberating armies against the royalists in Peru northwards through the Paraguay river system that provided the back door to the continent.

With the fall of Napoleon in 1814, Ferdinand VII was restored to the throne of Spain on a wave of national enthusiasm. But, true to his reactionary instincts, the new King promptly reverted to autocratic rule, overthrew the liberal Constitution of 1812, and viciously persecuted anyone who had supported it. In the Americas, his government went on the offensive. A Spanish army under General Manuel Morillo reoccupied New Granada, forcing Bolivar and his supporters to flee. Further south, the

Viceroy of Peru, Don Joaquin de la Pezuela, repelled three separate attacks by the United Provinces and crushed a rebellion in Chile. Meanwhile, at home, the Spanish Government began to assemble a huge military force in Cadiz aimed at the reconquest of the River Plate and the removal of the troublesome radicals who ruled it.

The only event that disturbed the rhythm of the Royalist reconquest was a Portuguese invasion of what is now Uruguay. It was done allegedly on behalf of Ferdinand VII, but was in reality an attempt to realise the historic Portuguese ambition of extending the frontiers of Brazil to the River Plate. But this was a matter of traditional power politics rather than a revolutionary threat – the Queen of Portugal and Brazil, the diminutive and malevolent Carlota Joaquina was, after all, Ferdinand's sister. Faced with these setbacks, republican confidence began to wane. And, understanding the realities of European politics, many patriot leaders – including Bolivar and San Martin – began to favour a compromise whereby the states of South America would become independent as monarchies ruled by minor European Royals.

The tide in South America began to turn in Spain's favour – but not for long. In 1817 there were two significant revolutionary gains. In the north, Bolivar returned, gathered support and began to roll back the Spanish positions. While in the south, a fourth liberating expedition against Peru was being prepared in the River Plate – this time under the command of the dominating figure of southern independence, General José de San Martin. Tall, dark and handsome, with bushy hair, thick black whiskers and piercing eyes, San Martin had been born in 1778 in the north of what is now Argentina, the fourth son of an army officer commanding a provincial outpost. Returning to Spain with the family, he had joined the Spanish army as a youth, eventually rising to become Lieutenant Colonel of the Walloon Guards and a staff officer with the Spanish forces fighting with the Duke of Wellington in the Peninsular War. Returning to the River Plate in 1812, San Martin joined the cause of independence and steadily rose to become its leading military strategist. He originally aligned himself with the Argentine Supreme Director Carlos Antonio de Alvear,[1] but the relationship soon went sour and when Alvear fell from power in 1816, it was San Martin who acted as 'king maker' and secured the appointment of Juan Martin de Pueyrredon as his successor.

That done, San Martin returned to his duties as governor of the remote state of Cuyo. But this was no provincial exile. He had long since concluded that the best way of attacking the royalists in Peru was to strike west across the snowy passes of the Andes and use Chile as the springboard for invasion. Cuyo was on the border, and its capital Mendoza commanded the crude post road that led to Santiago. It was here that San Martin organised and trained the invasion force, the Army of the Andes, which he led so dramatically across the Cordillera to victory in 1817. The planning and leadership shown by San Martin in the campaign were vital to its success, and Commodore William Bowles, who was then commander-in-chief of the British South America squadron, was so impressed that he wrote a special dispatch to London giving the details.[2]

Bowles knew San Martin well. He described him as well bred, pleasant in manners and conversation, but austere and abstemious in his private life – eschewing luxuries and preferring to sleep on a camp bed and share the hardships of his men. One of his most remarkable habits was his preference for taking his meals standing up, buffet style, rather than at a table. In the discharge of business he was hard working and conscientious, with no detail escaping his personal attention. San Martin's campaigns, however, had a bad effect on his health. He suffered from asthma and duodenal ulcers, and the opium he took as a remedy was later used by his detractors to give the impression he was an addict. As a soldier, San Martin was a hard disciplinarian but, unusual among Spanish officers, he was solicitous of the welfare of his troops and as a result was highly popular. Bowles saw San Martin as a dedicated patriot, but one who had no illusions about the potential for internal strife in South America and who therefore favoured an authoritarian – even monarchical – form of government. But he was not interested in political power for himself. Bowles found him 'entirely divested of personal ambition' and dedicated 'solely to the pacification and happiness of his country.'[3] Three years later, Captain Basil Hall of HMS *Conway*, formed exactly the same impression.[4] It was a judgement that was immediately confirmed when San Martin refused to accept the Supreme Directorship of newly liberated Chile, and stood down in favour of his friend and subordinate, General Bernardo O'Higgins.

Short and stout, with liberal principles he had acquired at school in England, O'Higgins was in many ways the opposite of San Martin. But he was a good choice, being a local boy and the illegitimate son of Ambrosio O'Higgins, one of the many Catholic Irishmen who had joined the Spanish royal service and risen high to become Governor of Concepción and Captain General of Chile. Unacknowledged by his father during his early life, Bernardo had had a penurious upbringing and was moved from one foster parent to another, until Ambrosio finally took an interest and sent him first to Spain and then to Richmond near London to complete his education. There – to the horror of his father who by this time had become Marquis of Osorno and Viceroy of Peru – he came under the influence of the veteran South American revolutionary, Francisco de Miranda. Inheriting a large estate on the death of his father, Bernardo returned to Chile and was inevitably drawn into the independence movement. And when the Viceroy of Peru invaded the country to reimpose royal authority in 1814, he found himself thrust into a leadership position in the military resistance. Defeated at Rancagua due to betrayal by his political rivals, the aristocratic and influential Carrera brothers, O'Higgins had joined the flood of refugees fleeing across the Andes and now returned as one of San Martin's subordinate commanders. As Supreme Director, O'Higgins became a popular figure, though subsequent events were to prove that he lacked the ruthlessness needed for survival in Latin American politics.

But before Chilean independence was finally secure there was a crisis. After Chacabuco, the shattered remnants of the Spanish army had fled south to Concepción and the Chiloé archipelago. There they were slowly reorganised and re-equipped, assisted greatly by cargoes of clothing, weapons and supplies found on board the American merchant ships *Beaver* and *Canton*, which had been seized by royalist privateers. Then in October 1817, the frigate *Esmeralda* arrived in Peru with a reinforcement of troops from Spain. This provided the Viceroy, Joaquin de la Pezuela, with the opportunity he needed to succour his colleagues in Concepción and attack the Chilean regime from the south. Three months later, ten transports carrying three regiments of infantry, one of cavalry and supporting batteries of guns landed at Talcahuana under the command of General Mariano Osorio. The united force struck north and inflicted a serious reverse on the unprepared Chileans at Cancha Rayada, midway between Concepción and Santiago, in which O'Higgins was wounded. There was momentary panic. The streets of the capital were once more filled with cargo mules and carriages as prominent citizens packed up their plate and valuables and prepared to flee over the Andes. But San Martin saved the day. Rallying the demoralised troops by sheer force of personality, he led

Bernardo O'Higgins, Supreme Director of Chile, Canning House, London

them back against the enemy and, on 5 April 1818, he secured a final and decisive victory at Maipú. Of the 10,000 men who began the battle, at the end of the day 2500 lay dead with a similar number of Osorio's men taken as prisoners.

Osorio's invasion had an unexpected side effect. For years the Carrera family, who arrogantly regarded themselves as the country's natural leaders, had been mounting a rival focus for Chilean independence, obtaining ships from the United States and raising men. At the beginning of 1818, two of the brothers, Juan José and Luis attempted to cross the border from the Argentine at Mendoza in disguise. Their purpose was to secure the overthrow of San Martin and O'Higgins by stirring up resentment at the growing dominance of the Argentine army in Chilean affairs and the secretive influence of the semi-Masonic Lautaro lodge to which San Martin, O'Higgins and most of their adherents belonged.[5] In the panic and confusion that followed, Cancha Rayada, Juan José and Luis were arrested and, at the instigation of San Martin's brutal and merciless aide Bernardo Monteagudo, were shot. It is said that letters from San Martin and O'Higgins ordering that the Carreras be reprieved were on the way, but their real wishes have never been satisfactorily established. The elimination of the Carerras was certainly convenient in removing the division within the patriot ranks and enabling them to concentrate on the final challenge – the campaign against Peru.

Among the officers of the Army of the Andes who were now enjoying the social life of liberated Chile were two young Englishmen – James Paroissien and William Miller. Both were to play supporting roles in the wars of independence, and both were to leave accounts of the campaign. Paroissien was the eldest. Descended from a respectable Huguenot family, he had been born on 25 November 1784 in Barking, where his father was a schoolmaster, and had later lived in Hackney where his half brother was the Anglican curate. He had had a general education, showing particular interest in natural science, but he also seems to have received some training in surgery and medicine. He certainly worked as a doctor in later life and frequently described himself as such. In 1806, Paroissien was one of the many Englishmen who rushed to the River Plate, dazzled by the British capture of Montevideo and Buenos Aires by Sir Home Popham and by the promise of imminent wealth. Alas, only months after Paroissien's arrival, the British were decisively defeated and forced to withdraw. Paroissien went to Brazil, where he became mixed up in one of Carlota Joaquina's intrigues to make herself Vice Reine of the River Plate as well as Queen of Brazil. Returning to Buenos Aires with secret papers, he was secretly denounced by the unspeakable Carlota Joaquina, arrested, and tried for treason. Fortunately for Paroissien, he was saved by the French occupation of Spain. One of the first acts of the newly appointed Junta of Buenos Aires was to release him and, with a probably undeserved reputation as a radical, he found himself welcomed in the United Provinces of the River Plate and awarded its citizenship. In 1811, he served as surgeon-in-chief in the first abortive expeditions against Peru. For the next four years, he was in charge of the state gunpowder factory in Cordoba. Then, in 1816, he was appointed surgeon-general to the Army of the Andes. In charge of the medical teams that accompanied San Martin's column, Paroissien crossed the Andes and distinguished himself at Chacabuco, the reverse of Cancha Rayada and the victory at Maipú. His stock stood high after these services, and he was decorated for his humanity and zeal for the injured. And the fact that he personally attended both San Martin and the wounded O'Higgins brought him into the inner circles of the patriot movement.

William Miller's fame is associated more with his activities in the liberation of Peru than with Chile – but he was there too. Born in Wingham near Canterbury, at the end of 1795, at the age of fifteen he had joined the Royal Artillery as an Assistant Commissary and soon acquired extensive experience on the battlefields of the Peninsular War and in the conflict with the United States. In fact he had been present both at the burning of Washington and the British defeat at New Orleans in 1815. After the war, Miller had rejected the idea of moving into the unexciting world of trade and had travelled to the River Plate where, in 1817 at the age of 22, he had been commissioned as a captain in the Buenos Aires Artillery. Posted to the Army of the Andes, he arrived too late to be present at Chacabuco, but during the debacle of Cancha Rayada had shown the first sign of his astonishing bravery by saving a battery of guns in the face of the enemy. San Martin had been so impressed by his performance that he promptly made him an aide-de-camp. It was the first achievement in a career that was to culminate in Miller's appointment as a Peruvian General.

Chacabuco and Maipú may have dealt shattering blows to the Spanish army's position in Chile, but the Spanish navy still commanded the Pacific. But this was due as much to patriot inaction as to the number of ships at its disposal. Indeed, the Napoleonic Wars had crippled Spain's once proud Navy, and the French occupation had destroyed the logistical base of its dockyards. There was therefore a woeful shortage of ships to counter the rebellion in South America. Commodore Bowles reported at the end of 1817, that 'the whole naval force of His Catholic Majesty in these seas consists of the *Venganza* and *Esmeralda* of 36 guns each, and three corvettes of 16 or 18 guns.'[6] In fact, Spain also had a dozen small gunboats and armed ships in the area, but these were of little military use except for port defence. In 1817, the Spanish Government estimated that it needed 20 ships of the line, 30 frigates and 40 lesser craft to meet its global commitments.[7] Only a fraction of these were available and, faced with a succession of budget deficits, the authorities found it impossible to provide many more. The government in Madrid made desperate efforts to do so and were not helped when, behind the backs of his ministers, Ferdinand VII bought five ships-of-the-line and three frigates from his friend the Tsar of Russia using, as a deposit, the entire £400,000 that had been paid to Spain by Great Britain in return for an agreement to suppress the slave trade. Alas, with two exceptions, the ships were found on arrival to be totally and embarrassingly rotten. However, one of the sound vessels, a big 18-pounder frigate renamed *Maria Isabel*, was hastily prepared for sea and, in May 1818, was sent to the Pacific with a convoy of twelve transports carrying 2400 men as a second reinforcement to the Viceroy of Peru.

The Spanish Government was still hopeful that the revolutionary tide in South America could be stemmed. In Cadiz, preparations for the great expedition against the River Plate went on apace. And in the Pacific, Spain still held two bases that would be crucial to any reconquest – one was the port of Valdivia in southern Chile; the other the heavily fortified arsenal of Callao – the port of Lima – in Peru. Valdivia was significant because it was the first place at which ships could now find refuge, supplies and repairs after the gruelling passage from Europe round Cape Horn. Callao was both Peru's major commercial port and the hub of Spanish naval activity on the Pacific coast. It was from Callao, that the Viceroy began to send warships and privateers to harry the rebels in newly independent Chile and to round up any merchant vessels trading with them. From June 1817, Valparaiso was blockaded alternately by the frigates *Venganza* or *Esmeralda* supported by corvette *Sebastiana* and the brigs *Pezuela* and *Potrillo*. With only two ships initially at its disposal – the brig *Aguila*, commanded by an enthusiastic but undisciplined Irish artillery captain from San Martin's army called Raymond Morris, and the tiny cruiser *Rambler*, under the former French privateer Juan José Tortel – there was little the Chileans could do about it.

Chapter 2

THE MAKING OF THE CHILEAN NAVY

Britain was generally favourable to the independence movements in South America. Radical opinion expressed both in the House of Commons and in the columns of the *Morning Post*, welcomed the end of autocratic government and the spread of political freedom. Ministers in the Tory Government were less enthusiastic. Their major concern was the preservation of British trade to the region, which had boomed during the Napoleonic Wars. As long as this was guaranteed they would have been perfectly content to see a continuation of Spanish rule. But even the Foreign Secretary, the aloof and icy Lord Castlereagh, realised that this was now impossible and that some form of self government was inevitable. Castlereagh expressed his willingness to mediate in the dispute, but made it clear that, while Spain was free to try a military solution itself, the British Government and Navy would stop the despotic monarchs of the European Holy Alliance from giving any assistance.

The spread of fighting on the ground and – more significantly – on the sea, posed a threat to British trade in the Pacific and to the commercial communities, merchant ships and whalers on which it depended. Faced with royalist embargoes, the creation of republican navies and the appearance of privateers on both sides, the Admiralty decided in August 1817 to increase its South American squadron to five vessels – the frigates *Amphion* and *Andromache*, and the sloops *Blossom*, *Tyne* and *Slaney*. But the commander-in-chief, Commodore Bowles, and his captains found themselves doing more than normal naval duties. Britain only had diplomatic relations with monarchical Brazil; so there were no diplomats in Chile and the River Plate where the revolutionary regimes were unrecognised, nor in Peru where the Spanish colonial system made it impossible. Naval officers therefore found themselves acting as floating ambassadors and consuls, reporting on political and military developments, intervening on behalf of individuals in difficulty and protecting British communities from forced loans or unfair commercial practices. Warships also played a vital function in safeguarding the profits of British trade by transporting remittances worth around a million pounds per annum to England. When, for example, the frigate *Owen Glendower* returned from the Pacific in October 1821, she carried $1.4m (£300,000) in cash and bullion packed into 600 bags, trunks and boxes. The list of contents covered 25 foolscap pages and required 287 separate Bills of Lading.[1] Since the captains whose ships carried such 'freight' were paid an average of 1 per cent of the value – the same amount being divided between the commander-in-chief and Greenwich Hospital – it was a much sought after duty.

The sending of more warships was however a precautionary measure. The British Government was determined to remain neutral in the conflict and to maintain good relations with both its old ally, Spain, and its new commercial partners; and it was made clear to naval captains that any kind of force or provocation should be avoided. In October 1817, Commodore Bowles was in

Lima, attempting to intervene with the Viceroy over the detention and looting of the British merchant vessels, *Justinian*, *Will*, *Mary Ann* and *Hydra*, by Spanish ships. Pezuela was unsympathetic and made it clear that they had been arrested not only under normal blockading rules but under the old Law of the Indies, which prohibited any form of trade by foreigners with the Spanish Empire. Bowles was further dismayed to be told that the blockade applied not only to merchant vessels but to warships as well, thus excluding his squadron from the haven of the Chilean ports.[2] This placed him in a dilemma since his orders stressed the need to maintain good relations with the Spanish authorities. Fortunately, the problem was solved by the Americans.

In the United States too, opinion on events in South America was divided. The public were vociferous in support of their fellow republicans in the region and there was considerable backing in Congress led by Henry Clay, Speaker of the House of Representatives. Secretary of State John Quincy Adams was less sure. He naturally favoured the establishment of sister republics in the region, but seriously doubted that the South Americans had the political maturity to operate a democracy. There was also the fact that the United States was doing very well by trading with both sides in the dispute. Nevertheless, with 40 merchant vessels, 60 whalers and property valued at a million dollars in the area, the American Government was concerned at the growth of naval activity and decided to establish a permanent presence in South American waters. Feeling that one ship was sufficient to protect its interests, in July 1817, the corvette *Ontario* was sent south with orders to defend American trade and shipping. She also carried an authorised diplomatic representative in the shape of Judge John B. Prevost to give official muscle to the efforts of the scatter of American commercial agents.

Ontario's captain, James Biddle, was a veteran of the campaigns against Tripoli and of the 1812–14 war, during which had had served on the *Wasp* when she captured HMS *Frolic* and commanded *Hornet* when she had taken HMS *Penguin*. Confident and politically well connected, Biddle was less tolerant than the tactful Bowles. Bold and arrogant by nature, he also belonged to a navy whose officer corps was notable for its personal rivalries and by elevated notions of personal honour that led to a culture of duelling. At the national level, its experiences in Tripoli had also led to the conviction that force was a far more effective way of settling disputes than weak diplomacy. Thus, when Biddle arrived off Valparaiso in January 1818, he refused to be warned off by the Spanish blockading squadron or to follow Bowles's example of trying to resolve the dispute through courteous correspondence, and sailed boldly into Valparaiso to succour the five American merchantmen – *Lion*, *Two Catherines*, *Enterprise*, *Rambler* and *Levant* – which had been caught in the port. With this act of defiance, the Viceroy's prohibition on the entry of foreign warships was broken and quietly forgotten.

With Chilean independence secured by the Battle of Maipú, San Martin began to prepare for the final show-down with the Spanish royalists in Peru. But the need to move his army northwards up the narrow strip between the Andes and the Pacific introduced a new element into the conflict – sea power. Up to then, the campaign had been dominated by land battles. Now it was clear that no invasion of Peru was possible until control of the Pacific was wrested from the Spanish Navy. The Chileans there-fore turned their attention to creating a navy of their own. In overall charge as Minister of Marine was José Ignacio Zenteno, a cold but dedicated man with the training and temperament of a lawyer, who had suffered all the ups and downs of the campaigns of liberation as an army officer and was high in the confidence of O'Higgins. His perform-ance as the architect of the new navy and later as Governor of Valparaiso more than justified the Supreme Director's good opinion. Zenteno's first task was to draw up the legal framework the new navy needed and, in November 1817, he promulgated a *Reglamento Provisional de la Marina* based on existing military codes, which – amongst other things – established the rules and procedures for the taking and adjudication of prizes, and laid down a rank structure for sea officers together with rates of pay and allowances. In Spanish American fashion, military designations were used, so that Chile's navy was initially commanded by a Brigadier, and its ships by colonels, majors, captains, lieutenants and ensigns.[3]

The Spanish blockade of Valparaiso made it difficult for Zenteno to procure ships locally. But a more acute problem was the absence of officers and sailors to man the new navy. In spite of its extensive coastline, Chile was a country of ranchers, miners and mountaineers: few people had any experience of the sea. Where therefore were they to find the men they needed? San Martin and O'Higgins had the answer – to send recruiting agents to the largest pools of maritime labour in the world, Britain and the United States. Accordingly, in June 1817, José Antonio Alvarez – the same discrete and trustworthy officer who had surveyed San Martin's invasion route across the Andes – headed for London and Manuel Hermanegildo Aguirre for New York, each carrying \$100,000 (the equivalent of £20,000) and orders to buy warships and to raise officers and men. Manuel Zañuarte went with similar orders to Buenos Aires, but with the general brief to maintain at all costs the Argentine alliance.[4]

The news that Chile was creating a navy and that Aguirre and Alvarez were looking for ships and recruiting men was received with excitement in naval circles in both countries. In England, the Royal Navy was in the depths of the depression that followed the Napoleonic Wars, which had seen the number of ships in commission fall from over 700 to 134, and the men in pay from 140,000 to 23,000. Almost 90 per cent of the 5250 officers on the Navy List were unemployed and living on half pay, and there were many more midshipmen and master's mates eking out a precarious living without even that. Among these thousands it was not difficult to find a few who were interested in the opportunities for pay and prize money offered by a South American war. Unemployed naval officers eagerly offered their services, some bringing fully armed and manned warships with them. Alvarez signed them up and sent them on their way. The first vessel, an 823-ton merchantman called *Windham*, previously licensed for the India and China trades, arrived in Valparaiso in March 1818 with a crew of four officers and 110 men. She was followed in May by the regular 1200-ton East Indiaman *Cumberland* under Captain William Wilkinson with five officers and 100 men. The Chileans were short of cash, but they managed to find $180,000 and $140,000 in order to buy the ships and took both, together with their officers and crews, into the new navy. They were renamed *Lautaro* and *San Martin*. Both were substantial, copper plated vessels capable of carrying artillery but, with a crew of 450 men and 64 guns on two decks, the *San Martin* was by far the largest of the two. When painted man-of-war fashion, these 1200-ton East Indiamen had often been mistaken for ships-of-the-line in the Napoleonic Wars, and the logs of vessels of the British South America squadron frequently described *San Martin* as 'the two-decker'.[5] *Lautaro*, on the other hand, was armed as a standard frigate carrying a crew of 310, a battery of 26 guns on her main deck, and another 14 lighter calibre cannon on her quarterdeck and forecastle.

Aguirre was just as successful in the United States. In November 1817, the 18-gun brig *Columbus* sailed from New York, fully manned and under Captain Charles W. Worster, a veteran of the war of 1812 in which he had commanded the privateer *Saratoga*. She reached Valparaiso eight months later to be purchased for $33,000 and renamed *Araucano*. Then, in July, Aguirre authorised the construction in New York of two fast 700-ton corvettes each mounting 28 guns. In keeping with the classical taste of the time, they were called *Horatio* and *Curiato*. The two ships were completed quickly and, after last-minute tussles with American neutrality laws, they were registered as the property of their captains Joseph Skinner and Paul Delano and sailed for the River Plate in September 1818. In the event, the Chileans were unable to find the money and could only afford to buy the *Curiato*. After a delay in Buenos Aires, Delano finally sailed her to Valparaiso in June 1819 to be incorporated into the Chilean Navy with the name *Independencia*. Her sister ship, *Horatio*, remained behind in the River Plate where she was later purchased by the Brazilians and christened *Maria da Gloria*.[6]

By the middle of 1818, the creation of the Chilean Navy was well advanced. And what it might be capable of had been shown in April, when, hot on the heels of San Martin's victory at Maipú, *Lautaro* sailed out of Valparaiso with orders to break the blockade. In command was former Royal Navy Lieutenant George O'Brian, supported by three British Lieutenants – James Argent, William Walker and Sam Fawkener – and William Miller who, after Maipú had been promoted to Major and sent to organise the Chilean Marine Corps. Posing as HMS *Amphion*, the *Lautaro* surprised the Spanish frigate *Esmeralda* on patrol outside the port, ran her bowsprit into the Spaniard's mizzen rigging and attempted to take her by boarding. Unfortunately for the Chileans, a heavy swell then separated the two ships and the boarding party, led by Captain O'Brian, was overwhelmed and killed. Both sides subsequently claimed a victory; but it was the Chileans who achieved their objective – *Esmeralda* and her consort, the brig *Pezuela*, were forced to withdraw and lift the blockade.

Meanwhile, the development of the new navy continued apace with the local purchase of an 18-gun corvette called *Chacabuco*, and the renaming of the brig *Aguila* as *Pueyrredon* in honour of the Director of Buenos Aires. The navy also acquired a new senior officer in the person of a 28-year-old army officer called Manuel Blanco Encalada. The son of a Chilean judge, Blanco had been educated in Madrid and had served briefly in the Spanish Navy as a midshipman where he was decorated for action against the French. Back in Chile after the war as an artillery officer, he had joined the independence movement, but had been captured and imprisoned on the island of Juan Fernandez. He had recently been released following a sortie by Morris in the *Aguila*. In June 1818, as the only senior Chilean with any naval experience at all, Blanco Encalada was given the key organisational post of Commandant-General.

Zenteno redoubled his efforts. In August, a spate of decrees changed the titles of the original ranks given in the *Reglamento Provisional de la Marina* to the more familiar naval ones of commodore, captain, lieutenant and midshipman, and added – in anticipation of the arrival of Lord Cochrane who had been recruited by Alvarez to be the new navy's commander-in-chief – the two senior posts of Vice Admiral and Rear Admiral.[7] They also laid down food and ration scales for the men, and established uniforms for the officers. Following the style of the British Navy, Chilean officers were to wear blue cut-away tail coats lined in white, blue stand up collars with anchor insignia, and gilt buttons stamped with anchors and stars on the cuffs and back pockets. In September, privateersmen were ordered to enrol on State ships; and, to encourage the recruitment of foreigners, pay scales were adjusted so that they would receive one-third more than their Chilean counterparts. Thus, foreign Able and Ordinary Seamen were paid $12 and $10 monthly – that is £2.40p and £2 – compared with the $8 and $6 paid to nationals.[8]

The development of the new Chilean Navy was given extra impetus by the arrival of two dramatic items of news – one bad, the other good. The bad news was that the Spanish were rushing out more reinforcements in the shape of a frigate (it was the *Maria Isabel*) and a convoy of 12 transports filled with troops. The good was that José Antonio Alvarez in London had recruited Lord Cochrane, one of the Royal Navy's most successful, but also most controversial officers, to be the Chilean Navy's commander-in-chief. Although Alvarez had done this entirely on his own initiative, O'Higgins and his government received the news with enthusiasm and began to wait anxiously for Cochrane's arrival. Temporarily, Blanco Encalada was appointed to the seagoing post of commander-in-chief and replaced as Commandant General by Luis de la Cruz. But time, tide and war wait for no man. In September 1818, a courier arrived hot-foot from Buenos Aires across the Andes carrying news that *Maria Isabel* and her convoy were nearing the Pacific. Their position had been revealed when one of the 11 transports that remained had mutinied and put into the River Plate, bringing news that the convoy had been severely weakened by sickness, and handing over orders, signals and rendezvous points. Commodore Blanco Encalada mobilised the Chilean squadron and on 19 October sailed south with the frigates *San Martin* (Captain William Wilkinson) and *Lautaro* (Captain Charles Worster) the corvette *Chacabuco* (Commander Francisco Dias) and the 18-gun brig *Araucano* (Lieutenant Raymond

Morris). His orders were to intercept the Spanish but also to keep an eye open for the ship carrying Lord Cochrane. It is said that O'Higgins watched them leave the bay with the words 'three little ships gave the King of Spain possession of the New World. These four are going to deprive him of it.' The story may be apocryphal, but it is a good one.[9] Other observers were less sure. Indeed local opinion was divided as to whether the squadron with its brand new ships and hastily assembled polyglot crews was sailing to victory or disaster.[10]

Blanco encountered contrary winds and lost touch with the *Chacabuco* when tacking against them at night. But the two frigates and the brig managed to remain in company and reached the latitude of Concepción on 26 October. There, the *Araucano* was ordered to reconnoitre the Bay of Talcahuana, while Blanco Encalada headed for one of the Spanish convoy's known rendezvous points at the Island of Santa Maria. There he learnt from a British whaler that the *Maria Isabel* had been in the vicinity five days earlier but had then left for Talcahuana. Even better, the *San Martin*, mistaken for one of the convoy, was boarded by members of the crew of the *Maria Isabel* who had been left behind to receive the transports as they arrived and hand over instructions and signals. Now fully aware of Spanish intentions, Blanco Encalada sailed east with *San Martin* and *Lautaro* to the Bay of Talcahuana where, on the morning of 28 October, they found the Spanish frigate at anchor disembarking her sick. Flying British colours until they were within musket shot, Blanco's ships made for the *Maria Isabel*, unleashed a broadside and boarded the enemy vessel in the smoke. In a brisk action in which Lieutenants Ramsey, Bell and Compton and Major Miller of the marines distinguished themselves, the frigate was taken.[11]

With the captured *Maria Isabel* in company, Blanco's ships returned to Santa Maria where they remained in the bay flying Spanish colours for a week until, one by one, the transports *Xavier, Dolores, Magdalena, Elena, Jerezana* and *Carlota* sailed innocently into their arms. On 9 November, a strange sail proved to be the *Galvarino*, formerly the 18-gun brig HMS *Hecate* which had arrived the previous month from England via the River Plate with Commander Martin Guise RN, Lieutenant J. T. Spry, and 140 officers and men.[12] She had been immediately incorporated into the Chilean Navy under the name of *Galvarino* and sent south to join Blanco Encalada. Then, three days later, the Argentine brig *Intrepido* arrived, sent to Chile by the Government of Buenos Aires as an act of solidarity with a largely British crew. She was commanded by Captain Thomas Wren Carter, a hot-tempered Irishman and veteran of the Royal Navy in which he had risen to the rank of Commander in July 1815. The timely arrival of *Galvarino* and *Intrepido* gave Blanco Encalada the additional men he needed to provide prize crews for the Spanish frigate and transports. That done, Blanco Encalada and the Chilean squadron returned in triumph to Valparaiso with their prizes. With only four of the original twelve transports eventually reaching Callao carrying a severely reduced numbers of troops, the action was a serious reverse for the royalists.[13] And the use by the Chileans, once more, of the British flag and the wearing of British uniforms caused a strong protest from General Osorio to Captain Hickey of *Blossom*. There was, however, nothing the Royal Navy could do about what was a legitimate ruse de guerre, except complain to the authorities in Valparaiso.[14] In Chile, Blanco Encalada's victory was a triumph and source of confidence. Some historians have suggested that it made some feel that they no longer needed foreigners to man their navy.[15] But it is difficult to accept such a suggestion. Although Blanco Encalada and Francisco Dias of the *Chacabuco* were South Americans, neither had much maritime experience at all, and the rest of the captains, almost all the officers, and the bulk of the seamen were British and North Americans.

November 1818 saw not only the Chilean Navy's first victory but an important increase to its strength when the frigate *Maria Isabel* was added under her new name, *O'Higgins*. The Chilean Navy now comprised three big frigates, one corvette, four brigs, a schooner and numerous small fry – an even match for the Spanish Navy in the Pacific. Recruitment had also gone well, and the service could boast 1200 sailors, 400 marines, and 40 sea officers. Although commanded by the Englishman William Miller, the marines were entirely Chileno, but two-thirds of the seamen and almost all the officers were North Americans or British, many of the latter with Royal Navy experience. All that remained to make it fully operational was the eagerly awaited arrival of its commander-in-chief, Thomas, Lord Cochrane.

Chapter 3

THE COMING OF LORD COCHRANE

When José Antonio Alvarez arrived in London on his recruiting mission, one of the most brilliant and talked about naval commanders of the Napoleonic Wars was Thomas, Lord Cochrane. Born to a noble but impoverished Scottish family in 1775, Cochrane entered the navy at the comparatively advanced age of 17 years through the agency of his uncle, Captain the Honourable Alexander Cochrane RN. He advanced rapidly in his profession, due partly to his skill and interest in technical matters, and partly to the 'interest' he enjoyed as a member of the navy's Scottish mafia. At an early age, through the patronage of Lord Keith, who was not only one of the navy's most distinguished admirals but its most senior 'Scotch' officer, he secured the coveted promotion to the rank of commander. Cochrane immediately showed his daring and ability when, in charge of a diminutive brig called *Speedy*, he captured the greatly superior Spanish frigate *El Gamo*. Promoted to post-captain and given command of a frigate called *Pallas*, on his first cruise Cochrane seized enemy ships and property worth £300,000 – perhaps £5 million in modern money – more than enough to satisfy those members of his crew who had been encouraged to sign on by the promise of Spanish silver contained in his famous recruiting poster. 'None should apply,' it had said, 'but SEAMEN and Stout Hands, able to rouse about the Field Pieces and carry an hundred weight of PEWTER without stopping at least three miles.' *Pallas* was then sent to operate in the Bay of Biscay, capturing coasters and gunboats, destroying shore batteries and burning signalling stations. Transferring to the more powerful frigate *Imperieuse*, Cochrane then proceeded to cause mayhem on the Mediterranean coasts of France and Spain, launching assaults from the sea against roads and isolated batteries before dramatically directing the defence of the city of Rosas against a French assault. With his reputation now established, in 1809, Cochrane was sent to apply his skills with pyrotechnics to an attack being planned against a French Fleet in the Basque Roads.

His adventures in command of the *Pallas* made Cochrane rich. Those in the *Imperieuse* made him famous. Newspapers sung his praises and a special biography was printed in the *Naval Chronicle*. In these operations, Cochrane established himself as a master of amphibious warfare. His tactical flare and ingenuity were ideally suited to keeping a coast in uproar by sudden and unexpected raids from the sea. They also confirmed that in battle Cochrane was a true leader of men. Fearless and cool under fire, he led from the front, personally leading the attack by fire ships and explosion vessels which successfully drove a panic stricken French fleet onto the mud at the Basque Roads and left it at the mercy of the British.

But the qualities that made Cochrane so successful in war made him a quarrelsome nuisance in peace. At sea, the speed with which he arrived at decisions, and his refusal to contemplate doubt or hesitation thereafter, made him invincible. On land, his hasty decision making, and his refusal to change his mind once it had been made up –

whatever evidence there was to the contrary – had the opposite effect. Indeed, Cochrane tended to assemble the facts to support what he wanted to believe rather than draw conclusions from the facts themselves. The result was a series of catastrophic misjudgements. This bloody-mindedness, combined with an instinctive mistrust of anyone in authority, an insubordinate streak, and an element of self-righteousness, regularly put Cochrane at loggerheads with his superiors. Ignoring, for example, the technical problems that prevented his immediate pro-motion to post-captain after the capture of *El Gamo*, Cochrane convinced himself against all the evidence that he was in the 'bad books' of the Admiralty and began a personal and political vendetta against the First Lord, Admiral Lord St Vincent. Again, after the Basque Roads, he almost single-handedly converted what was seen as a naval triumph into a missed opportunity, forcing the British commander, the worthy if over-religious Admiral Lord Gambier, to demand a court martial to clear his name. Cochrane's conviction that Gambier had no intention of attacking the stranded French, and had only been forced into doing so by the activities of *Imperieuse*, was unshaken by evidence to the contrary and he pursued Gambier to the bitter end. Meanwhile his campaign against St Vincent, the erstwhile First Lord, was gaining such a momentum that the Admiral gave vent to his famous phrase that Cochrane was 'mad, romantic, money getting and not truth telling.'

There was certainly a romantic streak to his personality. Indeed, at the age of 38, he had contracted a runaway marriage in Scotland with Kitty Barnes, a half-Spanish beauty of 16 who, to the dismay of Cochrane's relations, was not an heiress. They were to make a striking pair – Cochrane, tall and redheaded with sandy whiskers; Kitty, short and petite, with raven hair worn in fashionable corkscrew ringlets.

Lord Cochrane in his prime, with fireships burning in the background.
From the Mezzotint by Meyer

In other aspects of his personality, however, he was entirely practical. His father, the 9th Earl of Dundonald, had spent the family fortune on failed scientific experiments and Cochrane inherited his keen interest in technical matters. And, as regards money, St Vincent was right. All naval officers were keen to gain from the prize money that was the reward for capturing enemy ships and property, but Cochrane took it to extremes. He had been in the embarrassing position of being an aristocrat without money; and his youth was spent among financial crises and parsimony. It is therefore hardly surprising that money-making became a major obsession in Cochrane's life and that he was none too scrupulous about how he got it.

Lord Cochrane's fame in Britain was not, however, based solely on his naval achievements, for in his earlier years he also played a significant political role. Although he was an aristocrat, his hostility to the corruption of Georgian Britain and his feeling of personal alienation from the Establishment turned him into a radical politician. He served successively as Member of Parliament for the 'rotten borough' of Honiton in Devon, and then for the more 'democratic' constituency of Westminster. In the House of Commons, Cochrane became a thorn in the side of the government, delighting in exposing corruption in the prize courts and abuses in the establishment, and grinding a number of personal naval axes. He became particularly influential in the years after the Napoleonic Wars when an economic slump caused hardship, want and unrest throughout the land. There was an avalanche of working-class petitions and it was Cochrane and Sir Frances Burdett, his fellow Member of Parliament for Westminster, who ensured that they reached an unreformed House of Commons. It was a role that Cochrane relished.

Unfortunately for him, in 1814, Cochrane was implicated

in a Stock Exchange swindle engineered by the black sheep of the family, his uncle Andrew Cochrane-Johnstone, and some of his shadier associates. A fake colonel in a red uniform appeared at Dover, announced that Napoleon was dead and took a post-chaise to London spreading the good news and distributing gold Napoleons noisily on the way. Share prices soared at the promise of peace; and none rose higher than a volatile stock called Omnium. The conspirators – for Napoleon was still jauntily alive – had invested heavily in Omnium, which they now sold at a handsome profit. Unfortunately for Cochrane, as soon as he had arrived in London, the 'colonel' went straight to his house in Green Street where he borrowed clothes to cover his red uniform. Clearly implicated in the conspiracy – not only by this incident, but by the heavy purchases of Omnium he had made in the previous weeks and his intimacy with those who were clearly responsible – Cochrane was found guilty of fraud at the resulting trial, fined and briefly imprisoned. Stunned by the verdict, he vociferously protested his innocence; but his case was not helped by his refusal – or inability – to offer an explanation. He continued to enjoy the support of the electors of Westminster, but his public career was over and he was officially disgraced. His Knighthood of the Bath was stripped from him and he was dismissed from the Navy.

The year 1817 was a particularly bad one for Lord Cochrane. His naval career was over, he had been publicly humiliated, and he was becoming politically frustrated. Cochrane needed a change: he was depressed by what he regarded as the injustice of the Stock Exchange trial, and was short of money. He also needed a job, and he began to look around for a profitable way of using his military talents. A meeting with José Antonio Alvarez in London was therefore providential. On arrival, Alvarez had sought out leading radicals who were sympathetic to the cause of independence, many of whom – like Sir Francis Burdett, Henry Brougham and Sir James Macintosh – were intimates of Lord Cochrane. Alvarez had no orders to sign up a commander-in-chief for the new Chilean Navy, but learning of Cochrane's situation and finding his military and political credentials compelling, he offered him the post. To his delight, Cochrane accepted. On 12 January 1818, Alvarez passed the good news back to his masters in Santiago, writing:

> I have extreme satisfaction in informing you that Lord Cochrane, one of the most famous and perhaps the most valiant seaman in Great Britain, has determined to travel to Chile in order to direct our navy and cooperate decisively in the consolidation of liberty and independence. He is a person highly commendable, not only for the liberal principals with which he has upheld the cause of the English people in Parliament, but because he possesses a character superior to any ambition … and has been watching with enthusiasm the progress of South America. As a consequence, I have not hesitated one moment in using the plenary powers with which you honoured me, to offer him the rank of admiral and commander-in-chief of the naval forces of Chile; and to authorise him to select and nominate officers and men who will be capable of fulfilling their destinies in a manner satisfactory to the Supreme Director.[1]

The Chilean Government was quick to confirm Cochrane's appointment. Cochrane too was pleased. The offer was exactly what he was looking for and the cause of liberty in the Pacific fired his imagination. So much so, that he did not even ask how much money he was to be paid. Indeed so enthusiastic did he become that his second son, born on

8 March 1818, was christened William Horatio Bernardo in honour of O'Higgins.

And there was more. Alvarez announced that Cochrane intended to bring an armed steamship of 410 tons with him called the *Rising Star*. The vessel was already being adapted at Brent's Yard at the Greenland Dock on the Thames to a revolutionary design that included twin funnels and an internal retractable paddle wheel. She was driven by 60 horse-power engines supplied by a manufacturer called Galloway, although she was rigged to carry sail on two masts as a precaution. So great was Cochrane's confidence in the future of steam power, that he had put £3000 of his own money into the venture. Another £4000 had been supplied by a well-known South American trader, Edward Ellice, on condition that he was allowed to import 200 tons of goods into Chile free of duty.[2] Alvarez was keen on the project and had clearly been convinced by Cochrane that with such an example of modern naval technology at their disposal, the Chileans would make short work of their enemies.

Neither was Alvarez's enthusiasm confined to steamships. In January 1818, possibly reflecting Cochrane's influence once more, he wrote enthusiastically to Valparaiso reporting that he had gained access to the secrets of one of Britain's latest weapons of war – the incendiary rockets invented by Sir William Congreve – and was taking steps to send out a supply and to ensure that they could be made in Chile.[3] True to his word, the following month one of Congreve's assistants, Stephen Goldsack, accompanied by a subordinate called Taylor and a military adviser in the form of a Major James Charles, were on their way to the Pacific with their families charged with establishing a local factory for the manufacture of rockets. They were to arrive in Valparaiso on the *Ann* on 12 November.

To equip a war steamer on the Thames for a revolutionary

struggle against a friendly power was, nevertheless, a risky undertaking and efforts were made to conceal the *Rising Star*'s real purpose. Cochrane put it about for example, that her name was actually the *North Star*, and that she was to be used in an attempt to win the £20,000 prize offered to the first man who could sail to the North Pole. Attention was focused on the fact that her figurehead was a bear – presumably a Polar Bear – and that her stern was decorated with a painting of the constellation of the Bear rather than on the fact that she was pierced to carry ten guns.[4] The story may have deceived the readers of the *Naval Chronicle*, but it did not fool the Spanish authorities. Madrid was made fully aware of what Alvarez and Cochrane were up to by its ambassador in London.[5]

The adaptation of the *Rising Star* seemed likely to take some time and Chile needed Lord Cochrane urgently. Alvarez therefore persuaded him to leave the supervision of the project to Galloway and his brother Major William Cochrane and to leave without delay.[6] Cochrane agreed, concluded his preparations and wound up his affairs. In June, he made his last speech in the House of Commons. It comprised an expression of thanks to the electors of Westminster, a final swipe at sinecures and pensions, and a plea to the government for reform before it was too late. He then headed for Boulogne to embark on the merchant-man *Rose*. With him went his wife Kitty, his sons Thomas aged four years and William Horatio (nicknamed Horace) aged six months, a relation called Jane Frith Cochrane, the Argentine lawyer and politician Antonio Alvarez Jonte and a group of servants and secretaries. On 15 August 1818, the party set sail for Chile, on the other side of the world.[7]

Chile was the country cousin of the wealthy Viceroyalty of Peru. Wedged between the Pacific and the Andes, it was a long straggling country extending from the waterless

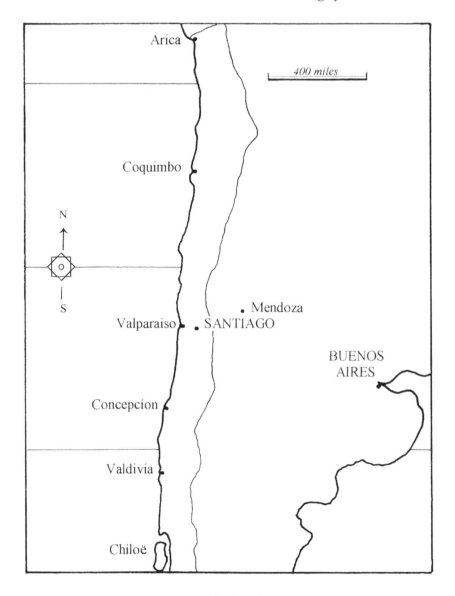

Chile 1818

Atacama desert in the north, to the wooded province of Concepción, beyond which was a dramatic wilderness of islands, mountains and fiords which stretched southwards as far as Tierra del Fuego and Cape Horn.

Within these limits, Chile – with its Mediterranean

climate, mountainous backdrop, gushing streams, lush central valleys and wooded coastal hills, which English travellers compared with Devonshire – was a delightful location. But there were no silver or gold mines to generate the same opulence and wealth as in neighbouring Peru. There was some copper mining, but the Chilean economy was based on agriculture and stock raising, and its society was made up of a small number of landed gentry and a mass of peasants. Its neatly laid-out colonial style capital of Santiago could boast some 30,000 people, but most of its towns were little more than big villages of only regional importance with populations of less than 6000.

One exception was the town of Valparaiso, located three days journey from the mountain capital of Santiago. The port had boomed following independence. Freedom from the old Spanish restrictions had brought foreign goods and merchants flocking to the city that became Chile's gateway to the world. Valparaiso was Lord Cochrane's destination and, at the end of November 1818, the *Rose*, having fought her way round Cape Horn into the Pacific, was in sight of the jagged white peaks of the Chilean cordillera. On the 29th, driven by a brisk sea breeze, the brig rounded a rocky headland, sailed into the bay on which the city was built, and dropped anchor in the cold, blue water before the port. Valparaiso was a straggling town wedged onto a narrow semi-circular strip of land between the sea and the slopes of the hills which rose precipitously all around. In this space were huddled shops, churches, the customs house, meat and fish markets, and rows of one-storey whitewashed houses with red tiled roofs that spread inland up a number of narrow ravines which cut into the hills. The most prominent of these was the suburb of Almendra, which occupied a sandy plain to the east and was named after the almond trees that grew there in such abundance. The whole scene was dominated by the governor's palace in the centre of the bay and a citadel that was perched on the dry slopes behind. The population of Valparaiso at the time was around 8000, of which 500 were British, mostly seafarers, merchants and their families. There were plenty of grog shops and other facilities for low life, but there were also two coffee houses to cater for the more respectable members of the community, and a school, run on the Lancaster model by a Mr Thompson.

The news that Lord Cochrane had arrived spread rapidly. Bernardo O'Higgins hurried down the coach road from Santiago to greet him and to inaugurate days of junketing and celebration. The Governor of Valparaiso offered a special dinner at which the newly arrived British were entranced by the beauty and style of the local ladies who had 'dark abundant hair falling to the shoulders adorned with jasmine and other flowers', although – according to Major William Miller – all were put in the shade by 'the two presiding belles … Lady Cochrane and Mrs Commodore Blanco, both young, fascinating and gifted'.[8] Lord Cochrane reciprocated by throwing a lavish party on St Andrew's night, appearing in kilt and the full highland dress that the Prince Regent and Sir Walter Scott had so recently made popular. There was infectious good cheer, food, champagne and good wine punctuated by innumerable toasts. Even Cochrane, who was impatient to get on with the job and who disliked parties, drank little and smoked less, seemed to enjoy himself.

Soon the partying was over and the Chileans got down to business. On 11 December 1818, Lord Cochrane became a Chilean citizen and was appointed Vice Admiral and commander-in-chief, while Commodore Blanco Encalada was promoted to the rank of Rear Admiral.[9] Both officers were happy with these appointments, which reflected exactly their respective ages and experience. There was never any chance of their positions being reversed (as was suggested later by Cochrane in his tendentious *Narrative of Services*)[10] nor is it true – as suggested by later biographers – that Blanco Encalada 'stepped down' in Cochrane's favour. Indeed, Cochrane's appointment as commander-in-chief of the Chilean Navy was known in Valparaiso before Blanco Encalada had even been appointed Commandant-General, and he expected nothing more. Cochrane also learnt for the first time that his pay and allowances in the Chilean service were to be $6000 a year – that is, the equivalent of £1200.[11] This was considerably less than the pay and allowances earned by a Vice Admiral in the Royal Navy, but at this stage Cochrane's preoccupation with money seems to have been overlaid by his pleasure in the appointment and his enthusiasm for the cause.

Cochrane was anxious to familiarise himself with the ships and men he was to lead. But first he had to find a house and see his family comfortably settled. Then he had to appoint a staff. To discharge his enormous responsibilities as commander-in-chief, Cochrane needed a staff that was experienced, efficient and trusted. He needed them to write his correspondence, do his accounts, handle his prize business and provide him with dispassionate information. In London, Cochrane had been authorised to recruit suitable people to accompany him to Chile, and he had brought with him a former Royal Navy Purser called Henry Dean who claimed to be an expert on naval administration and prize matters. William Jackson, who had served as his secretary for many years and was to work with him for the rest of his life, had remained behind, expecting to follow in the *Rising Star* whose departure was believed to be imminent. Once in Chile, Cochrane immediately appointed two more individuals. One was William Hoseason, a locally resident merchant who was to act as his prize agent and handle his finances. Unfortunately,

Hoseason had arrived in Chile only recently and had little experience of the country. Neither did he have much capital or credit to back his business activities. His only qualification for the job was that he was the father of Dean's attractive and popular wife. The second appointee was William Bennet Stevenson, who joined Cochrane's team in March 1819 as his adviser on local affairs. Hailing originally from Lincolnshire, Stevenson had been resident in Chile and Peru for decades where he was known by his middle name in the Spanish fashion as 'Don Luis Bennet'. Stevenson had a fund of local knowledge and was later to publish an account of his adventures called *A Historical and Descriptive Narrative of 20 years Residence in South America*. He was also well known as a raconteur and gossip, but his inexperience of legal or finance matters was to prove a problem.

The tone was set almost immediately when Cochrane was told by his entourage that two of his captains – John Tooker Spry and the American Charles Worster – had been criticising him for using his title when he was now in the service of a republic. It was later reported that they were 'caballing' against him under the slogan 'two commodores and no Cochrane.' In other words, that the Chilean Navy should have no single commander-in-chief but should be led by two equally ranking commodores. According to Stevenson, the idea was that Spry and Worster would then be able to 'control' Rear Admiral Blanco who was inex-perienced and spoke no English.[12] There was clearly not the slightest chance that a 'two commodores' arrangement could ever come to pass, and it is fanciful to see these comments – if they were true at all – as anything more that loose, tap room talk. Certainly, the republican atmosphere of Chile seems to have encouraged some officers to talk too much.

Cochrane's staff nevertheless had a cuckoo in the nest.

To solve the language problems inevitable in the command of the squadron and to provide advice on judicial and financial matters, the government appointed Antonio Alvarez Jonte to double as Cochrane's Secretary and Auditor of Marine. In view of the fact that Jonte was fluent in English and had got to know Cochrane both in London and on the voyage out in the *Rose*, it seemed a sensible decision. But the Vice Admiral was hostile from the beginning. Suspicious by nature, he saw it as an attempt by the authorities to control his activities and to deny him the freedom to pick his own immediate entourage. For six months he looked for an excuse to get rid of him. It finally came in July when Jonte innocently opened a box containing delayed dispatches from Cochrane and removed those addressed to O'Higgins and San Martin. Cochrane objected violently, accused him of being a spy,[13] and forced his resignation on health grounds. His place as Secretary was taken by the already available William Stevenson.

Before the organisation of the squadron was complete in January 1819, there was, however, another appointment to be made – that of Captain of the Fleet and therefore, technically, it's third in command. This caused a problem. Before Cochrane's arrival, the obvious candidate was Captain Martin Guise. Guise had arrived in Valparaiso too late to take part in the capture of the *Maria Isabel*, but the fact that he was the only senior officer with regular naval experience gave him an undisputed claim. Neither Wilkinson nor Worster, who ranked equally with Guise as captains-of-frigate, had this. Born in 1779 to a Gloucestershire family, Martin Guise had joined the Royal Navy on *Marlborough* at the age of 15. He had then spent three exciting and profitable years in Captain Charles Stirling's frigate *Jason* when it formed part of the commerce raiding squadron commanded by Sir John Borlase Warren in the Channel and off the east coats of France. He had then moved to the line-of-battleships *London*, *Ville de Paris* and *Foudroyant* where he had been promoted to lieutenant in 1801. Guise's career during the next eight years is unknown, but he reappears in 1809 as flag-lieutenant to Vice Admiral George Cransfield Berkeley when the latter was appointed to the Lisbon station to support the recently landed British expeditionary force under the future Duke of Wellington. Berkeley was a member of an influential West Country family and had political clout as Member of Parliament for Gloucestershire, so that Guise's links in the county may have had something to do with the appointment. However, it only lasted three months before he was replaced by the Vice Admiral's nephew, Maurice Frederick Fitzhardinge Berkeley. Guise then left on *Conqueror* for two years of duty on the Mediterranean coast of Spain and in the blockade of Toulon under the command of Sir Charles Cotton. Between 1811 and 1813, Guise was employed in the West Indies, where he commanded the cutter *Liberty* and the brig *Swaggerer* before returning to England. He was promoted commander on 29 March 1815 and spent the post-Waterloo period commanding the bomb vessel *Devastation*.[14]

Unfortunately for Martin Guise, Cochrane wanted one of his 'followers', Robert Forster, to fill the job of senior captain in the Chilean Navy. Forster too was a veteran with vast experience of both frigates and 74-gun ships. Born in Bamborough in Northumberland, one of ten brothers who all followed army or naval careers, Forster had entered as a First Class Volunteer in *Camelion* in 1795 and then served in Home waters and the Mediterranean on the frigates *Garland*, *Alceme* and *Leda*, the line-of-battle ship *Majestic*, and on *Kent* and *Ville de Paris* when they were flying the flags of Admirals Duncan and St Vincent. Following promotion to lieutenant in 1802, he had spent the next four years on *Nemesis*, *Charwell* and *Gibraltar*. Transferred to

Mars, he had been present when the squadron of which she formed part had captured four heavy French frigates leaving Rochfort for a commerce raiding trip to the West Indies; and, in 1807, had participated in Lord Gambier's attack on Copenhagen. Serving then in the Baltic as First Lieutenant of the frigate *Owen Glendower*, he had played a leading part in the capture of Anholt in 1809. In 1814, Forster had been appointed First Lieutenant of HMS *Tonnant*, the ship which – but for the Stock Exchange scandal – would have taken Lord Cochrane to North America, and had subsequently joined *Asia* commanded by the latter's uncle, Sir Alexander, where he had distinguished himself in land operations in the war against the United States. Forster had been recruited for the Chilean service in London, and had been promised the post of second-in-command by Cochrane himself, who at that time had no knowledge of what was going on in Chile. Unfortunately, Forster's seniority as a Royal Navy commander dated from only 13 June 1815,[15] making him junior to Guise by three months – a small but important difference since Chile had decided to use British rules to regulate its naval service. Nevertheless, Cochrane felt that his promise had put him under an obligation to Forster, and insisted that he got the job. As a result, Forster was made flag-captain of *O'Higgins* and Guise, the more senior man, was left without an appointment though, as compensation, he was promised command of one of the American built corvettes when they arrived from the United States.

With all these arrangements concluded, on 23 December, Cochrane hoisted his flag on the *O'Higgins* and to the thunder of salutes, took command of the squadron. Preparations for putting to sea went on apace. For days there was an endless coming and going of boats as desperately short supplies, cordage, canvas and munitions were ferried from the arsenal to the warships. Recruiting had also gone well and by 1819, the squadron had been able to find 1400 of the 1610 officers and men it needed. The manning of privateers was banned; and more and more foreigners were signing on, attracted by the magnet of Cochrane's name and by the preferential rates of pay being offered. There was, however, a down side. Desertions of sailors from British and American ships caused angry protests, and on the Chilean vessels resentment began to grow among national seamen at the higher rates of pay given to the foreigners. There was also a reshuffle in the senior ranks of the squadron. William Wilkinson was left in command of the *San Martin*; but Robert Forster was given the flagship *O'Higgins*, Thomas Carter – formerly of the Argentine *Intrepido* – of the corvette *Chacabuco* and John Tooker Spry and James Ramsey – erstwhile First Lieutenant of the *San Martin* – of the brigs *Galvarino* and *Araucano*. William Prunier, a native of the Channel Islands, was sent to the brig *Pueyrredon* as a replacement for the unruly Raymond Morris.

The Chileans were delighted at Cochrane's arrival, but their feelings were not shared by everyone. Life had been difficult from the beginning for resident British merchants whose commercial operations covered both Chile and Peru. Fortunately the two sides in the conflict were anxious to ensure a continuation of a trade that they needed as much as the British, and had been willing to permit a series of temporary arrangements to prevent instant seizure of ships off Chile and Peru on the grounds they had stopped in the ports of the other. Now Lord Cochrane had arrived. Commodore Bowles was well aware of his enthusiasm for both action and financial gain, and feared that there would now be an unscrupulous onslaught on neutral commerce in the interests of prize money. Reporting to the Admiralty from Rio de Janeiro in December 1818, he wrote 'It is not difficult to foresee that the class of foreigners entrusted with the principal naval commands are likely to use their power and influence for the gratification of their private interests. ... Their Lordships will judge what sort of conduct may be expected from Lord Cochrane.'[16] Later, he added gloomily,

I have little doubt, from the language used by Lord Cochrane that whenever a fair opportunity offers he will pay no more regard to neutral rights than to the orders of the government under which he serves. ... He has come to this country, as he himself expressed to Mr Worthington (one of the American commercial agents), to live. He has brought a prize agent with him and professes the determination to keep every-thing in his own hands and distribute the proceeds of all captures himself.[17]

Relations between the Chileans and the British neverthe-less remained good. One reason was the scrupulous neutrality that officers of the Royal Navy were required to observe. Another was the fact that Captain William Shirreff of the frigate *Andromache* – which, with the sloop *Blossom*, had been sent by Commodore Bowles to the Pacific in April 1818 – sympathised with the patriot cause and was an admirer of Lord Cochrane. Chilean relations with the United States were not so good. Almost as soon as he arrived, Biddle of the *Ontario* had lost the popularity he had gained by challenging the Spanish blockade by a stiff-necked dispute about salutes. And as the year went on the situation got worse. In addition to trade protection, Biddle's major task in the Pacific was to sail north and take possession of the Colombia River in the name of the United States. On the outgoing and return voyages, he visited Peru in July and October. There, the Spanish Viceroy

Pezuela went out of his way to court the American captain. Anxious to obtain information on events in Chile, and to counteract what he saw as inevitable American sympathies for the patriot cause, he received Biddle with ostentatious affability, offering hospitality, openly praising his efforts and presenting him with a sword. Biddle, who – unlike the British – did not appreciate that cool formality was more appropriate to neutrality than visible cordiality, responded in kind, and was rewarded when the Viceroy agreed to modify the enforcement of the blockade in accordance with American views on the subject,[18] to restore the *Beaver* and *Canton* to their owners, and to allow the watering and supply of American whalers in Peru.

Seen from Chile, all this good will looked distinctly suspicious, and when *Ontario* arrived back in Valparaiso in December 1818, she received a chilly reception. There were rumours that much of the huge quantity of bullion she had on board was not American property – which was legitimate – but Spanish – which was not – and that among her passengers were six Spanish military officers, one of whom was the Viceroy's own nephew. Tensions reached a climax when Biddle refused Cochrane's request to delay *Ontario*'s departure until the Chilean squadron had sailed against Callao and abruptly left for the United States on 31 December. Publicly, the authorities tried to minimise the dispute by claiming in the *Gazeta Ministerial de Chile* that it was nothing more than a minor disagreement between Biddle and Cochrane over the protocol of salutes;[19] but the cat was let out of the bag on 29 January 1819 when *El Sol de Chile* revealed that deserters claimed that the *Ontario* was carrying $800,000. For its part, the government sent a blistering complaint to Washington about Biddle's lack of neutrality, his transportation of enemy property and money, and his carrying of 'spies'.

Chapter 4
THE CALLAO CAMPAIGN

Foreigners may have been worried by Lord Cochrane's appearance in Chile, but the government and the public were delighted with their good fortune. The news of his appointment as commander-in-chief was made public in *El Argos*, *El Duende* and *El Sol de Chile* in October 1818 and, three months later, the *Gazeta Ministerial de Chile* confidently predicted that,

> The nomination of Lord Cochrane as commander of the naval forces of Chile promises us the complete destruction of the Spanish Squadron in the Pacific; and, as soon as a respectable expedition appears before Callao which will stimulate the feelings of patriotism of Peruvians, the consequent explosion will break our subordination to the Tyrant.[1]

O'Higgins and his colleagues had high expectations of Lord Cochrane. But they did not see him as a saviour who had come to take charge of the war. In many ways he was an unknown quantity. His brilliance as an aggressive naval leader had been well established, but in no higher rank than a captain and in command of nothing bigger than a frigate. Cochrane's sympathy with radical causes was also well known – but so was his preference for independent action and his impatience with any superior authority. This was worrying. The struggle for freedom in South America was dominated by land campaigns, and command of the sea was a subordinate part of an overall strategy. Tactically, therefore, while the Chileans were happy to rely on Cochrane's legendary ingenuity, what he did at sea had to be controlled and coordinated with what took place on land. Private letters from O'Higgins to San Martin make this clear.[2]

Thus, when Cochrane took command, he was not – as some biographers seem to think – given *carte blanche* to take on the Spanish Navy as he saw fit. His orders, when they arrived on 9 January 1819, were both specific and detailed. They began 'the principal objective of this expedition is to blockade the port of Callao, to cut off the maritime forces of the Viceroy of Lima … and by so doing enable them to be defeated in detail', and continued in 17 clauses to lay down exactly how this was to be done, with what forces, and for how long. They emphasised that the expedition was a preliminary foray intended to weaken the royalists through blockade (Article 1); to encourage patriot resistance (Article 6); to gather intelligence on military deployments (Article 7); to exchange existing prisoners of war and protest about their treatment (Article 9); and to seize all ships and property belonging to Spain (Article 12). And to ensure that nothing should put at risk the invasion planned for the following year, Cochrane was ordered to keep clear of shore batteries (Article 5), and to avoid action with superior forces (Article 13).[3]

Cochrane expressed satisfaction with these orders and concentrated on getting his ships ready for sea. It was no easy task. The Commandant General's Department was newly created and disorganised and the arsenal in Valparaiso was desperately short of naval stores, equipment and money. But with remorseless pressure from Cochrane and imperative orders from Zenteno it was done. It was planned that the Chilean squadron would sail in two Divisions – the first under Cochrane, comprising the heavier ships, which had received priority in the distribution of supplies, *O'Higgins, San Martin, Lautaro* and *Chacabuco*; and the second, consisting of the three brigs, *Galvarino, Pueyrredon* and *Araucano*, which would follow under Blanco Encalada as soon as it was equipped. On 14 January 1819, the first division was ready and the signal for departure was hoisted. It was a typical summer's afternoon, with a bright blue sky, a fresh breeze, and the waters of the Bay alive with the last minute bustle of pulling to sea. Cochrane was anxious to leave before dusk, and no sooner had the boats carrying Lady Cochrane and other visitors left the ship's side for the pull to the shore than the *O'Higgins* manned her capstan and began heaving the cable short. By the time the boats returned, the flagship had weighed anchor and was heading slowly seaward. But they contained one unexpected passenger. In the confusion on the dockside, Cochrane's five-year old son had somehow escaped from his mother, had been swept up in the excitement, deposited in the launch and returned to the flagship. It was now too late to send him back, so Thomas stayed on board as the squadron worked its way out of the Bay, turned into the cold blue rollers of the Pacific and headed north for Callao.

But there was a last minute problem. *Lautaro* had been unable to put to sea with her consorts before nightfall on 14 January. Now, the following morning, the resentment of the Chilean seamen in the frigate over pay boiled over: they refused duty, and the marines declined to force them to do so. Captain Worster was unable to control the outbreak and resigned, to be replaced by Martin Guise. Strong measures and the personal influence of Blanco

The departure of the Chilean Squadron of Independence by
T. Somerscales, Club Naval de Valparaiso

Encalada finally restored discipline, and at noon *Lautaro* finally sailed to join Cochrane at sea.[4]

Cochrane's Division made good time in reaching the coasts of Peru. The voyage proceeded smoothly, the only disruption being that no sooner had *Lautaro* been reunited with the flotilla than *Chacabuco* disappeared. When the corvette eventually rejoined off Callao six weeks later, it was revealed that the delay had been caused by a mutiny that had broken out on board over pay grievances on 23 January. After four days, the officers led by Lieutenants Robinson and Morgell had managed to regain control and had taken *Chacabuco* into the port of Coquimbo on the Peruvian border where the ringleaders had been dealt with, and 16 of their confederates sent back in chains to Valparaiso for trial.

In the middle of February, Cochrane's ships began to enforce the blockade of Callao, seizing the occasional

Spanish prize and searching neutral vessels approaching the port. On the 15th, the lookout ship *Lautaro*, investigating strange sails on the horizon found them to be the British merchant vessel *Alexander* escorted by two ships of the South America squadron, *Andromache* and *Blossom* which had been sent by Commodore Bowles to keep an eye on the blockade and protect British ships and property in Callao valued at a million dollars.[5] Captain William Shirreff of *Andromache* was impressed by the courtesy shown by Captain Guise and was further relieved when he went aboard the *O'Higgins* to be assured by Lord Cochrane that he had 'not forgotten that he was an Englishman' (*sic*) and that he would ensure that British vessels were treated fairly.[6] Shirreff was also given the outline of Cochrane's first intended sally against the heavily fortified port of Callao. The Vice Admiral had been generally content with his orders, but their cautious tone was not to his taste. Believing that the enemy should be hit hard and fast he therefore decided to stretch them to the limit. For his initial attack, he planned to take advantage of a local carnival on 23 February when the defenders would be distracted by drink and partying, to slip into Callao with *O'Higgins* and *Lautaro* flying American colours and posing as the American ships *Macedonian* – which had just replaced *Ontario* – and *John Adams*. Once inside Cochrane intended to board and carry off one of the Spanish frigates *Venganza* and *Esmeralda* which were anchored within the port. Captain Shirreff had anticipated such an assault and had issued precise instructions to British merchant ships that, if an attack did take place, they were to raise national colours and move to a position at least one mile out of gunshot.[7]

Callao, the port of Lima, was situated some five miles away from the capital and linked with a straight tree-lined road. Unlike the splendour of the capital with its baroque churches, convents, ornamental walks, triumphant arches, plazas and regular, intersecting streets, Callao was a scruffy low-lying town built at sea level against a backdrop of hills, which rose in successive ranges as far the distant peaks of the Andes. Its buildings and defences were scattered round the curve of a semicircular bay, the seaward arm of which was dominated by the Castles of the Real Felipe and the entrance blocked by a massive chained boom. It was this heavily protected position that Cochrane planned to penetrate. Leaving *San Martin* off the adjacent island of San Lorenzo, he prepared *O'Higgins* and *Lautaro* for action in accordance with his plan of attack. But on the chosen morning, 23 February, the approaches were suddenly blanketed by fog and the attempt had to be abandoned. It lasted for a week, dense and impenetrable. Then, during a clearer spell of hazy sunshine on 28 February, there was the sound of guns from the shore. It was only the firing of salutes to mark a visit by the Viceroy but the Chileans, mistakenly thinking that one of their ships was in trouble, headed for Callao only to find the fog rolling in once more. When it lifted, Cochrane's ships discovered themselves huddled together near the entrance with a Spanish gunboat caught in their midst. The gunboat was easily taken, but the Chileans were within range of Callao's formidable defences – 160 fixed guns on land plus a similar number on the broadsides of the Spanish armed ships that had been anchored in a semi-circle to protect the merchant vessels sheltering behind. Sighting the intruders, the Spanish batteries erupted in thunder and smoke, and with shot whistling about their ears the Chileans turned and laboriously worked their way out of the bay to safety. It had been a bad moment for Cochrane – made worse by the fact that, in his miniature midshipman's uniform, little Thomas had escaped from the after cabin in which he had been locked and had made his way to the quarterdeck where he was found splattered with the blood and brains of those killed by the Spanish cannonade.

Cochrane had now experienced at first hand the difficulties of operating off Callao. First there were fluky winds and the sudden frequent fogs, which could act as a cover to the odd blockade runner or enemy warship sneaking in or out. Then there were the batteries, which guarded the port – so massive that he must have begun to understand why his orders had urged caution and the avoidance of any engagement with them. His initial foray against Callao may have been frustrated, but with typical resilience Cochrane was already planning another attack. It came on 2 March, when the boats of the squadron led by Captain Forster and Major Miller seized San Lorenzo. Although the island was little more than a dreary outcrop of sand and rock without a scrap of vegetation, it was three miles from Callao and an ideal base from which to blockade the port. Cochrane also established a laboratory there to experiment with the explosives and primitive torpedoes with which he planned to harass the enemy. The first victim, however, was William Miller, who was dreadfully burned preparing charges for an explosion vessel. It took him six weeks to recover.

The liberation of 29 Chilean soldiers who had been kept on the island in chains for eight years reminded Cochrane of Article 9 of his orders. Two days later, he sent a letter in to Spanish Viceroy Joaquin de la Pezuela under flag of truce, proposing an exchange of prisoners and complaining about the ill treatment meted out to those who had already been captured after skirmishes ashore or from the patriot privateers *Maipú* and *Ariel*. Pezuela, accustomed to the stately courtesies of Spanish official correspondence, was annoyed by Cochrane's undiplomatic tone and reciprocated by expressing surprise at seeing a British nobleman in the company of a bunch of rebels! But in doing so, Pezuela made a big mistake. Cochrane loved paper disputations, and for the next fortnight the two men indulged in an orgy of verbal point-scoring over the justice of the Chilean cause, the neutrality of Great Britain, and the right of a British nobleman to fight on behalf of aggrieved humanity wherever he chose.[8] The correspondence ended with Cochrane pleased that he had won the argument. But alas, the real objective was overlooked. There was no exchange of prisoners.

On 22 March, Cochrane tried another destructive foray against Callao, this time using three prizes *Victoria*, *Barbara* and *Lucero* – the first two converted into fire ships, the last into an explosion vessel packed with gunpowder. With *O'Higgins* providing protection, the three ships advanced against the port covered by Forster in a bomb vessel and Lieutenant Wynter in a gunboat when the wind suddenly dropped to the lightest of breezes. Reluctantly, Cochrane called off the attack. Unfortunately, the explosion vessel under Lieutenant Nicolas Lawson of *Lautaro* had gone too far and was hit by fire from the shore batteries before she could get away. Cochrane was now convinced that further action against the Spanish base was impractical. At the beginning of April therefore, leaving *Chacabuco* on patrol off Callao, he withdrew with the rest of his ships to Huacho to fill his water casks. It was there that Blanco Encalada and the brigs found him on 4 April.

The Rear Admiral's arrival gave Cochrane the opportunity to broaden his attacks on Peru so, sending Blanco Encalada back to Callao to renew the blockade, Cochrane sailed north with *O'Higgins*, *Galvarino* and the recently captured schooner *Montezuma* to raid the settlements scattered along the long desert coast. Here, Cochrane was in his element. With the same skill he had shown when commanding the *Imperieuse* in the Mediterranean, he fell on the unsuspecting villages, distributing proclamations to inspire the patriots and seizing ships, property and money to dismay the royalists. At Patavilca on 5 April, he seized

$67,000 together with quantities of sugar and rum. The following day at Huarmey, Cochrane sent the marines under Miller to ambush a mule train carrying $120,000 in gold and silver, then took a schooner called *Macedonian* that was obviously waiting to load the money. On 10 April at Gumbacho, he caught up with a French brig called *Gazelle* carrying $60,000, which he suspected belonged to the Philippines Company. Alas, the ownership of this booty was claimed by an American called Elphalet Smith, who was not only the owner of the *Macedonian* but of some of the money taken from the mule train. Smith, who was in the vicinity, furiously confronted Cochrane with a pistol but was disarmed and hustled away. But he had powerful friends in both the United States Congress and the Navy, and the seizures were to cause the Chilean Vice Admiral a great deal of trouble. Three days later, Cochrane captured and plundered the town of Paita, though – to the astonishment of the foreign sailors – he returned silver crosses, chalices and other religious objects that had been looted from a church and flogged the offenders.[9] The rest of the booty was loaded onto the Spanish schooner *Sacramento*, which had been seized in the bay.

On 5 May, Cochrane returned to Callao. There was no sign of the blockading squadron, so, after waiting three days, Cochrane sailed back to Supe to pick up *Galvarino* and the prizes before sailing south for home. Behind him, the Spanish advanced to reoccupy the towns he had liberated, inflicting heavy punishments on those who had shown support for the patriot cause. In Huacho and Supe alone, 13 sympathisers were shot and 15 imprisoned. On 19 June Cochrane arrived back in the middle of the raw, cold northerly gales of the Valparaiso winter, joining Blanco Encalada and the rest of the squadron, which had been forced to raise the blockade of Callao at the beginning of May by shortage of supplies. The Chilean Government had done its best to avoid this, but unfortunately, the American ship *Helen Mary*, which had been sent north loaded with provisions, had been captured when, in Cochrane's absence, the powerful frigate *Venganza* had driven off *Chacabuco* and *Pueyrredon* and carried out a foray into the Pacific. With the blockade now lifted, the royalists in Callao appealed for naval reinforcements from Spain, attributing much of Cochrane's success to the support given to the patriot cause by the United States and Great Britain.[10]

Back in Valparaiso, Cochrane received a hero's welcome. Whatever its initial caution, the Chilean Government fully approved of the aggressive approach he had taken. From the beginning, news of his triumphs had been published in the *Gazeta Ministerial de Chile* – indeed whole editions were filled with his dispatches.[11] The National Institute of Santiago issued a eulogy of his operations off Callao, and the public responded with enthusiasm. Nine months before, Chile had been entirely at the mercy of the Spanish Navy, which had blockaded its coasts and seized its ships at will. Now Cochrane had turned the tables and taken command of the seas, putting the Spanish on the defensive, driving their warships into harbour, and even attacking without hesitation their most powerful fortress in the Pacific. Judge John B. Prevost, who was now living in Santiago as American diplomatic agent to the region, caught the mood of the moment when he wrote to John Quincy Adams in July 1819, to say:

> The changes brought about in one short twelve-month [period] are almost incredible. On my arrival all was dismay and consternation, the Flag of Chile was not known at its Ports, the Squadron of the Enemy was in sight and five thousand Spaniards were penetrating the Heart of the Country; At this period all is confidence, the patriot Flag waves triumphant on the

ocean and upwards of forty large vessels at Valparaiso proclaim its success, while an equal number of troops are prepared for the invasion of Peru.[12]

Cochrane himself was more guarded in his assessment. In his view the purpose of the voyage – which had been to 'reconnoitre, with a view to future operations when the squadron should be rendered efficient, but more especially to ascertain the inclinations of the Peruvians in regard to their desire for emancipation' – had been achieved, and as a bonus, he had been able to 'restrict the Spanish naval force to the shelter of their forts, defeat their military forces wherever encountered, and capture a not inconsiderable amount of treasure'.[13] Further success had, however, been frustrated by the Spanish 'passive system of defence' and the refusal of their naval forces to come out and fight.

Nevertheless, O'Higgins was satisfied and hurried down the coach road from Santiago to offer personal congratulations and to raise a loan so the squadron could be supplied and paid. Cochrane's offer to use his prize money for the purpose was politely declined. His proposals for the next stage of the campaign were also agreed. This time, there was to be an attack on the shipping in Callao in true Cochrane fashion using the latest military technology in the shape of Congreve rockets and explosion vessels. Goldsack's factory had begun to produce the necessary rockets and bombs, and the various devices were successfully tested before they left.

Cochrane's attitude was entirely positive at this time. His studies of Spanish were also making progress, helped by volumes of Chilean history books sent to him by a helpful Zenteno. In letters to his brother William, he reported that things were going well, and that he had expectations of large amounts of prize money. 'Suffice it to say', he wrote on 9 August, 'that I have every prospect of making the largest fortune which has been made in our days save that of the Duke of Wellington.'[14] He even urged William to give up his life as a half-pay major in England and follow him to Chile, telling him that Captain Forster had married Jane Frith Cochrane in July, and that not only were there excellent brides to be found but any of his friends who had spare daughters were likely to find husbands as well![15] At a more mundane level, Cochrane asked William to contact Francis Place, the Charing Cross tailor who was one of Cochrane's radical friends, and to order a gross of admiral's brass buttons – without crowns – and a supply of blue cloth suitable for uniforms. Cochrane was also getting on well with the Supreme Director. Bernardo O'Higgins was half Irish himself and had been educated in England with the result that he understood Lord Cochrane and Cochrane understood him. It was to prove a profitable relationship.

On the social side, Cochrane's domestic life also seemed contented. Lady Cochrane was certainly enjoying herself, being the belle of many balls and gaining the admiration of John Downes, Captain of the USS *Macedonian* which had relieved the *Ontario* in early 1819. Downes had good contacts in Chile and was familiar with the country having been First Lieutenant of the USS *Essex* – and commander of the *Essex* Junior – when they had been captured by HMS *Phoebe* off Valparaiso in 1814. He had already done much to erase the poor impression left by Biddle, welcoming visitors aboard the American frigate and throwing a party to celebrate Washington's Birthday on 22 February where he met Lady Cochrane. It was rumoured that he had been smitten by the dynamic Kitty, who was in the process of refurbishing her new house regardless of expense, and that he had sent the *Macedonian*'s carpenters ashore to help with the work. The frigate's Clerk, a straight laced New Englander called Charles Jarvis Deblois, was highly critical, writing in his Journal that Downes spent far too much time with her, socialising, riding on horseback and going for long walks.[16] Lady Cochrane was then 22 years old, a petite, vivacious brunette who loved parties, company and pretty clothes. Fortunately for her husband, she was also spirited and adventurous, and had determined to make the most of her new home by mastering the Spanish language. She was also enjoying the social life of Valparaiso and indulging in some adventurous travelling with her two children in the mountains and countryside around.

Alas, Cochrane's optimism was already being undermined by money problems. As usual, his expenses – with Kitty's assistance – were running ahead of his income. The costs of finding a house, of repairing it, of employing servants, and of providing the level of entertainment expected of an admiral on his flagship were well in excess of the $6000 he was being paid. Cochrane explained the problem to O'Higgins and described the Royal Navy's system of command pay or 'table money' for official entertainment, which effectively doubled the income of British flag officers. The Supreme Director saw the point. He and Zenteno sidestepped the question of table money, but got the Senate to agree that Cochrane's annual emoluments should be increased to $10,000, or £2000. It was made clear however that the extra $4000 was a personal gratuity payable only to Cochrane in recognition of his special circumstances and experience.[17]

But Cochrane was also worried about prize money. In Chile, the value of captured ships and property was shared among the captors as in Britain – the commander-in-chief receiving one-eighth; the captain of the ship concerned, two-eights; the sea officers, warrant officers and petty officers one-eighth respectively; and the rest of the ship's company the remaining two-eights. Unfortunately, in Chile only half of the value of prizes was distributed in this way, the rest being retained by the state. This was bad news for

Cochrane, whose share of prizes not only went down to one-sixteenth of the value, but was reduced further since he had to pay one-third of the flag's share to Rear Admiral Blanco Encalada! Cochrane wrote again to O'Higgins, pointing out that prize money was 'the liberal reward for enterprise and exertion which has brought the Royal Navy to the pitch of Glory', and recommending that Chile adopted British practice.[18] Once more, O'Higgins was sympathetic, and agreed that, in addition to his normal one-eighth share of prize values, Cochrane should receive one-eighth of the government's half as well – thus doubling his receipts and putting them on a par with what he would have received in the Royal Navy. Indeed, in their desire to win the confidence of the navy and reward its success, O'Higgins and Zenteno persuaded the Senate to agree that during the next cruise the state would forego its claim to half of the prizes taken, and would hand over the complete value of armed ships and equipment – though not of cargoes – to the captors.[19]

Pleased with both his reception and the government's generous response to his requests, Cochrane prepared the squadron for the next campaign. There were only minor adjustments to be made. With Martin Guise now in command of the frigate *Lautaro*, Robert Forster went to the corvette *Independencia*, which had now arrived from the United States; and a red-headed former Royal Navy Lieutenant, Thomas Sackville Crosbie, was given command of the *Araucano* in place of James Ramsey who was moved to *Chacabuco*. Forster's new appointment meant that the flagship lost its captain, but Cochrane declined to fill the vacancy and decided to do the job himself as well as acting as commander-in-chief. That done, on 12 September 1819, Lord Cochrane led the squadron out of the Bay to renew the attack on the royalists in Peru.

The orders Cochrane carried were as detailed as those he

had received for the first cruise. The object of the expedition, he was reminded, was to secure the command of the Pacific that was so vital for the forthcoming invasion. But this time there was additional urgency, for news had arrived that a third Spanish reinforcement had left Cadiz in May. With its initial plan for maritime supremacy foiled by the capture of the *Maria Isabel* and half of its convoy, the Spanish Government had decided to send a substantial force to the Pacific. This time it comprised the 74-gun ships *Alejandro I* and *San Telmo* and the frigate *Prueba*, whose arrival would clearly mean a sharp swing of maritime power in favour of Spain. Cochrane therefore had two objectives – one to find and destroy the Spanish ships; the other to attack Callao and its shipping using rockets. The Chilean Government laid great store on achieving success and had ensured that the squadron lacked nothing in terms of supplies. Indeed, the squadron carried a battalion of marine infantry commanded by James Charles – now a colonel – to mastermind the rocket attacks. O'Higgins estimated that the cost of the expedition was no less than $400,000 or £80,000.[20]

Cochrane's orders contained a third element. The Chileans had approved of his aggressive approach during the first cruise but were unhappy at the assaults he had made against the coast of Peru. Cochrane, of course, simply saw it as enemy territory, which should be attacked by any means. O'Higgins and his colleagues did not agree. To them, Peru was a friendly country whose inhabitants were oppressed by an occupying army. In their view, seizures of their towns and assaults on their commerce made no real contribution to ultimate liberation and, as had been shown in the first voyage, only put local patriots at risk once the Chilean forces had withdrawn. All this was carefully explained in Cochrane's orders and led to the delicately expressed conclusion that 'you will expressly forbid the forces under your command under any pretext to undertake incursions or hostilities of any kind against the coasts of Peru.' Only parties filling water casks, gathering intelligence or contacting patriot elements were permitted to land, and then with only minimum numbers of men.[21]

Cochrane reached the Peruvian coast on 27 September. With the blockade reimposed and no sign of any enemy, he began to prepare the rocket and mortar rafts needed for the great assault on Callao. But first, he wrote to the Viceroy suggesting that he send an equal number of ships out of Callao so the fate of the port could be decided by some kind of duel between the two squadrons at sea. Puzzled by such a bizarre request, Pezuela refused.[22] Rebuffed, on 1 October Cochrane prepared for the first attack. As night fell, the rafts were towed into position by the brigs *Galvarino*, *Araucano* and *Pueyrredon* and began to fire into the anchorage. Each was commanded by a marine officer – the mortars by Major William Miller; and the rockets by Colonel James Charles and Captain Henry Hind. They were answered by a hail of cannon fire, the shore batteries using red-hot shot. After a vigorous exchange, the Chileans withdrew. They had suffered only slight damage, principally when Captain Hind's rocket raft had blown up and a stray shot had killed Lieutenant Bealy of the *Galvarino*, but the performance of the mortars had been poor and the rockets had performed erratically.[23]

The days that followed saw more skirmishes, while Cochrane prepared for a second attack scheduled for 5 October. With the rest of the squadron left waiting outside, the three brigs once more towed their rafts into position and opened fire, while a fire ship commanded by Lieutenant Morgell was sent in to break the boom and flush out the vessels in the harbour. Alas, a lack of wind prevented him from gaining his objective before his ship was destroyed, while the rockets once more missed their targets, going wildly off course or plunging into the sea. The attempt was a failure. When writing the *Narrative of Services* in old age, Cochrane – then anxious to denigrate the Chilean authorities in any way – blamed them for the malfunction of the rockets in the two attacks because, for reasons of parsimony, they had used Spanish prisoners for the work who had 'embraced every opportunity of inserting handfuls of sand, sawdust and even manure at intervals in the tubes ... so that the charge would not ignite'.[24] There is reason to doubt this. In the letters he wrote at the time, Cochrane made it clear that the failure had nothing to do with the explosive charges, but was due to 'the poor and hasty work of welding the tubes and cylinders of the rockets ... and because some broke at the tail because the sticks had been made of knotty or imperfect wood'.[25] In other words, the technology was in advance of its time. He was also anxious that the Chileans should not lose faith in the system, and explained that Britain had had exactly the same teething troubles when it had first used these weapons. Likewise Zenteno, replying to one of Cochrane's compendium letters of complaint on 14 May 1820, denied completely that prisoners-of-war had been used at all, writing that the rockets were 'constructed exclusively by the same artisans who had come to make them; and since only they were sufficiently skilled it was necessary to put the work in their hands notwithstanding the cost'.[26] Unfortunately for Mr Goldsack, it was he who became the scapegoat.

Cochrane was now convinced that further attacks on Callao would be doomed to failure. The defences had been reinforced and all element of surprise had been lost. Cochrane now concentrated on the simple matter of blockade, but was anxious to find other ways of continuing the campaign. On 7 October, he wrote to Zenteno, discussing how the necessary pressure on the Spanish in Peru could be maintained while preventing incursions into Chile. One option he ruled out was an attack on Valdivia, the last royalist base in southern Chile. 'Although the taking of Valdivia would be useful,' he wrote, 'it is doubtful whether its surrender would achieve these objectives, since there are many smaller maritime locations which could be used by any naval force present in the area.'[27]

Turning his attention to Peru, the carefully expressed paragraphs in his orders that banned incursions on the coast were soon forgotten. The following day, he wrote urgently requesting that a special force of troops be put under his command to facilitate amphibious expeditions. 'A war of gentle means and half measures can gain no partisans,' he explained, and even if no reinforcements were available, the men he already had could keep the coast of Peru in constant uproar.[28] O'Higgins's reply was cool. He reminded Cochrane that no force of fewer than 4000 men would make the slightest impact, and that nothing of military consequence should be risked while the Spanish reinforcements were still at sea. But there was good news. Intelligence from Gibraltar had reported that the poor condition of the *Alejandro I* – one of the worthless ships foisted on Ferdinand VII by the Tsar – had forced her to turn back before she even reached the coast of Brazil, so that the force now only consisted of the *San Telmo* and the *Prueba*.[29]

Keen to make his point and replenish his supplies, Cochrane reimposed the blockade with *San Martin*, *Araucano* and *Pueyrredon* while Captain Guise was ordered with *Lautaro* and *Galvarino* to attack the fort at Pisco and seize the shipping and supplies sheltering under its guns. Unfortunately, contrary winds delayed their arrival so that the attack took place in broad daylight on 7 November.

Guise carried out his mission successfully, but Miller was wounded, taking three musket balls in the body, and another senior officer was killed – this time it was Colonel Charles, the commander of the marines. Charles was a Woolwich trained officer who had served with Sir Robert Wilson's irregulars in Portugal during the Napoleonic Wars and had later been seconded to the Russian army for the campaigns in Germany. As Maria Graham subsequently wrote, 'he was a brave and excellent officer but deserved a better fate than to be killed at the taking of so paltry a fortress.'[30] She could have added 'against the Chilean Government's orders'. Charles was later to receive a hero's funeral in Valparaiso.

Then there was another cause for frustration. Fortunately for Chile, the naval reinforcements sent from Spain had by this time shrunk to a fraction of their original size. Not only had the condition of the *Alejandro I* forced her to turn back, but the second two-decker, the *San Telmo* was hit by a severe storm rounding Cape Horn and was lost with all hands.[31] Only the *Prueba* was now left to reach the Pacific and get as far as Peru. The Spanish frigate was actually sighted by the Chilean blockading squadron off Callao, but she turned and headed north pursued by *Araucano* before she could be identified. Later Lord Cochrane heard rumours that she had been seen to the north in Guayaquil. He immediately sailed in pursuit with *O'Higgins*, *Lautaro*, *Galvarino* and *Pueyrredon*. But on arrival they were disappointed. Leaving the flotilla outside, Cochrane entered the bay with the *O'Higgins* and after a brisk action seized two prizes, *Begonia* and *Aguila*, hiding behind the Island of Puna loaded with timber. Of the *Prueba* there was no sign. The Spanish frigate had in fact been lightened, taken up river and moored for repairs under the guns of the batteries. Cochrane had no choice but to abandon his quest and return to Callao.

Chapter 5
THE CAPTURE OF VALDIVIA

Cochrane had not been satisfied with the campaign of 1819. The Chilean Government too was disappointed with the failure of the rocket attack on Callao. But, as O'Higgins pointed out in a letter to Lord Cochrane, no one blamed him.[1] As far as the Chileans were concerned Cochrane had done all that had been asked of him. True, his attempts to destroy the shipping in Callao had failed, but he had effectively driven the Spanish Navy from the seas, imposed a crippling blockade on the Peruvian capital, and taken a useful bag of prizes. It was an impressive achievement for a navy that had existed for only a year. The government had already doubled his salary and prize money in recognition of his efforts. Now it featured his dispatches and achievements in the fortnightly *Gazeta Ministerial de Chile*.[2] O'Higgins wrote repeated personal notes of support, and in a long letter dated 26 November 1819, Zenteno praised Cochrane's audacity and tactics, confirmed that he had the Supreme Director's total confidence, and demonstrated it by giving him a free tactical hand, concluding:

> while reiterating that the squadron should (i) not return unless faced with an emergency it cannot overcome, and (ii) that it should operate in such a

way as to avoid compromises but take advantage of any chance to destroy all, or part, of the enemy's forces – the Government does not wish to restrict you with any rules. It leaves you free to operate in its interests according to circumstances.[3]

Cochrane, however, was his own sternest critic. Although in public he was resentful of any outside criticism and incapable of admitting mistakes, in private he was deeply depressed by anything he saw as a failure. The events of his early life had given him a strong sense of insecurity. The death of his mother when he was no more than a child, and his father's preoccupations with inventions and money problems, had left him desperate for the approval of his superiors, and full of foreboding that it might not be forthcoming.

Thus, he was genuinely dejected by what he regarded as his failure off Callao and – in spite of ample evidence to the contrary – was convinced that O'Higgins and his colleagues felt the same. Cochrane had hoped that the capture of the *Prueba* would compensate for his lax blockade of Callao – but in that too he had been frustrated. What he needed now was a victory to restore his reputation and defy his supposed detractors in Chile. Then he picked up a rumour that *Prueba*, or one of her consorts, had made landfall in the southern fortress of Valdivia.[4] This gave him an idea. Forgetting that he had previously dismissed the base as an unimportant target, Cochrane came to the conclusion that the best way to frustrate his enemies was to seize Valdivia by *coup de main*![5] It was a plan of astonishing – but typical – audacity. It was also totally against his orders, which were to remain off Callao. The blockade had already been weakened when *San Martin* and *Independencia* had been forced to return to Valparaiso by an outbreak of typhus. Now, leaving only the heavily outgunned

Galvarino and *Pueyrredon* to watch the port and intercept blockade runners, Cochrane sailed over the horizon in the *O'Higgins* to Valdivia – 2000 miles away from where he should have been! He told the Chilean Government nothing of his movements or plans. The flow of weekly dispatches simply ceased.

Cochrane reached Valdivia at dusk on 17 January 1820. His first task was to assess the chances of a successful attack. There are two alternative versions of how he did this. Cochrane himself, in his *Narrative of Services in the Liberation of Chile, Peru and Brazil*, claims that – sacrificing the element of surprise – he boldly entered the bay in *O'Higgins* flying Spanish colours, learnt what he needed to learn, and sailed out again taking prisoners with him.[6] William Bennet Stevenson who was there, however, gives the more likely description. According to him, Cochrane left the *O'Higgins* standing off the entrance of the bay flying the red and gold of Spain to avoid alarming the defenders, and carried out a personal pre-dawn recon-naissance of the harbour in his gig.[7] After he had returned, the intelligence he had gathered was supplemented by four Spanish soldiers and a pilot who had innocently boarded the Chilean warship while he was away deceived by her false colours. *O'Higgins* then made sail and disappeared over the horizon. Cochrane now had two objectives – the first to capture the Spanish brig *Potrillo*, which he learnt had evaded the blockade off Callao and was heading for Valdivia carrying money and supplies for the garrison; the second to head for the nearest Chilean base at Talcahuana in search of reinforcements for his attack.

Potrillo sailed straight into Cochrane's arms without the need for a search and, though she attempted to escape, she was dismasted in a squall and captured. On board Cochrane seized $20,000 in silver and $40,000 worth of stores and munitions. With the prize in company, he then headed for Talcahuana, arriving on 22 January 1820. There he found himself in luck. In the harbour were two Chilean warships, the *Intrepido*, under the command of Thomas Carter, and the schooner *Montezuma*. Cochrane took both under his orders. Likewise, on hearing his plans for the capture of Valdivia, the Governor of Concepción, General Ramon Freire, willingly supplied 250 infantrymen under Major Jorge Beauchef to supplement the flagship's marines and provide Cochrane with an adequate landing force. The final adjustments were quickly made. The troops were embarked, and *Potrillo*, with its cargo of money was sent off to Valparaiso under Henry Cobbett, the First Lieutenant of the *O'Higgins*. With all now prepared to Cochrane's satisfaction, the flotilla weighed anchor, and on 29 January, headed into the open sea.

But almost immediately, there was a crisis. On the first night out, the ships became separated, and the progress of the *O'Higgins* was suddenly interrupted by a grinding shudder as she went aground on a reef off the remote island of Quiriquina. There was momentary panic as her false keel was torn off, her pumps failed, and she began to take in water from the damage to her underwater timbers. Cochrane immediately rallied his men, led them below, carried out repairs to the pumps and hull with his own hands, and saved the day. Fortunately, the wind was light so that the Chileans were able to heave the *O'Higgins* off the reef using the kedge anchor until she floated again. That done, and with pumps going continuously to stem the inflow of water, the frigate headed once more for Valdivia. It took more than a minor accident and a damaged ship to deflect Cochrane from a mission!

For a sailing ship to run aground at night in poorly charted waters was not an uncommon event. But Cochrane's inner circle soon realised that the incident did not reflect well on their patron. It was necessary therefore to manufacture a defence. The excuse that subsequently appeared in Stevenson's book, and that has been repeated by biographers ever since,[8] is that Cochrane was exhausted with carrying out the duties of both commander-in-chief and captain, and went to bed giving orders to the officer of the watch, Lieutenant Nicholas Lawson, to call him if the wind rose. Lawson, however, was negligent and retired himself, leaving the deck to an inexperienced midshipman. He in turn failed to rouse Cochrane as ordered, and could not cope with the crisis when it arose. Thus, Cochrane's partisans were able to convince themselves that he was blameless for the accident. Alas, this carefully devised excuse does not hold water. The responsibility for allowing the flagship to become so seriously deficient in officers was Lord Cochrane's. It was he who decided that *O'Higgins* did not need a captain while he was on board. It was he who allowed the complement of lieutenants to fall to two by putting the rest aboard prizes. And of those who remained, Cochrane had arrested one – an American called Edward Brown – so that only Lawson had been left to carry out watch keeping duties. He, no doubt, was as exhausted as his Vice Admiral. The grounding of the *O'Higgins* showed Cochrane's powers of leadership, his strength of character, his technical skills and his seamanship at their best. It is a pity that his constant need for self-justification did not allow him to leave it at that.

Valdivia was Spain's last remaining stronghold on the Pacific south of Callao. Located on the seaboard of the mountains and fjords of southern Chile, it was the first landfall for ships coming round Cape Horn from Europe and was an important base and a major depository of supplies, arms and munitions. The town, in a sheltered spot surrounded by apple trees and with an ample harbour, was located on the low, heavily wooded banks of a long river running into a flask shaped bay with a narrow fortified entrance 1200 yards wide running from west to east. Stevenson described it as 'the Gibraltar of South America', defended by 2000 men and more than 100 guns. This was, however, an exaggeration. Unlike Gibraltar, the troops and guns defending Valdivia were not located in a single fortress, but were scattered between five different forts and four smaller gun emplacements perched on the rocky heights that dominated the bay on every side. Thus, an enemy ship entering the harbour would first have to pass the guns of the Fort of Ingles on the right command-ing the approaches; then those of San Carlos and Amargos, with Niebla on the opposite side; then, further down on the right, those of the Castle of Corral, which formed the centrepiece and dominated the interior of the bay.

The defences of Valdivia appeared formidable, but Cochrane knew their weaknesses. Not only was the garrison scattered, but the guns were positioned so as to resist an attack by sea. To a man of Cochrane's tactical gifts, the answer was clear. It was to attack unexpectedly by land at night, and to roll up the forts and batteries one by one before a central defence could be organised. And this is exactly what he did. Late on the afternoon of 2 February, Cochrane's flotilla approached to within striking distance of Valdivia. Leaving the damaged *O'Higgins* out of sight of the shore, Cochrane embarked the landing parties on *Intrepido* and *Montezuma* and, in a heavy sea, they headed for a cove at the foot of the heights on which Fort Ingles was built. To gain time the Chilean ships flew the Spanish flag – and even communicated with the shore posing as friendly vessels fresh from Cape Horn. The bluff was eventually called, but by the time the fort opened fire it was too late. With Miller and the marines in the lead, the boats battled through a rising wind and crashing surf to reach the beach and drive off a picket of enemy skirm-ishers. Then, with the light fast fading, the rest of the

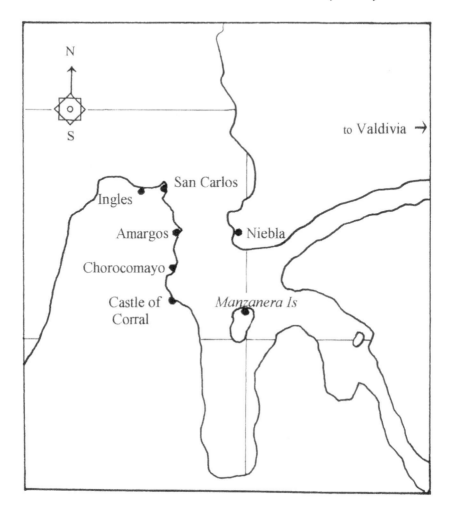

Valdivia showing the principal forts

troops landed and began to file up a steep goat track to the heights. When they reached the top it was night.

With the defenders of Fort Ingles firing blindly into the darkness, Ensign Francisco Vidal of the marines managed to bridge the defensive ditch and the Chileans stormed it in a two pronged attack, driving the defenders out at bayonet point. Fleeing in panic the Spaniards collided with a column of reinforcements and threw them too into disorder. And when the fort of San Carlos opened its gates to admit the refugees, a horde of pursuing Chileans followed them in and promptly captured that as well. The attack surged on, with Fort Amargos falling with equal ease.[9] The Castle of Corral was the objective of the Chilean infantry under Major Beauchef, and the regulars of the Cantabria Regiment, who formed the garrison, could have been expected to put up serious resistance. But by this time, so great was the confusion and demoralisation among the Spanish forces that when Beauchef attacked, the defenders rushed for the boats and escaped, leaving Colonel Fausto de Hoyos, his officers and a handful of men to surrender.[10] By daybreak, the whole of the western side of the bay was in Chilean hands.

Next day, taking advantage of the unexpected success of the previous night, *Intrepido* and *Montezuma* were ordered to carry the landing force from the castle across the bay to attack the Fort of Niebla and the batteries on the eastern side. But at that moment the menacing bulk of the *O'Higgins* appeared under a pyramid of sails from the seaward. Ignorant of the frigate's condition, alarmed at the thought of her heavy guns and assuming that she carried further Chilean reinforcements, the remaining Spaniards abandoned their defences and retreated up river to Valdivia while the *O'Higgins* entered the bay and was hastily beached before she could sink. By 6 February it was all over. Cochrane reached the town to be met by a flag of truce and to receive the surrender of the remaining Spanish forces.[11] The mopping up operation, however, was not without its brutal side. The conflict in South America, as in so many essentially civil wars, had been marked by cruelty on both sides – indeed the south of Chile was at that moment being ravaged by a band of royalist irregulars commanded by a bloodthirsty warlord called Benavides. Valdivia was no exception. Captain Francisco Erezcano of the *Intrepido*'s marines, who had acted so bravely in the attack on Fort Ingles, sullied his record by killing two unarmed Spanish officers; while Ensign Latapia, left in charge of the Castle of Corral, thought nothing of shooting prisoners to enforce his authority and would have killed more if Stevenson had not intervened.

The taking of Valdivia was a major victory and a confirmation of Cochrane's extraordinary daring and military prowess. Its fall not only removed the last potential threat to Chilean independence but put a vast amount of military equipment in the government's hands. All told, Cochrane had seized 50 tons of gunpowder, 10,000 cannon shot, 170,000 musket balls, huge quantities of small arms, 128 pieces of artillery and a prize ship, the *Dolores*. His men also looted the town, the churches and the Governor's Palace, seizing tobacco worth $9000 and ornaments and plate to the value of $10,000; and on his own account, Cochrane took possession of $20,000 worth of crockery.[12] The debit side of the capture only amounted to the *O'Higgins'* underwater damage and the loss of the *Intrepido*, which had grounded on a mud bank going upriver to Valdivia. Emboldened by his success, Cochrane decided to try his luck against Chiloé, a large archipelago 150 miles to the south which dominated the approaches to the fjords and mountains of southern Chile. But this time the Spanish garrison, under the redoubtable Colonel Quintanilla, was ready and waiting. The initial foray by 150 troops was beaten off by defenders of twice that number and Miller who, as usual, was in the vanguard of the attack against the strong point of Fort Aguay, was badly wounded by grape shot and had to hand over command to the Argentine marine Captain Erezcano. Faced with this rebuff, Cochrane called off the attack, justifiably content with what he had achieved so far. For the rest of the war, Chiloé was to remain as a minor irritant and a base for royalist privateers.

Chapter 6
'HEARTFELT GRATITUDE AT THAT SIGNAL ACHIEVEMENT'

News that Lord Cochrane had left the blockade of Callao and disappeared over the horizon was received with concern in Chile. From the beginning some had feared that the Vice Admiral might ignore his orders and go off on some scheme of his own, and now their fears seemed justified. But, on 16 February, letters arrived from General Freire revealing not only that Cochrane was in Valdivia, but that he had achieved a stunning and unexpected victory. The Chilean authorities were relieved and delighted. Next day they published an Extraordinary Edition of the *Gazeta Ministerial* carrying the momentous news, and followed it two days later by another that triumphantly reprinted all of Cochrane's dispatches.[1] A week later the government signified its pleasure by ordering that medals be struck for the victors[2] and by issuing a public letter from Zenteno on 22 February, which began:

> If victories over an enemy can be estimated according to the resistance offered and the national advantages gained, then the conquest of Valdivia is, in both senses, inestimable – encountering as you did the natural and artificial strengths of that impregnable

fortress ... the memory of that glorious day will occupy the first pages of Chilean history and the name of Your Excellency will be transmitted from generation to generation by the gratitude of our descendants.

His Excellency the Supreme Director, highly gratified by that noble conquest, orders me to inform you that he feels the most heartfelt gratitude at that signal achievement. The meritorious officers ... and soldiers who, in imitation of Your Excellency, encountered such vast dangers, will be brought to the notice of the Government in order to receive a distinctive medal in gratitude for their gallantry and in proof that Chile rewards the heroes who advocate her cause.[3]

In his own letters to O'Higgins, Cochrane was keen to rub in the significance of Valdivia and the lesson to be learnt writing, on 10 February, that the capture of Valdivia 'was felt more by the enemy ... than burning the ships in Callao. ... I hope your Excellency will approve what I have done without orders; if so, I care little about the opinions of those who gave me the last orders with a view to prevent me doing anything.'[4] In other words, the cause of Chilean freedom was best advanced if he was left to do what he liked rather than what he was told! It had an ominous ring.

On 6 March, the Vice Admiral returned to Valparaiso in the *Montezuma*, having left *O'Higgins* in Valdivia to be hove down and repaired under the supervision of Secretary Stevenson. He was given a hero's welcome. The City Council and the National Institute of Santiago published messages singing his praises to amplify those already given by the government. Minister Zenteno repeated these congratulations in a private interview. But he was inevitably obliged to point out that the Vice Admiral *had* acted against orders, and that it had been a risky enterprise. Alas, in so doing, Zenteno made a serious mistake. In Cochrane's simplistic view of the world, anyone who was not for him was against him, and anyone who offered the slightest criticism must be motivated by malice. Henceforth Zenteno was cast in the role of an enemy. Out of delicacy, the minister's comments had been made in private. It was Cochrane and his entourage who made them public. The Cochrane version of the interview was retailed in the books subsequently published by his business associate, John Miers, the travel writer, Maria Graham, and in his own *Narrative of Services*. In these accounts, the minister is accused of being abusive, of railing that Cochrane had acted like 'a madman ... and that I even now ought to lose my head for daring to attack such a place without instructions and for exposing the patriot forces to such a hazard'.[5] From this point on, Cochrane sees Zenteno as 'my bitter opponent, obstructing all my plans for the interests of Chile'[6] and all the while secretly plotting against him.

It would be naive to expect a revolutionary official to be an angel of virtue, but there is no supporting evidence to back this vilification of Zenteno. Indeed, Cochrane's portrait of the man in no way conforms to his record as the creator and organiser of the infant Chilean Navy. As one Chilean History puts it, 'with no personal knowledge of naval affairs, with inexpert and impromptu assistance, and with little aid from an empty treasury and an impoverished people, Zenteno, without ostentation and without friction, maintained and supplied the fleet, paid the officers and sailors, and transported the army to Lima relying solely on the resources of his own department.'[7] It is difficult to believe that a man with Zenteno's reputation and dedication would be distracted by malice towards a subordinate – particularly one whose victories reflected credit on the department he led.

Cold and austere by temperament, Zenteno was clearly no charmer. Indeed, he was well known for his lack of civility. But the written record does not substantiate Cochrane's accusations that he was treated with malice and obstruction. Rather the reverse. During their four-year association, Zenteno sent Cochrane hundreds of orders, supplemented by scores of personal letters discussing the strategic situation, praising Cochrane's actions, and trying to anticipate his complaints. Frequently when sending an order he knew would be uncongenial, Zenteno attempted to mollify him by adding a personal note of explanation.[8] Even allowing for Latin American courtesy, these communications are amiable and friendly. Indeed, the tone of Zenteno's letters is so at variance with the depiction given in the *Narrative of Services* that even Cochrane realised it and tried to explain away the discrepancy.[9]

Cochrane's suspicions of Zenteno were soon directed at the Chilean Government as a whole. This is not surprising. Cochrane had a lifelong mistrust of anyone in authority, especially politicians, and in Chile it was no different. Only O'Higgins was immune. Cochrane depicts him as an honest and well intentioned patriot, but his ministers are described as corrupt, hostile, and so jealous of a foreigner achieving military glory that they deliberately undermined his efforts. Written in bitter hindsight, Cochrane's *Narrative of Services* claims that this animosity existed from the beginning. The sensible precaution in his original orders to avoid action with the batteries of Callao in order to preserve the squadron for the forthcoming invasion of Peru is denounced as a ploy by jealous ministers to stop a foreigner gaining military glory. And, at the moment Cochrane was capturing Valdivia, Zenteno is accused of plotting to have him court-martialled for insubordination[10] – a charge that Zenteno's biographers strongly deny.

The Cochrane version of events was retailed in John

Miers's book *Travels in Chile and La Plata*. Here, the events that followed the taking of Valdivia are described in the following terms:

> Lord Cochrane on his return instead of being hailed by the government for the services he had rendered was annoyed by every vexation. ... This Minister (Zenteno) carried out a series of intrigues the object of which was to degrade the Admiral and lessen the glory which his brilliant services so well deserved. He did not even receive public acknowledgement or thanks for the brilliant exploit ... and it was only when Lord Cochrane's indignation was roused at the ingratitude of the Government of Chile and it was feared that he was about to retire in August that the requisite form of thanks was conceded and medals were distributed to the victorious troops and a nominal reward was granted in the form of the grant of an estate to lord Cochrane for his brilliant services.[11]

This description clearly bears no resemblance to what really happened: yet Cochrane seemed to believe it. In letters to San Martin about events at the time, he later wrote 'plans and intrigues were set afoot for my dismissal from the Chilean service ... for no reason other than certain influential persons of shallow understanding and petty expectations hate those who despise mean acts accomplished by low cunning'. San Martin's version of the letter adds, 'the conduct of the Senate and of Zenteno merits no other description.'[12] Cochrane never convincingly explains why, if they were so anxious to get rid of him, Zenteno and his colleagues refused to accept his numerous resignations. Likewise, the accusation that Zenteno and the Ministry – still engaged in an uncertain revolutionary struggle on which their careers and even lives depended – would deliberately hamper the naval effort because of jealousy of a foreigner defies common sense.

The reality of the matter was very different. O'Higgins and the Chilean Government were pleased with Lord Cochrane's activities, and said so frequently and publicly as in Zenteno's letter of 22 February. They expressed the same views in private. In a confidential letter sent by O'Higgins to the Senate at the end of March, for example, he stressed the importance of the capture of Valdivia to the Chilean nation, and concluded 'the government finds itself necessary for reasons of policy, gratitude and justice to show to Lord Cochrane – the one and only author of this reconquest – due recognition that we are indebted to him for its success. He has gloriously extended himself beyond the purely naval sphere and has rendered the fatherland a truly extraordinary service.'[13] The Chilean Government had already shown its appreciation by almost doubling Cochrane's pay and prize money: now it awarded him the Chilean Order of Merit, a Gold Medal and an estate of 20,000 acres at Rio Clara in the south.

The Chileans gave Cochrane all he craved for in terms of recognition, reward and approval, yet it is astonishing to find that he could not believe it. Driven by a restless and suspicious temperament, he persuaded himself that, in spite of all appearances, he was being secretly criticised by his superiors and was surrounded by people who were plotting to get rid of him. Cochrane began to develop psychosomatic symptoms, complaining of palpitations of the heart.[14] Not even the joy of becoming the father of a baby girl in March 1820 seemed to relieve his mounting inner tensions. The child was christened Elizabeth Josephine with O'Higgins standing as Godfather and Cochrane wrote personal letters to his closest acquaintances telling them the good news.[15]

From the perspective of O'Higgins and his government, Cochrane's victories shone with even greater glory against the background of what was happening in Argentina. During 1819, there had been disturbing signs of political disintegration and of a struggle for power between the centralisers of Buenos Aires and the federalist warlords in the provinces. Indeed, in the states of Entre Rios and Santa Fe only the proximity of the Northern Army under General Belgrano was preventing a revolt. Private armies roamed the pampas causing fear and disruption. One of the worst was the so-called 'Chilean Legion' led by the last of the Carrera brothers, José Miguel. The government in Buenos Aires, exhausted by a succession of wars and with trade at a standstill, seemed powerless to prevent it. Not even the threat of the Great Expedition preparing at Cadiz stimulated any closing of ranks. At the end of 1818, Director Pueyrredon had been replaced by the weak and vacillating General Rondeau, whose first act was to recall San Martin and the Army of the Andes from Chile! San Martin reluctantly returned with half his men, but stayed at Mendoza, just over the border, preferring to remain as a distant, brooding presence while events played themselves out in the south. It was only in February 1820 – at the same time as Cochrane reached Valparaiso after the taking of Valdivia – that a compromise agreement was hammered out in Buenos Aires, allowing San Martin to return with reinforcements to prepare for the final assault on the royalists in Peru. In these circumstances, the pleasure with which O'Higgins and his ministers received and acknowledged Cochrane's achievements is hardly surprising.

There were some matters of course on which disagreements between the Chilean Government and its Vice Admiral were inevitable. There were, for example, long running tensions due to the different traditions of the British and Spanish navies. In the former, admirals enjoyed considerable freedom of action, while individual captains exercised almost untrammelled authority within the ships they commanded. In the Spanish tradition, which Chile largely inherited, not only was control from the centre more rigid, but the representatives of the different shore based departments on board had authority that was independent of the captain. Neither Cochrane nor his British commanders seemed sensitive to this and acted in the way to which they were accustomed. One result that was significant and alarming to the Chileans was the imposition of fierce and brutal British ideas of discipline on their crews.

A major problem was that of prize money. By the middle of 1820, Cochrane had already been paid $19,244 (that is, £3850) for enemy ships and property taken during the blockade of Callao and off Valdivia.[16] But a serious disagreement arose when it emerged that prize money would only be paid in respect of ships and property captured afloat or in transit. Cochrane was used to a system whereby the captors retained the booty when an enemy town was taken and expected the same rules to apply to the taking of Valdivia. The South Americans, however, had a different view. They believed that the liberation struggle was about the replacement of the Spanish regimes by independent ones, and that the ownership of public property would simply pass from one government to the next. The idea that their continent and its cities were 'enemy' territory, whose riches belonged to whoever captured them, was unthinkable. As a result, there was no massive hand-out of prize money following Cochrane's capture of Valdivia. And since he was unable or unwilling to understand the Chilean position, he nursed a permanent grievance.

Pay, however, was the greatest problem. Not Cochrane's of course. The Chileans knew the Vice Admiral's reputation well enough to know that it was wise to ensure that he received his emoluments promptly. Thus, by October 1820 he had already been paid $17,462 – the equivalent of £3490 – in addition to his prize money. As usual, however, with the assistance of Kitty, his expenditure was running out of control and already amounted to $71,052, much of it was related to acquiring and developing a second estate at Quintero on the Bay of Herradura, a few miles up the coast from Valparaiso.[17] Although set in a delightful location, Cochrane's interest in the place was largely commercial. He had noticed – and surveys by his captains had confirmed – that Herradura was an ideal location for a naval base, being sheltered from the northerly gales that could hit Valparaiso with such devastating force during the winter. It also had the advantage of being near enough for easy official communications while being sufficiently distant to ensure that the crews were neither distracted by the town's grog shops nor tempted to desert to the merchant ships that filled the port.[18] Cochrane intended to run Quintero as a huge cattle ranch and his partner John Miers – the son-in-law of his erstwhile radical comrade Francis Place – had already begun to assemble in nearby Concon the machinery needed to produce salt beef in barrels, flour and biscuit with a view to becoming the principal supplier of the Chilean Navy and of visiting merchant ships.

Lord Cochrane may have received all his pay, but others were not so lucky. The problem was that the perpetual poverty of the Chilean Government made it difficult for them to produce the large sums of ready cash needed to pay the officers and men of the squadron. This was especially so in 1820, when they were preoccupied with finding the resources needed to fund San Martin's invasion of Peru. Thus, when Cochrane returned to Valparaiso he found the squadron unpaid and increasingly resentful. The foreign seamen, whose annual engagements had come to an end in February, were leaving in shoals, disgusted with their treatment and at the end of their patience. In April, the lieutenants, surgeons, midshipmen, warrant and petty officers of the fleet petitioned in a body for their pay. Cochrane himself backed the protest and threatened to resign unless something was done. His letter was one of the compendium sort he favoured, complaining not only about pay, but about delays in prize money, the poor quality of the provisions, the government's use of Spanish prisoners who had sabotaged the manufacture of the rockets, and the rigid nature of his orders, which had hampered the squadron's operations.[19] Zenteno replied in detail, firmly correcting Cochrane's wilder claims. He pointed out that all cash seized during 1819 had already been distributed; that prize money for the *Maria Isabel* and for ships taken before January 1819 had been fully paid; that the hold-up relating to ships captured after that date was entirely due to the fact that Cochrane's staff – Dean, Stevenson and Hoseason – had failed to submit the proper paperwork; that prisoners of war had *not* been used on the skilled work of making rockets; and that Cochrane had in fact been given full authority to act independently within the spirit of his instructions.[20] As was their custom, Cochrane's entourage ensured that his letter received wide circulation. Zenteno's reply did not. Then, while the two men argued, on 8 May the officers of the *San Martin* downed tools and refused duty, being supported by a round-robin signed by 33 officers representing all six warships that were in harbour at the time.[21] Cochrane dealt sternly with the outbreak and put the *San Martin*'s officers under temporary arrest. But the petition, plus Cochrane's threat, must have helped to do the trick, and by 30 May the government had managed to raise enough money to pay the squadron's arrears up to the end of the previous December.

During 1820, the priority of the Chilean Government was to prepare for the forthcoming invasion of Peru – the last, and long awaited, showdown with the Spanish Empire in the Americas. San Martin – now back from the Argentine – O'Higgins and Zenteno were preoccupied with raising huge amounts of money, assembling troops, finding equipment, guns and supplies and impelling the inefficient and under-funded marine departments to ensure that the navy was mobilised, manned and ready. Indeed, the challenge of organising and supplying the transport needed for the troops was so obviously beyond the competence of the Commandancia of Marine, that a private company had to be created to do the job. In these circumstances, the manner of Lord Cochrane's protests can hardly have been welcomed: but the navy would play a crucial part in the invasion, and it must have been clear that its effectiveness depended on the distribution of pay. Thus, in spite of its hectoring tone, Cochrane's intervention was accepted as a positive element in the planning of the invasion.

Chapter 7
PLOTS AND PARANOIA

By the middle of 1820, the Chilean Navy's pay problems may have been settled, but to the dismay of the government, Lord Cochrane's complaints did not stop. This time they were caused by personality clashes within the officer corps which the Vice Admiral seemed to be stimulating rather than containing. The leadership challenge facing Lord Cochrane was certainly not easy. In creating a navy, the greatest problem for O'Higgins and his government had been to find officers and sailors to man and fight their ships. Chile was a continental country, few people were seafarers, and there was little maritime tradition. Filling the gap with experienced British and American sailors seemed an ideal solution. But there were disadvantages. These men were fighting principally for pay and, although many were attracted by the cause of freedom, there was no shared patriotic tradition. The principal focus of their loyalty therefore became the ships in which they served and the captains who commanded them. American Consul General Prevost bluntly summarised the situation – and Cochrane's achievements – in a dispatch sent in September 1819. 'When I take into view', he wrote:

the materials with which he had to operate, I think he

deserves infinite praise for having maintained the Sovereignty of the Ocean. He had difficulties to encounter in the organisation of the marine and in the discipline of the crews that would have appalled a less determined character – men of every grade and description assembled from different parts of the Globe for the purpose of plunder as of promoting the cause of freedom have by his address, firmness and perseverance been subdued into perfect order.[1]

Prevost painted an over-optimistic picture. As time went on, the difficulties of managing such heterogeneous crews increased, and the lack of cohesion in the officer corps became clear. True there were some 40 foreign sea officers who were present for the whole of the campaign: but there was an equal number who came, served for short periods, and then went. To unite such a group and instil a common ethos required extraordinary qualities.

At first, Cochrane did wonders for the newly formed Chilean Navy. His social position as the son of an earl and his reputation as a fighting captain gave him an unquestioned authority. Under his influence, the Chilean Navy adopted the regulations, signals and behaviour of the British Navy; and his aggressive tactics soon gave the squadron successes and achievements of which it could be proud. But as time went on, the negative side of his character became more and more pronounced. Maria Graham was later to write 'the state of the Chilean Navy required a man of prudence as well as courage, of temper as well as firmness ... and (Lord Cochrane's) gentle and courteous manner ... was admirably calculated to conciliate all parties'.[2] Alas, there is no evidence she was right. Cochrane may have exerted great personal magnetism on those immediately around him, but he seemed unable to inspire those who were not. With close friends or inferiors he was affable and interesting, but others remember him as being tall and round shouldered with an awkward manner and a monosyllabic mode of speech that was uninspiring.

The officers of the Chilean Navy came from a variety of backgrounds and had been appointed in a variety of ways. Cochrane's first task in imposing his authority was to take control of the appointment of officers and to insist that all communication between individuals and the Ministry of Marine went through him. There was some resistance to this; but by August 1820, it had become accepted that the appointment of all officers to the fleet had either to be proposed or approved by Lord Cochrane. Unfortunately this was not enough. To ensure the loyalty and cohesion of the squadron when it was not engaged in warlike operations required qualities of leadership that Cochrane did not seem to possess. Indeed, things were made worse by his personal style of working – notably his favouritism towards his followers, his lack of interest in routine administration, and his consequent reliance on a widely mistrusted staff. As a contemporary observer, John Thomas, so delicately put it Lord Cochrane's 'extraordinary mind does not appear formed for those small details, a strict attention to which is indispensable to good discipline'.[3] The position was not helped by an unease in the squadron about the fairness with which Cochrane was distributing prize money. There were constant rumours that he was more concerned with getting his own share than with securing the rights of others.[4] Thomas again put it in a nutshell when he wrote of Lord Cochrane that 'to pronounce an accurate opinion of a character full of inconsistencies and, under the greatest extremes, of all that is good, and all that is bad, is no easy task. ... He is brave to excess, kind and indulgent to his followers ... and most fertile in snares and plans for entrapping and defeating the enemy. ... With these extraordinary talents he possesses those of the keenest calculator in money matters, and pecuniary calculations maintain an ascendancy in his thoughts.'[5]

The result of all this, was that the Chilean officer corps did not behave like a Nelsonian 'Band of Brothers'. As reflected in the words of contemporary observers like John Thomas, they had ability and experience as fighting seamen, but standards of reliability and discipline could be poor. There were many examples of captains trying to act independently, disobeying orders to go in search of prizes unless under Cochrane's immediate supervision, and of leaving their ships without permission – often in order to lobby for promotion ashore. There was also constant bickering between individuals. Off Callao, Lieutenant Bealy publicly accused Wilkinson of the *San Martin* of cowardice; Claudius Charles, recently appointed to command the *Rising Star* when she arrived, had two blazing rows with Captain Ramsey in front of the whole crew when he was a passenger on *Chacabuco*, during which he denounced him as a drunkard and challenged him to a duel; Lieutenant Woolridge, on receiving orders to help water a transport, told Captain Delano to go to hell; and Lieutenant Ford Morgell, at regular intervals, was censured no less than three times by Captains Carter, Cobbett and Crosbie for insolence and insubordination.[6] None of these incidents provoked more than a mild reprimand from the commander-in-chief. At times, Cochrane's own behaviour was little better. Almost as soon as he arrived, he was involved in an altercation with Captain Carter when he attempted to move members of the *Intrepido*'s Argentine crew to the *O'Higgins*. In the public row that followed, Cochrane accused Carter of 'learning his logic in the bogs of Ireland', to which Carter – who was well known for both his rowdy socialising and hasty temper –

snapped back that he at least 'had understanding and firmness enough not to be made a dupe in a Stock Exchange fraud' and put his hand on his sword hilt.[7] There was even an argument with his 'follower' Robert Forster when Cochrane resumed command of the blockade of Callao in July 1821 and ordered him away on a cruise. A furious Forster boarded the flagship and confronted Cochrane, accusing him of sending him away after six months of blockade duty so as to deprive him of the prize money that would accrue when the port fell.[8]

Cochrane was not helped by the system of patronage he operated at the time. In the Royal Navy it was common for senior figures to attract groups of adherents, or 'followers', round them – men on whom they could rely, and who received special favours in return for their loyalty and support. In Chile, Cochrane acquired such a group. Some were excellent men – like Thomas Sackville Crosbie who later followed him to Brazil and Greece; John Pascoe Grenfell, who became a Brazilian admiral; and William Miller of the marines who became a Peruvian General. Others were not. There were people like Henry Cobbett – nephew of Cochrane's old radical ally William Cobbett – who browbeat his subordinates in Chile just as he had bullied Marryat in Cochrane's frigate in 1809; Ford Morgell, a brave, even rash officer, but one who was notorious for his quarrelsome nature and his addiction to gambling; and, of course, Cochrane's staff – Stevenson, Dean and Hoseason. The last two were to cause Cochrane endless difficulties and were eventually to sue him for huge sums of money. Dean was always on the lookout for ways of adapting Cochrane's financial affairs to his own advantage, and was later described by John Miers as 'a complete swindler who has proved to be a monster of ingratitude for your friendly services towards him'.[9] Admittedly, Miers never had a good word to say about anybody, but by the time he wrote these words, Dean had provided ample evidence of the devious way in which he operated. Stevenson's problem was that he was a gossip and inexperienced in naval matters and procedures. Indeed, his handing of the squadron's prize affairs was partly responsible for the general discontent.

Likewise, while Cochrane treated followers such as Morgell and Dean with indulgence – and seemed to find it difficult to dismiss or reprimand even the most inept – his attitude to others was cold and distant. And, after the initial euphoria of his arrival in Chile, the restless and suspicious elements in his personality began to assert themselves. Essentially Cochrane saw the world and its inhabitants in terms of black and white – those who were not for him must be against him. It took little for a person to be put in the latter category, and his inner circle kept him fully informed as to likely suspects. Cochrane, who was depressed by the reverses off Callao, began to believe that he was being secretly criticised by disloyal subordinates. As early as December 1819, he was writing 'I know to the marrow all who are about me; as well as the conduct and character, and the secret acts and plots, of others who little suspect it.'[10]

Outside the writings of Cochrane's intimates, there is no evidence to support these suspicions. Indeed, the performance of the squadron in action off the coasts of Peru had been admirable, and the chief suspects – Captains Guise and Spry – had taken leading parts in the various engagements. Guise had been wounded in the initial foray against Callao and had led the attack on Pisco, while Spry had been praised in Cochrane's dispatches for the attempt with rockets and explosion vessels. But once his suspicions were aroused, Cochrane was always able to find evidence to justify them. Guise, for example, had been disappointed when the job of senior captain went to Forster. Cochrane soon convinced himself that Guise was so resentful that he and his followers were plotting to get him the supreme command.[11] This was actually an astonishing allegation since Blanco Encalada was clearly the only possible successor.

Likewise, Guise was neither secretive nor a plotter. If anything he was too open and honest. A proud man, who was accustomed to mixing with senior and aristocratic officers, he was neither overawed by Lord Cochrane nor afraid to speak his mind. Towards the end of 1819, for example, Guise was unwise enough to question Cochrane's allocation of prize money. He was concerned that during the blockade of Callao and the raids on the Peruvian coast, Cochrane had appointed no captain to the *O'Higgins*, and was therefore claiming not only the commander-in-chief's one-eighth share of prizes taken, but the captain's two-eighth's as well! The brig *Potrillo*, for example, captured at Valdivia, carried $19,360 in specie of which $9680 was retained by the Chilean Government and the remaining $9680 paid to the captors. From the government's half, Cochrane received the agreed admiral's share of $1210; and from the captors' half he claimed both the admiral's and captain's shares – that is, $3630. In other words, the prize money payment Cochrane received totalled $4840 – the same amount as was shared between all the other officers and men put together.[12] Guise thought this was unfair and reminded Cochrane that as a British Member of Parliament he had denounced officials for holding two jobs and two salaries simultaneously.[13] This touched a raw nerve. It was also a sensitive area, since the shortages of money and delays in pay that had caused trouble on the *Lautaro* and the *Chacabuco* in Cochrane's first months of command continued to haunt the squadron until the end.

Guise's plain speaking on the subject did him no good. Cochrane resented any kind of criticism – and remembered it – so that 35 years later, when writing the *Narrative of Services*, he added Guise's name to those whom Stevenson's book had accused of disaffection and plots. But at the time, no one saw him in this way. Contemporary descriptions of him are favourable, John Thomas noting that, in addition to being a good seaman, his manners and civility made him respected and admired by all who met him.[14] Even Cochrane's partisans, Stevenson and Maria Graham described him as 'a good natured, gentlemanlike man'.[15] As a result, they refused to believe he could be the villain of the piece, and found it more comfortable to believe that his follower, the humbly born Captain Spry, was his evil genius. John Tooker Spry was from an obscure branch of a Cornish family who had joined the Royal Navy as a Second Class Ship's Boy on *Nimrod* in 1803, and had eventually risen to Midshipman. After service in the Channel, Spry arrived in the West Indies in 1805 but, lacking influence, had spent the next four years being passed from *Nimrod* to *Wolverine*, *Pelouis*, *Neptune* and then *Slatira* without promotion. His luck, however, changed in 1810, when he was posted to the cutter *Liberty*, then commanded by Lieutenant Martin Guise. Guise made Spry a sub-lieutenant and encouraged him to take the lieutenant's examination and achieve promotion on 17 July 1813. He finished the war with commissioned service in various vessels on the North America station.[16] From this time on, Spry accepted Guise as his patron, and accompanied him to Chile as commander of the former *Hecate* in 1818.

Neither Spry's lowly background nor his equally lowly stature seemed to have endeared him to the inner circle of the aristocrat Lord Cochrane. Reflecting their view, Maria Graham (who never met him), described him as an adventurer and 'a low minded man'.[17] Unfortunately, the republican atmosphere of Chile had made Spry free with his views, and his private conversations had been reported back. At the time, Lord Cochrane had shrugged off the allegations that Spry and Worster had criticised his use of his title, and that they had 'caballed' over 'two commodores' – but the seed of suspicion had been planted and Spry had been identified as one of those who were 'against' him. The reputations of both Guise and Spry were subsequently damned in the memoirs of Cochrane and his partisans and the animosity was soon extended to cover all the officers who served under them in *Lautaro* and *Galvarino*.

It is difficult to read the details of Cochrane's campaign against Guise, Spry, Worster, Alvarez Jonte and other subordinates without a feeling of unease and sympathy for them. On the other hand, it is difficult not to feel sympathy for Cochrane himself. His self doubt and his suspicious temperament not only compromised the careers of others; it destroyed his own peace of mind and made it impossible for him to enjoy his own undoubted achievements. Indeed, in the period following Valdivia, Cochrane's obsession that there were plots and dissension within the squadron made it impossible for him to relax and bask in the glory of an astonishing victory. Instead he convinced himself that his supposed detractors – notably Spry – were part of the Zenteno-inspired conspiracy to have him court-martialled, and that only news of the capture of Valdivia had prevented it. There is no evidence for any of this, nor any likelihood that it is true. Indeed, it would have been physically impossible for Spry to have been involved as he was absent on blockade duty in Peruvian waters from September 1819 until 24 February 1820 – well after news of Cochrane's triumph at Valdivia had arrived in Valparaiso.[18]

Matters came to a head on 11 July 1820, when Cochrane had Guise arrested and demanded a court martial. He was charged with 'endeavouring in ... various acts of disobedience ... to set at defiance and bring into contempt the authority of his superior officer, the commander-in-chief'. The papers relating to the case, however, reveal little of substance. What is clear is that Cochrane's entourage had been watching Guise for months in order to accumulate complaints against him. These were then assembled into a dozen charges, the most serious being – that 'on a certain date' he had failed to report the arrest and release of an American brig; that he had been negligent in discharging a lieutenant; that he had allowed an officer ashore without reporting it; that he had been slow in sending boats to a vessel in difficulties; that he had allowed his crew to be paid before that of the *O'Higgins*; and that he had detained a ship although '*Lautaro* did not have the guard'. And with Guise under arrest, Cochrane's men were able to search the frigate's books for mistakes. This led to two more charges – failing to report deficiencies in carpenters' stores, and 'falsifying', that is, miscalculating, crew numbers.[19]

Whatever it thought of the charges, the Chilean Government was not prepared to be distracted from its preparations for the invasion of Peru. They had better things to do than become sidetracked by the court martial of an experienced and able captain. They therefore refused Cochrane's request and restored Guise to command. Cochrane again threatened to resign. But the Chileans had no intention of losing their greatest maritime asset either, and urged the Vice Admiral to remain. Zenteno wrote :

At a moment when the services of the State are of the highest importance and the personal services of Your Lordship indispensable, the Supreme Director with the profoundest sentiments of regret has received your resignation which, should it be admitted, would involve the future operations of the army of liberty in the New World in certain ruin, and ultimately replace in Chile, your adopted home, the tyranny which Your Lordship abhors. ... HE the Supreme Director commands me to inform Your Lordship that should you persist in resigning command of the squadron which has been honoured by bearing your flag – the cause of terror and dismay to our enemies and to the Glory of all true Americans – it would be a day of universal mourning in the New World.[20]

Cochrane decided to stay, and agreed with Guise to let bygones be bygones. Indeed, Guise was further mollified by being promoted to the rank of captain-of-navío. But the atmosphere immediately deteriorated once again when Cochrane's entourage excluded *Lautaro* from a prize money distribution made to the rest of the squadron on 25 July![21] Rumours that their chief had offered his resignation had, however, been received with dismay by many officers, and his followers quickly rallied in support. Although they presumably assumed that there was a nobler reason for the threat than annoyance at the government's refusal to court-martial Guise, on 18 and 19 July, five serving captains and 15 lieutenants signed petitions pledging support and threatening to resign in sympathy with their commander-in-chief. They even put their commissions in his hands to surrender with his own.[22] This was gratifying for Cochrane, although he could not have failed to notice that four captains and eight lieutenants had not added their names.

Then came another distraction. The proposed Guise court martial had accidentally entangled John Tooker Spry. Ironically, when Cochrane arrested Guise, he had moved Spry – who had recently been promoted – to *Lautaro* to replace him. But when, two days later, Guise was restored to his ship, the unfortunate Spry had to be moved again. Spry was now a captain-of-frigate and there was only one post at this level of seniority which was vacant and, indeed, had been for over a year – that of captain of the *O'Higgins* and therefore Flag Captain to Cochrane himself. The Minister of Marine – probably knowing nothing of Cochrane's antipathy to Spry and anxious to get on with the invasion – innocently thought he could kill two birds with one stone by moving him into it. But Cochrane was furious, seeing it as part of the great Zenteno inspired conspiracy against him. In the *Narrative of Services*, he disingenuously writes 'I had nothing against Captain Spry personally ... but had great doubts as to the reason for the appointment ... perhaps to prevent me doing anything beyond keep the Spanish in check.'[23] In fact, when Spry boarded the flagship to take up his post, he was astonished when Cochrane publicly denounced him for being a spy like Alvarez Jonte.[24] Once again, the government, anxious to get on with the invasion preparations, bowed to Cochrane's wishes and agreed to replace Spry with one of his followers, Commander Thomas Sackville Crosbie – even though he had to be specially promoted to captain in order to fill the post.

It was now August, and preparations for the invasion were at last reaching their climax. Valparaiso Bay was alive with launches, water hoys and supply boats. On the ships the final touches were put to paintwork, rigging and sails, while tons of supplies and munitions in kegs, barrels and casks were rowed to the side, swayed on board and stowed away in the hold. Finally, San Martin's troops marched down to the dockside with their bands and equipment to be ferried across to the hired transports. A special landing stage was built to speed their embarkation. Physically, the squadron itself was in good shape. The appearance of pay and prize money had done wonders for the remaining officers and men and recruitment had gone well. Aided by a hot press, a wave of patriotic fervour and proclamations from San Martin promising bonuses to the men on the liberation of Lima, Cochrane's warships were almost completely manned. The only difference was that now, three-quarters of the sailors were Chilean – many of the foreign seamen having packed their bags and left.[25]

Chapter 8
INVASION AND BLOCKADE

On 20 August 1820, amid noisy celebration, the great expedition against Peru sailed from Valparaiso. In command as Captain General was José de San Martin at the head of 4500 troops, with the Argentine General Las Heras, who had forced the western route during the crossing of the Andes three years before, as his chief-of-staff. It was a multinational army with units from Chile and the Argentine and volunteers from various other South American and European countries. It was also multiracial, with white, mulatto and black troops. The men, with their supplies, artillery and 800 horses, were packed into troop transports under the supervision of Paul Delano, the American captain who had delivered the *Curiato* to Chile the year before. There were 13 ships altogether – *Potrillo* carrying powder and munitions, and *Argentina*, *Magueña*, *Gadiana*, *Empenadora*, *Santa Rosa*, *Perla*, *Galandrina*, *Aguila*, *Dolores*, *Begonia*, *Peruvana* and *Jerezina* with troops. The last five were prizes that Cochrane's agent had freighted to the transport company. The escort was provided by Lord Cochrane's squadron and comprised the flagship *O'Higgins* (Captain Thomas Sackville Crosbie), the frigates *San Martin* (Captain William Wilkinson), and *Lautaro* (Captain Martin Guise), the corvette *Independencia* (Captain Robert

Forster), the brigs *Galvarino* (Captain John Tooker Spry), *Araucano* (Captain Thomas Carter) and *Pueyrredon* (Lieutenant William Prunier) and the schooner *Montezuma* (Lieutenant George Young) for San Martin's personal use. For the first three days the wind blew foul, making the task of assembling the convoy difficult; but after that it blew from the southeast bringing the invasion force to within striking distance of Peru in a fortnight.

As well as his military commanders, San Martin's staff included the civilian aides who were to assist in the political task of liberation. There was the sinister Bernardo Monteagudo, a talented but ruthless Argentine radical in the fanatical mould of the French Revolution. The difference was that in South America, opponents were shot not guillotined. O'Higgins's rivals, the Carrera brothers, had been two victims of Monteagudo's policy: there were to be many more. At the other extreme was the diplomat Juan García del Rio. Born in Cartagena in New Granada, but educated in Europe and England where he had absorbed the principles of the Enlightenment, García del Rio was a minor philosopher and the pioneer of a free press in both Chile, where he founded *El Telegrafo* and *El Sol de Chile*, and in Peru. At a less influential level were two other staff figures – the self effacing and tactful Tomas Guido, who was San Martin's devoted follower and acted as principal aide de camp; and the Englishman James Paroissien, whose journal and correspondence recorded the events of the invasion.[1] The accuracy of this journal has been questioned, and Paroissien's criticisms of Cochrane have been discounted by at least one biographer as reflecting little more than the envy of the son of a Barking schoolmaster towards an aristocrat.[2] But the document gives an invaluable insight into San Martin's reactions to the antics of the brilliant but wayward Vice Admiral and is given credibility by the fact that Paroissien – rather than being a distant detractor – was a friend of both Cochrane and his wife.

Some biographers have suggested that the command of the expeditionary force was divided – with San Martin being in charge of the military campaign, and Cochrane responsible for what happened at sea. This was not the case. Cochrane's instructions made it clear from the beginning that San Martin was in command, and that he was under the Captain General's orders. They began:

> The object of the present expedition is to free Peru from her odious vassalage to Spain and to elevate her to the rank of a free and sovereign nation. ... The Captain General of the army, D José de San Martin, is the Chief to whom the Government and the Republic have confided the exclusive direction of the operations of this great enterprise. ... I have consequently the satisfaction to advise Your Lordship that ... you should act precisely according to the Plans that General San Martin shall order in regard to both the point of disembarkation, and the succeeding movements which Your Lordship may have to make with the squadron; and that Your Lordship should not act on your own account with either the whole or any part of the vessels of war which you command.[3]

The Chilean Government knew that Cochrane would find this subordinate position uncongenial. Indeed, they had already had a taste of his preference for independent action and of the insubordinate streak in his character. In an attempt to mollify him and head off trouble, O'Higgins concluded Cochrane's orders with the pious hope that,

> It is unnecessary to recommend most earnestly to Your Lordship the most exact observance of my

resolution in all your areas of responsibility. Your Lordship has given sufficient proofs that your military conduct has followed no other course than that indicated by the Government, and I flatter myself that Your Lordship, conforming to this, and to your own principles, will present yourself to the gratitude of America as the hero of its liberty.[4]

The purpose of the liberating expedition had been decided early. Peru was not seen as enemy territory but as a sister South American country whose independence had been prevented by the presence of occupying Spanish military forces. In addition to tactical flare, San Martin had the ability to think at a high strategic level and fully understood that Peru could not be liberated without the active support of the population. He did not therefore see himself as launching a simple invasion of the country. His purpose was to neutralise the Spanish army so that the Peruvians could liberate themselves. He made this strategy clear on many occasions. San Martin was optimistic of his chances of success, and his confidence had been reinforced when news arrived that the Great Expedition assembling at Cadiz to impose Ferdinand VII's rule on the Americas was no more. In January 1820, a mutiny led by Major Raphael Riego, had spread like wildfire through the ranks and had destroyed it as a military force.

And there was more. The mutiny had triggered a series of events that resulted in the overthrow of Ferdinand's government of reactionaries and the re-adoption of the liberal Constitution of 1812. Led by the well-meaning Augustin Arguelles, the new ministers believed that the patriot struggle in South America – like their own – had been stimulated by opposition to despotic rule from Madrid, rather than rule from Madrid as such, and they

naively assumed that with the coming of constitution-
alism the problem would go away. They therefore became
preoccupied with the task of enacting a series of pro-
gressive laws for an Empire which, in fact, no longer
existed. Spanish generals were ordered to talk rather than
to fight, and commissioners were sent to the four corners
of South America to negotiate the terms on which, it was
confidently expected, the revolutionaries would return to
their allegiance. Unfortunately, this policy was based
upon a totally false premise and got nowhere. The
commissioners met no one – except San Martin – and
achieved nothing. All it did was to deny Viceroy Pezuela
in Peru any hope of reinforcement, to lower the morale of
the Spanish armies in the field, and to cause splits and
dissension. San Martin knew all this, and was convinced
that the position of the Viceroy and his generals would
get worse once they were faced with a liberating army on
the ground. He was therefore in no hurry, and believed
that, even without spectacular victories, it was only a
matter of time before Peru fell into his hands like a ripe
plum.

As military preparations gathered momentum during the
first half of 1820, the royalists in Peru knew exactly what
was going on in Chile. Sympathisers in Valparaiso and
Santiago and the captains of visiting merchant ships kept
them fully informed. The only details that were unknown
were the exact date and place of the invasion. The failure of
Cochrane's attacks by rockets on Callao had, however,
been presented as a great victory by the Spanish authorities
who had showered medals on the defenders. Cochrane's
efforts were mocked in the press, and Lima was treated to
a theatrical performance called *Drama Naval sobre el ataque
del Callao*, which starred San Martin and Cochrane, and
portrayed a lecherous O'Higgins entering into a pact with
the Devil to gain Kitty's favours.[5]

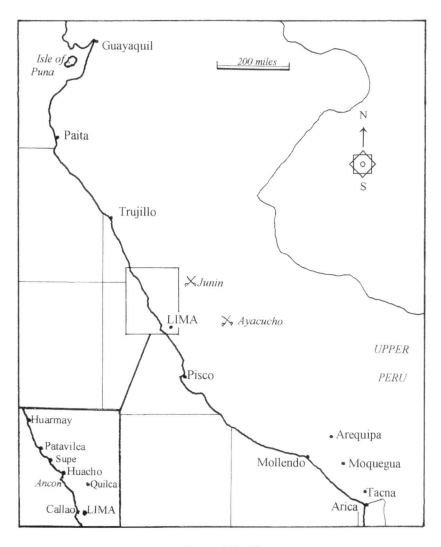

Peru 1819–23

With the disappearance of Cochrane at the end of 1819 and the lifting of the Chilean blockade, ships of the Spanish navy were at sea once more, searching for enemy privateers and transferring men, powder and arms to the more vulnerable outposts. In February the frigates *Esmeralda* and *Venganza* sailed to visit the northern ports and collect the *Prueba*, which was completing her refit in Guayaquil.[6] On 2

April – a week after she had arrived from the north – *Prueba* herself sailed with the brig *Manipur* and the armed ship *Javeria* carrying reinforcements back to Guayaquil. The flotilla returned to Callao on 8 August having sighted and driven aground the patriot privateer *Rosa de los Andes* commanded by Captain John Illingworth on the way. It was Illingworth and this ship, then named *Rose*, that had delivered Cochrane to Chile 18 months before in November 1818. Meanwhile, *Venganza* and *Esmeralda* waited in idleness in Callao. It was not until June that there were sufficient stores and money to prepare the two frigates for sea, and even then – to Pezuela's annoyance – their captains seemed defeatist and unwilling to take active measures against the enemy.[7] In such circumstances, there was little the Viceroy could do but wait for the patriots to strike.

He did not have to wait long. On 8 September, San Martin's liberating army disembarked at Pisco, 100 miles southeast of Callao and Lima. The town was secured and enough rum and provisions were seized to keep the army and the squadron supplied for months. San Martin then slowly began to occupy the surrounding lowlands while a force of 1000 men under Colonel Juan Antonio Alvares de Arenales pushed northwards to threaten Lima from the east and raise rebellion in the interior.

Relations between the Captain General and the Vice Admiral were strained from the beginning. Routine naval work like escorting a convoy made Cochrane bored. It also made him careless, so that on the voyage from Valparaiso he managed to lose two transports, the *Aguila* carrying the 4th Infantry Regiment and the *Santa Rosa* loaded with artillery.[8] Paroissien's journal reflected San Martin's concern when he complained 'the ships-of-war are spread about in all directions but to no purpose. Everybody who pretends to know about naval affairs on board the *San*

Martin says that the business of the convoy is conducted in a very unsailorlike manner.'[9] As a result, when San Martin arrived at Pisco he found himself without any artillery and lacking a fifth of his infantry.[10] He was not pleased. Neither was the atmosphere improved by the knowledge that the slow sailing *Aguila* had been one of the five prizes supplied by Hoseason as a business speculation on Cochrane's behalf at a charge of $8 a ton! The missing *Aguila* appeared the following day, but the *Santa Rosa* did not arrive until 16 September.

Meanwhile Cochrane, whose instincts were totally aggressive, was scathing about San Martin's choice of a landing place, and argued that he should have dis-embarked nearer to Lima and launched an immediate attack on the city.[11] He had even had a good natured bet with Paroissien, wagering a crate of champagne that Lima would be taken quickly and with ease.[12] Other military observers took the opposite view. Captain Basil Hall, who had recently arrived on the scene in HMS *Conway*, thought that the landing at Pisco was a masterstroke.[13] The town lay to the southeast of the capital and, with the wind blowing constantly northwards in this latitude, a re-embarkation and landing further along the coast could be made at any time. The possibility that the final attack might fall somewhere else, and the distraction caused by Colonel Arenales and his troops, threw the Viceroy into a state of uncertainty about San Martin's intentions and left him undecided as to whether to march against Pisco, or against Arenales, or to remain in position to defend Lima. This confusion, plus the impact of the new orders from Madrid, was enough to make the Viceroy offer an armistice in the middle of September. Guido and García del Rio hastened to Miraflores near Lima to discuss terms, but the Viceroy had no authority to discuss any kind of autonomy and the talks broke down after a week. Nevertheless, with his strategy apparently working, San Martin re-embarked his army on 28 October and headed for Ancon to begin operations north of Callao.

During all this time, the Chilean ships had patrolled the adjacent coastline, their commander-in-chief fretting at what he saw as enforced inactivity. The transfer of the army and squadron further north was a welcome move. As before, Cochrane's handling of the squadron and convoy at sea was worrying. On only the first day of the voyage, Paroissien confided to his journal:

> The Admiral has as usual left them (the warships) to run a great distance ahead and it was in vain that the General made signals to order the headmost ships to lay to and await the convoy. ... Not a day passes but brings some proof of (Lord Cochrane's) unfortunate selfish disposition and there is not a man in the fleet who does not lament his carelessness in not keeping the convoy together, although we are within a few miles of the enemy's port. He has not given the least order about the actions of the transports in case of action, nor do the ships of war know what they should do. The Admiral cheerfully neglects this and seems to suppose that his only duty is taking prizes.[14]

The convoy was off Lima on 29 October. Leaving *San Martin* and *Galvarino* to escort the transports carrying the army the remaining 25 miles north to the scruffy little port of Ancon, Cochrane turned aside with the rest of the squadron and began to enforce the blockade that the Chilean Government had declared on 20 August. Unfortunately the blockade was to create more problems for the Chileans than it solved. At the end of 1818, Viceroy Pezuela had decided to increase the flow of supplies and expand his revenues by allowing foreign ships and goods to enter

Peru. It took time for neutrals to respond, but by 1820, dozens of British and American ships were arriving in Peruvian waters. As far as Cochrane was concerned, all those carrying contraband of war or Spanish cargoes were liable to seizure. Indeed, immediately on arrival he took the British *Rebecca* and the American *Canton* in the harbour of Pisco. Cochrane's actions came as an unpleasant surprise to British merchants. Only a month before, they had written to Captain Shirreff of *Andromache* expressing satisfaction at the way Cochrane had gone out of his way to avoid interfering with their trade.[15] Now he began to round up British as well as Spanish merchant vessels.

Official Protests from foreign naval commanders in the area quickly followed. No one disputed the fact that Chile had the right to declare a blockade and arrest any vessels that broke it. Indeed, the decrees that laid down the conduct of the blockade closely followed international practice. But for a blockade to be legitimate, there was a basic rule that the number of warships enforcing it had to be adequate to the task. The problem was that the Chileans had declared the Peruvian coast under blockade from 21° 48′ to 2° 12′ south – a distance of 2000 miles! Sir Thomas Hardy – Nelson's old flag captain at Trafalgar who had now replaced Bowles as British commander-in-chief – protested, pointing out that Cochrane's force was too small to be able to control such a vast area, and that the Chilean blockade could not therefore be accepted as legitimate.[16] The Americans took the same view. *Hyperion*, *Conway* and the USS *Macedonian* had been providing escorts for merchantmen for some time. Now the maritime powers began to increase their presence in the area. Sir Thomas Hardy rounded the Horn in the frigate *Creole* to be on hand personally and ordered the 74-gun *Superb* to follow. The American consul made it known that the 74-gun ship *Franklin* was on its way. Then, in January 1821, a French squadron comprising the 74-gun *Colosse*, the *Galathée* and *L'Echo* appeared. This caused some alarm until Rear Admiral Julien innocently assured the Chileans that his ships were only on a training and fact-finding cruise.

In theory, the British commander-in-chief, Sir Thomas Hardy, robustly rejected the legality of the Chilean blockade of Peru. But in practice, his orders to treat the Chilean authorities with kid gloves and to avoid any kind of provocation stopped him taking decisive action. The unfortunate Captain Searle of *Hyperion* fell a victim to this policy after a furious confrontation with Cochrane over the seizure of the *Rebecca* at Pisco – the second time Searle had found himself in conflict with the Chilean Vice Admiral.[17] The first occasion had been in May 1820, when Searle had arrived at Valparaiso to find Cochrane detaining a number of British ships on the grounds that their departures had been embargoed. He had immediately taken the post road up to Santiago and had received reassurance from O'Higgins personally that no embargo existed and that the ships were free to leave. Returning to Valparaiso with the news, Searle had been astonished when Cochrane still refused to allow the ships to sail. After a frustrating week in which all his overtures were rejected, the British captain took matters into his own hands and escorted the *Inspector* out with *Hyperion* cleared for action.[18] On that occasion, Searle had received a rap over the knuckles from the Admiralty for his undiplomatic conduct. After the second, he and his frigate were recalled to England. From the perspective of the British captain, however, even this cloud had a silver lining. According to Thomas Collings, the crippled clerk of HMS *Owen Glendower*, when *Hyperion* returned round Cape Horn she carried remittances of 'freight' from British merchants worth $3 million (or £600,000) in coin and bullion, half of which had been loaded at Callao.[19]

The percentage that Captain Searle received for providing this service would have been around £6000!

From the viewpoint of local British merchants, Hardy's position seemed legalistic and unhelpful. Particularly when compared with that of the United States Navy, whose reaction to finding an American ship in Chilean hands was to take it back by force! In letters to his local merchant community, Hardy told them quite clearly that the Chilean blockade of Peru was illegitimate, but advised them that to avoid trouble it should not be challenged, and that ships and cargoes should keep well clear of the ports in question.[20] Hardy had good reason to give this advice, for he knew that many of the ships involved were liable to seizure because they were indulging in dubious commercial practices. He phrased it delicately in letters to the Admiralty, writing 'the employment of British capital is obliged to be coloured and introduced in various shapes.'[21] What he meant was that, faced with complicated Spanish colonial import regulations on the one hand, and novel Chilean blockading rules on the other, British ships were resorting to a number of shady devices in order to disguise the true origin of their cargoes. These included unloading and reshipping goods at Gibraltar, and carrying two different sets of manifests and papers. O'Higgins and the Chilean Government knew this too, and its blockading decrees explicitly prohibited such practices. But the last thing they wanted were international complications over the arrest of foreign merchantmen. Naval officers who were sensitive to the complications – like Commodore Robert Forster who commanded the blockade from February until July 1821 – realised it too and refrained from scrutinising their papers too closely. Unfortunately, Lord Cochrane was incapable of exercising such subtlety and, to the embarrassment of the Chilean Government, seized neutral vessels without inhibition, exposing with relish the irregularities he found.[22]

By this time, the position of the royalists in Peru was becoming desperate. Foreign observers were struck by the contrast between the prosperity of liberated Chile and the impoverishment of Peru. In Valparaiso, the harbour was packed with shipping, the customs wharfs were piled high with goods, and the anchorage filled with ships unloading foreign merchandise and loading wine and corn. In Peru it was a different story. In Callao, the customs houses were empty, the wharfs were neglected and the few ships at anchor were corralled by gun-boats. The countryside was impoverished after years of war, and the population was depressed, gloomy and suspicious.[23] There was also a general hostility to foreigners, especially the British whose nationals could be seen manning the Chilean warships and whose government was widely believed to be helping the rebels in order to advance its own sinister intentions in the region. In January 1821, Captain William Shirreff, who had arrived with *Andromache* to replace *Hyperion*, even proposed that all British merchants in Lima, together with their property should seek sanctuary on his frigate until the conflict was over. After assurances of protection from the Viceroy, the offer was declined.[24] A month later, two officers from *Conway* were arrested and accused by five sworn witnesses of being members of Cochrane's squadron. Although the charge was blatantly false, the authorities were so frightened by the mob that it took Captain Basil Hall weeks to get them released. The upshot was a ban on officers of the Royal Navy from setting foot ashore.[25]

Chapter 9

THE CAPTURE OF THE
ESMERALDA

In directing naval operations off the coast of Peru, Cochrane was not content with routine blockade duties. As usual, he wanted to achieve something more spectacular. Callao, as before, bristled with guns and was defended by a squadron of warships and gunboats headed by the 40-gun frigate *Esmeralda*, which was armed with a mixture of 12- and 24-pounder cannon and equipped with sufficient stores for a three-month voyage. The other two major Spanish units, *Prueba* and *Venganza*, had sailed on 10 October and had been in Arica embarking troops when news was received of Cochrane's arrival off Callao and of the resumption of the blockade. After a council of war, the two captains had decided to head north for San Blas and Acapulco rather than risk a confrontation with the Chilean squadron.[1] *Esmeralda* therefore became the focus of Cochrane's attention. The destruction of the Spanish frigate would be both a major blow to royalist morale and a triumph for the revolutionary forces. How could he do it? Cochrane's answer, in a plan of typical audacity, was for the squadron's boats to enter the heavily fortified anchorage under the cover of darkness and carry her off in typical Royal Navy style.

Cochrane chose the night of 5 November for the attack, and made his preparations with his usual skill and attention to detail. Some 240 volunteers were selected, all wearing white with blue armbands to aid recognition and carrying pistols, cutlasses and boarding axes. Groups of men were given specific tasks to perform after the frigate had been captured – topmen to release the fore, main and mizzen topsails; axemen to cut the anchor cable; and keepers to secure the squadron's boats. Of these, 14 were to be used in the assault, operating in two divisions. The first, which was to board the *Esmeralda* on the starboard side, was under the command of Cochrane and Captain Crosbie, supported by Lieutenants Esmond, Brown, Morgell, Robertson and Wynter of the *O'Higgins*. The second, which was to attack the frigate's port side, was under Captain Guise, seconded by Lieutenants Bell and Freeman of *Lautaro*, and Lieutenants Grenfell and Gilbert of *Independencia*.

With night well advanced, at 10.30 p.m. the boats pushed off from their mother ships and headed under muffled oars for the gap in the heavily chained boom that sealed off the harbour. Overwhelming an unwary guardboat on the other side, the attackers slid silently through the black water to where the unsuspecting *Esmeralda* lay anchored. They reached the frigate undetected in the darkness, clambered up the sides and launched themselves at the startled defenders, Lord Cochrane in the lead being knocked back into his boat by the butt of a sentry's musket. Many of the *Esmeralda*'s crew had been sleeping on the deck so, although initially taken by surprise, they were able to give a good account of themselves. But the momentum of the Chilean attack was irresistible. After a bloody hand-to-hand struggle on the quarterdeck with swords and pistols against parties led by Guise and Cochrane who had boarded at the port and starboard sides, and those of

Grenfell and Bell who had climbed up the frigate's quarters and over the poop, the Spaniards were forced back to the forecastle where they held out until Guise and Crosbie rallied their men and charged along the gangways. Guise then cleared the lower deck of troops who were firing upwards through the hatches. The *Esmeralda*'s surviving crew dropped their weapons, and Captain Coig surrendered his ship.

Unable to make head or tail of what was happening in the darkened harbour, the shore batteries had been initially confused by the lights Cochrane hoisted into *Esmeralda*'s yard arms in imitation of those shown by neutral warships in the harbour. But the deception had not lasted long. Guided by the clash of steel and the flash of small arms, the Spanish guns began to lay down a heavy fire to prevent the ship's removal. Cochrane had announced that he intended to use the captured frigate as a platform from which to attack other vessels in the harbour and had ordered that, as soon as *Esmeralda* had been secured, Lieutenants Esmond and Morgell of *O'Higgins* should board the brigs *Pezuela* and *Maipú*, while Lieutenants Bell and Robertson of *Lautaro* and Grenfell of *Independencia* cast adrift the nearest hulks and merchantmen.[2] Whether he seriously believed that such a difficult feat was possible is difficult to say. At least one experienced observer, Captain Basil Hall of *Conway*, doubted it, and thought it was just rhetoric to inspire the men.[3] In the event, it proved an impossible ambition: fired by the adrenalin of victory, the British seamen broke into the spirit room and – not for the first time – became dead drunk; while their Chilean comrades began to loot the ship. Indeed, when John Pasco Grenfell and the other lieutenants tried to coax their men into the boats to attack the other ships, they flatly refused, saying that they had done quite enough.[4] In these circumstances Martin Guise, who had taken command when Cochrane was shot in the thigh during the final stages of the struggle, decided to cut the frigate's cable and sail her out. This he did, passing on the way HMS *Hyperion* and the USS *Macedonian*, which had been admiring witnesses to the whole episode – the former silently observing the studied neutrality that Captain Searle's orders required; the latter ringing with cheers and encouragement.

Their pro-Chilean demonstration did the Americans no good. The royalists were convinced that Cochrane could only have carried off the *Esmeralda* with some form of help from the British and Americans. Spanish historians think the same today, and a recent study still maintains that 'the contribution of the cited frigates (*Hyperion* and *Macedonian*) which were anchored within the chains securing the port was to provide intelligence, avoid raising the alarm, rescue patriot seamen who got into difficulties, and raise recognition lights so they could be copied by the captors of *Esmeralda* in order to confuse our ships and shore batteries.'[5] As a result, Captain Downes, who was ashore at the time, was forced to seek refuge in the Governor's Palace, while a boat's crew from the *Macedonian* landing next day to buy provisions was attacked and murdered by a vengeful mob.

The cutting out of the *Esmeralda* was one of Lord Cochrane's finest achievements. Captain Searle called it 'a most brilliant affair … commanded by Lord Cochrane in person, in which he carried (*Esmeralda*) together with a gunboat, from under the batteries and out of the line of defence, and in less than half-an-hour and under sail. This was done so quick and in so masterly a style that I had scarcely time to get out of the line of fire.'[6] It was also a deadly encounter, with the Chileans losing 11 killed and 31 wounded including Cochrane and Grenfell. Spanish losses were estimated at 56 dead, 70 wounded and 204 prisoners. Paroissien, who was no stranger to the aftermath of battles,

The capture of the *Esmeralda* by L. Colet, Club Naval de Valparaiso

boarded the prize two days later to arrange an exchange of prisoners and found the decks still bloody and littered with remains. It was, he wrote, 'a sight too horrible to describe'.[7]

The capture of the *Esmeralda* left Lord Cochrane undisputed master of the coast. The Spanish frigates *Venganza* and *Prueba* were still at large in the Pacific, but after the

115

affair in Callao they played no further role and went entirely on the defensive. San Martin immediately recognised the significance of the event and reported the cutting out of the *Esmeralda* to O'Higgins in glowing terms, writing:

> It is impossible for me to eulogise in proper language the daring enterprise of 5 November, by which Lord Cochrane has decided the superiority of our naval forces, augmented the splendour and power of Chile and secured the success of this campaign. I doubt not that His Excellency the Supreme Director will render the justice due to the worthy chief, the officers and other individuals who have had a share in that successful action.[8]

Six weeks later, San Martin went further, and decreed that the name of the *Esmeralda* should be changed to *Valdivia* in honour of Cochrane and of his victory in capturing that stronghold.[9]

Chapter 10
THE *VALDIVIA* COURT MARTIAL

The news that *Esmeralda* was to be renamed *Valdivia* came as a surprise to Captain Martin Guise who had been moved with his crew to the captured frigate from *Lautaro*. He was also disappointed. Guise expressed his regret when he was told the news by Lord Cochrane himself on the flagship's quarterdeck, explaining that the new name did nothing to commemorate the victory that the capture of the frigate itself represented. In his reply, Cochrane seemed to agree.[1] His officers were also disappointed and, on 2 February 1821, wrote to Guise, lamenting that the new name did nothing to recognise their efforts, pointing out that half of those who had captured the frigate had not been present at the attack on *Valdivia*, and asking him to use his influence with Lord Cochrane to obtain a reconsideration. Likewise, while they approved of Chilean ships being named after revolutionary heroes like San Martin and O'Higgins, they objected to the name of Pedro de Valdivia, one of the most oppressive of Spanish conquistadors!

Cochrane later claimed in his *Narrative of Services* that San Martin had proposed calling the ship *Cochrane* and that the officers wanted *Guise*.[2] There is no evidence or likelihood that either assertion is true. The letter was

signed by all the surviving wardroom officers – Lieutenants Robert Bell and Henry Freeman, Purser James
Frew, Surgeon James Michael and Assistant Surgeon Hugh
Kernan.[3] Guise could detect nothing disrespectful in the
letter, but to be on the safe side, he asked the opinion of
Lieutenant Colonel Miller, an intimate of Cochrane who
had also overheard his conversation with the Vice Admiral
on the *O'Higgins*. Miller said he could see nothing wrong
either[4] – so Captain Guise sent the letter on with a covering
note.

But Lord Cochrane was furious. Still convinced that he
was surrounded with plots and disaffection, Cochrane saw
the letter as part of a conspiracy masterminded by Spry.
Reporting the incident to O'Higgins, he wrote

> No sooner has Captain Spry returned to the squadron
> than the old plotting commenced again. ... I am quite
> vexed to be placed again in a position by this
> meddling, malicious little man in which I must either
> support my challenged authority as an officer or
> renounce the command. Captain Spry thinks I have
> kept him too long at Huacho and has taken this mode
> to induce others to insult me.[5]

The fact that Spry and *Galvarino* were miles from Callao at
the time did not dent Cochrane's conviction that he was
behind the protest. And, given the chance, Cochrane seized
on the opportunity to strike at what he saw as a conspiracy
and ordered that the officers of the *Esmeralda* be court-
martialled. Stunned by the over-reaction, Guise wrote
assuring the Vice Admiral that no disrespect had been
intended and that he would never have sent on the letter if
he had thought it to be the case. In reply, Cochrane
denounced the officers' 'real' intentions, adding that if
Guise was 'resolved to defend, or make party, with persons

who have so conducted themselves, then either you or I *must* resign'.[6]

Guise repeated that his officers were innocent of any insubordination or lack of respect and pleaded with Cochrane to see them personally and to delay any court martial until after the attack on Callao planned for the end of February. When that failed, he wrote to say that it would be impossible for him to serve further if he was to be 'deprived of those officers with whom I have long served, and who have all distinguished themselves under my command' and forced to accept unknown men in their place. But Cochrane refused to budge so, taking him at his word, Guise resigned.[7]

Guise had gone, but Cochrane's attitude to his officers remained implacable. He was unmoved by either protestations of innocence or their service records. All had taken part with Guise in landings on the Peruvian coast and in the cutting out of the *Esmeralda*, and Bell had been present at the capture of the *Maria Isabel* in 1818. Likewise Freeman, who had been a master's mate in the Royal Navy during the Bombardment of Algiers by Lord Exmouth in 1816, had played a prominent role in Cochrane's attack on Callao with rockets and explosion vessels. Many were surprised that at such a crucial moment, time was being wasted on an apparently trivial matter. Cochrane knew that the court martial would disrupt his plans for the next attack, but he still refused to postpone it. His followers ensured that Guise was unjustly blamed for the delay.

The court martial took place on 2 March 1821 before Captains Wilkinson, Crosbie, Prunier and Cobbett, with Robert Forster acting as President. The result had been fixed in advance by Cochrane's entourage who had drafted the charges so as to make a guilty verdict inevitable. There were three – first, sending the letter of 2 February, which excited disrespect to the commander-in-chief by denigrating the victory at Valdivia and which, second, tried to spread dissatisfaction by misrepresenting the name *'Valdivia'*; and, third, by 'insolently' interfering in the renaming of the frigate and holding conversations derogatory to Cochrane. Thus, to prove the charges, all the prosecution had to do was to show the letter had been written.

It was not Cochrane's finest hour. Indeed, the transcript of the court martial reflects the triviality of the incident and hardly disguises the embarrassment of all involved. The cross examination of Martin Guise is illustrative:

Question – On your receiving the order from the Admiral on his first making known to you that the name of *Esmeralda* was to be changed to that of *Valdivia*, did you make any remarks to his Lordship on the subject?

Answer – In the presence of Lt Colonel Miller I told the Admiral on his informing me the ship's name was to be altered to that of *Valdivia* that I was sorry for it for I thought *Esmeralda* was a pretty name and that if it was altered, the manner of her being captured would be forgotten; he answered me by saying "so was he" or words to that effect.

Q – Have you reason to think that the officers of the *Valdivia* were aware that his Lordship coincided in that opinion?

A – Yes, because I informed them myself.

Q – Did the order state that the name of *Valdivia* was changed by the order of the Captain General San Martin?

A – I cannot quite recall but I think it did.

Q – From what passed between you and the Admiral, did you have reason to think that it (the letter) would give any offence to his Lordship or show any disrespect?

A – No certainly not.

Q – Do you consider the letter sent to you a respectful representation on the subject?

A – I do consider it perfectly so.

Q – After forwarding the letter to his Lordship, when did you see him?

A – I think it was two or three hours after.

Q – Did his Lordship express himself displeased on the subject of the letter?

A – Yes.

Q – Did you express your approbation of the letter before this Lordship?

Q – Yes, I did, and apprised him that it had no intention of giving offence.

Q – Did you state your conviction that you were quite satisfied that, from your knowledge of your officers, they could mean no disrespect to his Lordship?

A – I have done so repeatedly.

Q – Was the letter in question such a one as you could have sent to an Admiral in the service of England on a similar subject?

(*The Court directed that this question should not be put.*)

Q – Did that explanation to his Lordship on behalf of your officers appear unsatisfactory?

A – Yes, it did not appear to satisfy his Lordship at all.

Q – When did you next see his Lordship?

A – The same evening, as soon as I heard the officers had been put under arrest.

Q – What was the nature of your conversation with his Lordship on your going on board the *O'Higgins*?

A – We spoke of many things, but the first was upon endeavouring to impress upon his Lordship's mind that the officers of the *Valdivia* had a high regard and respect for him.

Q – Did you remonstrate with his Lordship on the inconvenience to which the service would be exposed by the measure his lordship had adopted?

A – Yes I did state that my conviction was that the said officers intended the letter rather as a compliment than otherwise and apprised him that I would on no account appear to justify disrespectful conduct in my officers to their superiors.

Q –Did you at any time solicit that his Lordship

should see these officers whose wish it was to remove the unfavourable impression made on his Lordship's mind in consequence of their representation?

A – I asked him if he would see them.

Q – Did his lordship refuse that request?

A – Yes, his lordship's answer was 'I have seen too much of the world not to see their real intentions'.

Q – Did his Lordship say what that intention was?

A – No, I think not.

Q – Will you be good enough to state to the court your opinion of the character of your officers?

A – I take great pleasure in stating to the court that during the period in which the officers were under my command, they conducted themselves entirely to my satisfaction; and I have to express that on all occasions they were foremost in showing their zeal for the service and were always most anxious and ready to volunteer on every occasion, however hazardous, in which they might render service to the state and raise the character and reputation of their gallant commander-in-chief; and, as I had before stated to the Admiral, if I had my choice of officers there are none in the fleet on whom I should fix in preference to them. I further advised the Admiral that I was ready to undertake any plan of his Lordship, having seen them with me on service of a similar nature before. [8]

During the court martial proceedings the defendants tried to defend themselves, insisting that no disrespect had been intended, and complaining that Cochrane's entourage had pried into private conversations in order to try and prove the last charge. But their efforts were pointless. The five men freely admitted that they had written the letter, and the framing of the charge left no alternative but a guilty verdict. Purser Frew and Surgeon Michael were cashiered, while Lieutenants Bell and Freeman and Assistant Surgeon Kernan were severely reprimanded and dismissed from their ship.

But it was not over. John Tooker Spry had watched the moves against Guise with growing alarm, aware that Cochrane's antipathy made him the next target.[9] So, on 22 February 1821, when *Galvarino* was ordered to sea, Spry accepted the inevitable and asked to be replaced in command. Cochrane demanded a further explanation. Spry obeyed and replied in writing that he had come to Chile under Guise's patronage, and that if Guise were forced to resign, he too would have to go.[10] Cochrane promptly ordered a court martial and moved the *Galvarino* under the guns of the *O'Higgins* claiming that the ship was in a state of mutiny.[11] In fact this was untrue. As his successor, Crosbie himself testified, Spry had handed his ship over in good order with no sign of any insubordination on board.[12] Indeed, contemporary observers described Spry as 'a very skilful naval officer and a brave and zealous officer', adding 'there is no ship in the Chilean Navy in a better state of discipline than the *Galvarino*.'[13] Cochrane had then boarded the brig and told the crew contemptuously from the quarterdeck that he did not want their services and that he could execute his plans without them and without their ship.[14]

Spry's court martial sat on 3 and 5 March. Lord Cochrane preferred three charges – one, that Spry had refused to put to sea when ordered; two, that he had threatened to resign in sympathy with Guise; and three, that he had incited his ship's company to protest. Spry objected to the appointment of Cochrane's follower Henry Dean as Judge Advocate on the grounds that his neutrality was compromised by attempts to pump the *Galvarino*'s officers for complaints against him. But to no avail. Spry was found guilty of the second charge and part of the third, was dismissed from his command and put at the bottom of the list of captains.

Although to an impartial observer the whole affair was a storm in a teacup, Cochrane seemed genuinely to believe that there had been a conspiracy against him. He also felt that Guise had betrayed him. Cochrane told him bluntly that his elevation to command of *Valdivia* had been intended as a sign of favour, a compliment to Guise's qualities as a gentleman, and proof that he had drawn a veil over past disagreements. He ended the letter with the rueful reflection that 'these differences would never have existed had it not been for the evil influence of Captain Spry and the malevolent pen of Dr Michael.'[15] Guise replied that the real problem had been caused by Cochrane's own staff who had been intriguing against him from the beginning. 'Look around you', he replied, 'and amongst those who share your confidence, patronage and protection ... you cannot be ignorant of the means that have been resorted to against me.'[16]

Guise and the others then made an appeal to San Martin. The Captain General was on amicable terms with Cochrane and had been careful to avoid difficulties with the prickly Vice Admiral. This was one of the reasons that had led him to praise effusively the capture of the *Esmeralda*, and to rename the frigate in his honour. San Martin therefore decided that he could intervene without causing offence. At the end of March, the officers returned with a letter from the Captain General asking that Guise be restored to command and the officers appointed to his ship. There then followed an exchange of correspondence in which Cochrane – who relished written disputations – cleverly frustrated all their efforts. After a few days, Guise and his men realised that they had been outmanoeuvred.[17] Guise's last words were bitter, provoking Cochrane to reveal his true motive by writing:

> you are pleased to notice that had I no object but personal injury it could not have been more success-fully completed. I am convinced that this expression … arises from that irritability of mind for which I have more than once told you you are most remark-able – stimulated by disappointment in your endeavour to force back upon the service a club of officers who have so scandalously misconducted themselves; and who vainly hoped that union would be the best means to place you, their patron, in the chief command of the squadron.[18]

Spry did better. Needing a naval aide-de-camp, and knowing Spry was available, San Martin appointed him to the post. It was only afterwards that he received Cochrane's letters reporting on Spry's alleged insub-ordination and complaining of a further incident when the Admiral had accidentally met him dining ashore with Colonel Miller and Major Hind. The two marines had promptly leapt to their feet and removed their hats, leav-ing Spry seated and defiantly covered. When challenged by Cochrane, he had walked out.[19] San Martin was embar-rassed but felt unable to sack Spry without further reason. And in spite of what is said in the *Narrative of Services*, Cochrane made no objection to the appointment beyond pointing out that Guise was a more experienced candidate for the post.[20] Nevertheless, to persist in the appointment showed poor judgement by San Martin who by this time was fully aware of Cochrane's sensibilities. Indeed, to some outside observers it looked like a studied insult.[21]

In the months following the capture of the *Esmeralda*, Cochrane settled back into the routine of the blockade, seizing ten Spanish-flagged coasters and eight more British merchant ships, some of them – to the dismay of local merchants – taken within sight of ships of the Royal Navy. The new detainees comprised the *Edward Ellis* and *Lord Suffield* carrying wine, hardware and quicksilver from Europe, *Catalina* and *Colombia* with general cargoes, *Indian* with earthenware and *Diadem*, *Robert* and *Walsingham* loaded with flour. They were sent to an assembly point at Huacho to join *Rebecca* and *Speculator* – the latter detained not by the navy but by the commander of the fort at Pasamoyo. In accordance with their instructions, the Royal Navy's captains did nothing beyond issuing formal protests and trusting that the Chilean prize courts would rectify any illegal detentions. Indeed, they not only declined to use force to protect British merchant ships, but actually told the Chileans that they had no intention of doing so.[22]

Officers of the United States Navy followed a more vigorous line. When the USS *Macedonian* left Callao at the end of November, she passed Cochrane's blockading line with five American ships under the protection of her guns – *Zephyr*, *Pallas*, *Dick*, *Panther* and *Savage*. By arrangement with Captain Searle of *Hyperion* – who fired a salute to underline this instance of Anglo-American solidarity – she was also accompanied by the British ships *Egham*, *Matilda* and *Royal Sovereign*. With the American frigate cleared for action, Cochrane's blockading squadron refrained from interfering and let them pass even though they believed that Downes was carrying Spanish as well as neutral money. On her way home to the United States, *Macedonian* stopped off at Huacho on Christmas Day and, finding American merchantman *Louisa* detained in the anchorage, promptly forced her release as well. Her replacement on the station, the USS *Constellation*, followed exactly the same policy. Indeed, the first act of Captain Charles Ridgley on his arrival off Peru in May was to retake the American ships *Chesapeake* and *Warrior* from the Chileans in the port of Coquimbo. The captains and owners of detained British merchantmen were dismayed that warships of their own navy were not taking similar action![23]

While all this was going on, there were significant changes taking place in Cochrane's domestic life. Following her husband's departure with the Great Expedition to Peru, Kitty had continued to enjoy herself, both in terms of the socialising she enjoyed so much and of satisfying her curiosity about the fascinating scenery of Chile. In Santiago, she had been a welcome visitor at the homely residence in which O'Higgins lived with the female members of his family. For the Supreme Director never married but lived in simple, unostentatious style with his mother Dona Isabella, to whom he was devoted, and his formidable sister Dona Rosa who acted as First Lady. Kitty's courage and spirit also led her to explore the wild foothills of the Andes with children, nanny and servants in tow. Indeed, on the very day Cochrane was capturing *Esmeralda*, Kitty was battling her way through snowdrifts on the high mountain passes that linked Chile with Argentina heading for Mendoza, just over the border. All this was exciting: it was also dangerous and on a least one occasion the party was threatened by robbers.

Lord and Lady Cochrane's time in South America was the first occasion on which they had been separated for any lengthy period since they were married; and the absence seemed to take its toll. Kitty's letters to her husband at this time were full of both longing and concern – for Cochrane's own communications were beginning to reflect the stress he was under and the persecution and betrayal from which he was convinced he was suffering. In one passage she referred to 'that tendency to despair which is now so strongly depicted in your letters'. In another she begged him to 'Keep your mind at rest my dearest and most beloved Cochrane, and for my sake take care of yourself and remember that absence strengthens and not diminishes love.'[24] But by the end of 1820, the strain of separation had become too great and, on 9 December, Kitty embarked with her three children on HMS *Andromache* bound for Peru.

Andromache reached Callao on 29 December, and a fortnight later, the Cochrane family were reunited when *O'Higgins* and *Esmeralda* rejoined the blockade after an unsuccessful search for *Venganza* and *Prueba* on the high seas. But Kitty had not wasted her time. She had always been worried about the validity of the ceremonials that had punctuated their unorthodox lifestyle and had, for example, insisted that their runaway marriage was later confirmed in no less than two religious ceremonies – one according to the rites of the Church of Scotland, the other by the rites of the Church of England. Now Kitty took the opportunity to have baby Elizabeth and little Horace christened, or rechristened, by the *Andromache*'s Anglican Chaplain, the Rev Henry Thomas Taylor.[25] Finally, on 16 January 1821, Kitty and the baby were transferred to the *O'Higgins* and, leaving the boys behind in the care of Captain Shirreff, she sailed with the Chilean squadron to Huacho. In his memoirs, Cochrane described one occasion when Kitty, then on board the *O'Higgins*, fired cannon at a 'treasure ship' and promptly fainted. If this incident ever happened, it must have been at this time, although the vessel in question was probably nothing more than a blockade runner. Cochrane, like so many of his contemporaries, seemed to believe the legends originating from the time of Drake that South American waters were filled with treasure galleons!

The excitement continued when they reached Huacho, a small port 70 miles north of Callao commanding the fertile valley of the Huera, which San Martin had selected as his headquarters and base for the army. It was there that Colonel Miller, now in command of the 8th Buenos Aires Regiment of black infantrymen and a squadron of cavalry, was disembarking with his men for an incursion into the interior. Kitty went ashore and was invited to inspect the troops. She was a sensation. As Miller recorded in his memoirs, when he introduced her as their 'Lady General', the men greeted the vision of the young and vivacious brunette on the back of an enormous horse with cheers and wild enthusiasm.[26] Cochrane then put to sea, leaving Kitty to go off on a brief tour of Peru in which she soon established – not withstanding her husband's position – warm personal relationships with the local Spanish aristocracy. Escorted by James Paroissien, she left Huacho on the afternoon of 28 January, and headed north on the first leg of a journey inland to Quilca. Once more she enjoyed crossing mountains and deserts and swinging over precipitous ravines on rickety rope bridges. But, while staying at the palace of the Marquesa de la Placer at Quilca, she heard rumours of a plot to kidnap her and her child and hold them hostage. Borrowing a palanquin from the obliging Marquis of Torre Tagle, Kitty made a dash for the coast, passing through an area where an epidemic of typhus was raging. She reached Huacho on 14 February and immediately joined her sons in the welcoming sanctuary of HMS *Andromache*. But alas, for baby Elizabeth Josephine – less than a year old and already ailing – the rush through the fever infested coast of Peru proved to be too much and, on 20 February 1821, Captain Shirreff sadly noted the baby's death in the frigate's log.[27] The body was put in spirits to preserve it until Christian burial could be arranged. For Lord Cochrane this blow added to the strain he was already under. In March, he wrote sadly to tell O'Higgins the news, and prepared to send Kitty and the children home to safety in England on the *Andromache*.[28] The frigate was at that moment loading gold and bullion worth some $1,500,000, for *Andromache* had been given permission to carry remittances from British merchants in Peru back to England. In view of the notoriously extravagant lifestyle of Captain Shirreff and his wife, the £3000 he received for carrying this 'freight' would come in handy.[29]

Andromache sailed for England on 10 April 1821. Happily, Kitty and the children were to have company on the voyage, for also on board was the former Vice Reine of Peru, Dona Angela de la Pezuela, who was returning to Europe with servants, baggage and – on the authority of Thomas Collings – the silver viceregal chamber pot.[30] Captain Shirreff's men spent a week building a special cabin for her. Cochrane says that when he was introduced to Dona Angela at this time, he was gratified when the Vice Reine expressed surprise that he was a quiet gentleman and not the vicious brute she had imagined. The exit of Dona Angela's husband, the former Viceroy, was not so easy. Don Joaquin de la Pezuela had to be smuggled out of Peru in the American merchantman *General Brown*, joining the ship in an open boat after she had left Callao and had passed through the Chilean blockading squadron escorted by the USS *Constellation*. San Martin was seriously annoyed at this American breach of neutrality but could do nothing about it.

Chapter 11

THE LIBERATION OF PERU

On land, San Martin's campaign against the royalists in Peru followed its slow and relentless course. With little hope of help from Spain, and unable to bring the liberating army to action, the royalists began to bicker among themselves. For political reasons, Viceroy Pezuela was determined to hold Lima. His generals objected, arguing that the defence of a static position prevented them from concentrating their forces and going in search of the enemy. At the end of January, Pezuela was overthrown in a palace revolution and replaced as Viceroy by the army commander, General José de la Serna. Then in May, Manuel Abreu, the Peace Commissioner sent by the government, arrived at last from Madrid. De la Serna, in spite of his better judgement, was forced to ask for a 20-day armistice and even approached Captain Spencer of the *Owen Glendower* to ask if the British would act as guarantor of any agreement with San Martin.[1] The talks in fact got nowhere, due partly to the fact that self-government was not on the royalist agenda, and partly to divisions on the Spanish side. Abreu was impressed with San Martin's support for the idea that the South American republics should become monarchies ruled by members of the Spanish Royal Family and wanted to take a conciliatory line, whereas de la Serna, confident of a victory, was eager to concentrate the 20,000 troops he commanded, take the offensive and smash the rebels once and for all. The talks broke down with acrimony on the royalist side – de la Serna angrily denouncing Abreu for acting 'more like an agent of the dissidents than a deputy of Your Majesty' and Abreu accusing the new Viceroy of being uncooperative and abusive.[2]

Ironically enough, many of San Martin's subordinates – including Lord Cochrane – were critical of San Martin's 'softly softy' tactics and also yearned to settle the fate of Peru on the battlefield. They argued that the best way to win Peruvian hearts and minds was a quick victory not a prolonged political debate. But the Captain General stood firm, knowing that the enemy's numbers were greater than his own and confident that his political strategy would work. And he was right – up to a point. The arrival of the liberating army on Peruvian soil had the effect San Martin had anticipated. In October 1820, the northern province of Guayaquil declared its independence. A month later, the Marquis of Torre Tagle brought the fortified town of Trujillo into the patriot camp. At the beginning of December, the desertion of the Royal Numancia Regiment to the patriot side was the first in a steady stream of defections. True, there was no widespread national uprising, but the royalist regime in Peru slowly began to unravel. Trade was at a standstill; starvation threatened as food supplies were cut by Cochrane's blockade; and, to cap it all, the coast was swept with an epidemic of fever. In fact it did more damage to San Martin's army than the Spanish and at the end of February 1821 Paroissien estimated that 900 men, including the Captain General who was spitting blood, were sick.[3]

Right as he so frequently was in matters of military strategy, San Martin's hopes for a national rising in support of Peruvian independence were unrealistic. Like O'Higgins, his expectations had been formed in the liberation struggles of the semi-rural societies of Chile and the Argentine. Peru was different. Since its foundation, the development of the Viceroyalty had been conditioned by the huge wealth of its silver mines, which had allowed it to import all the trappings of church and state from aristocratic Europe. It was a country of sharp social contrasts between the wealthy merchants and titled officials of Lima and the impoverished Indians and Negro slaves who lived in the countryside. Geographical contrasts were just as great, with barely accessible forests and mountains dominating the interior, while the bulk of the population lived along a narrow coastal strip, the green areas of settlement and cultivation separated by waterless deserts or mountainous outcrops. The whole was dominated by Lima, the 'City of Kings' with its domes and spires, baroque churches and convents, public parks, triumphant arches and neat grid of streets and plazas. But neither the wealthy minority of merchants and aristocrats, nor the poor and impoverished majority, were fruitful breeding grounds for a revolution. The former had too much to lose, and the latter were more concerned with survival.

After *Andromache* had sailed away carrying Kitty and his family, Lord Cochrane handed over the blockade of Callao to Robert Forster – now a commodore – and turned his attention to raiding the isolated settlements scattered along Peru's long coastline. To satisfy Cochrane's continual demand for military action, San Martin had eventually supplied him with a newly raised Peruvian regiment commanded by Colonel William Miller and given him a free hand. On 20 March 1821, he attacked Pisco, which had been reoccupied by the royalists after San Martin's withdrawal the previous October, seizing cattle, horses and much-needed supplies. On 21 April, Cochrane evacuated the town once more and, with his flag now flying in the *San Martin*, headed south. On 6 May, he bombarded and sacked Arica, seizing $110,000 in coin and silver. With orders to raise the Provinces of Arica and Arequipa,[4] Miller and his men advanced into the interior in the direction of Tacna, swinging northwest to head off the three detachments of Spanish troops sent from Arequipa, Puno and La Paz before they could combine to confront him. He met and defeated the first in the valley of the Mirave, then forced-marched his troops 100 miles north to Moquega where he routed the other two detachments, pursuing them into the high mountains. Only the armistice of 23 May prevented further activity.

Cochrane was pleased with these military adventures, which were just the kind of thing he had excelled at when invading enemy territory in France during the war.[5] But occupied Peru was not France, and it was not enemy territory. Certainly, Cochrane took supplies and booty for the patriot forces and Miller's operations diverted Spaniard troops away from San Martin's army, but in the longer run his adventures damaged the country's economy and caused hardship to many Peruvian citizens. The orders Cochrane had been sent on 9 September 1819 had discussed the issue and explained that short-term incursions like these could be nothing more than a side show that put local patriots at risk once he had left. Indeed, Arica had to be evacuated as soon as the armistice was over and Spanish forces returned in strength. Behind him Cochrane left a ghost town, its population driven away, its shops and storehouses pillaged, and its houses looted with furniture smashed with shattered doors hanging from their hinges.[6] It was not the way to win hearts and minds.

Meanwhile, Cochrane's bag of prizes increased. As he made his way down the coast he seized seven more British merchantmen in Peruvian ports – *Admiral Cockburn, Joseph,*

Robert Fuge, Mary, Rebecca (2), *Robert* and *Lord Cathcart*, though the last was not taken over by a Chilean prize crew and escaped on the first dark night.[7] Captain Basil Hall, who was patrolling the coast in HMS *Conway*, sent details of these fresh detentions to Sir Thomas Hardy in Valparaiso. Hall had also discovered that Cochrane had changed his style and that, instead of detaining alleged blockade runners, he was freeing them on purchase of a trading 'licence' costing 18 per cent of the value of the cargo.[8] *Joseph, Robert Fuge* and *Admiral Cockburn* paid Cochrane's licence fee and were released – the latter supplying, in place of cash, much needed cordage and rope for the Chilean Squadron. Sir Thomas Hardy, now in Chile, made an official protest to O'Higgins who was dismayed to hear what was going on and totally disowned Cochrane's activities.[9] Hardy then sailed for Peru with *Creole* and the 74-gun *Superb* to sort out the problem personally.

There was, however, little Hardy could do in relation to the merchantmen that had been seized by Cochrane's ships except to lodge an official protest.[10] The British Government's policy of strict neutrality and the dubious nature of the practices being used by British merchants to disguise the true origins of their cargoes tied his hands. All he could do was to pass his concerns on to the Admiralty, complain about the anomaly of a situation where illegal 'acts of hostility ... are daily committed by His Majesty's natural born subjects serving in the Chilean squadron against others of His Majesty's trading subjects on this coast, without benefiting much the patriot cause,'[11] and exchange letters with Lord Cochrane over the right and wrongs of his actions. Meanwhile, the USS *Constellation* had no hesitation in releasing the handful of American ships that had fallen into Cochrane's hands by force.

Meanwhile, on land, the army of liberation waited for events to unfold, while San Martin lived aboard the schooner *Sacramento*. Basil Hall visited him at this time and was impressed with the Captain General's personality:

> At first sight there was little that was striking about his appearance; but when he stood up and began to speak, his superiority was evident. He received us on deck very simply, dressed in a loose coat and a large fur cap. He was seated at a table made from several board planks and placed over some empty barrels. He is a handsome man, tall, erect, well proportioned with a large aquiline nose, abundant black hair and long black whiskers. He is highly courteous and simple, unaffected in mannerisms, excessively cordial and unassuming and possessed of a kindly nature. ... In conversation on important topics, he disliked wasting time on details, he listened attentively and answered with clarity and brilliance of language, showing admirable resources of argumentation and a ready abundance of knowledge.[12]

Hall was equally impressed by the logic behind San Martin's intention to liberate Peru rather than conquer it and by his patience in waiting for the collapse of Spanish power. His plans, wrote Hall, 'certainly appeared to many people to be very judicious at the time as they were uniformly followed by the success which he anticipated; and I am free to confess that ... his measures at this juncture, seemed to me to be marked with sagacity, prudence and foresight.'[13]

San Martin did not have long to wait. Spanish rule continued to crumble and, on 6 July 1821, Viceroy de la Serna and his men carried out their plan to abandon Lima and regroup in the mountains of Upper Peru – what is now Bolivia – to the southeast. When the troops marched out they left the capital apprehensive and deserted, many of the population having fled to take refuge in the Castles of Callao, which still held out, while the rest waited apprehensively with boarded up shops and windows for the orgy of pillage and looting they thought would follow. But nothing happened. San Martin surrounded the capital with his Army of Liberation but did not advance. His forbearance paid off. The local authorities regained their confidence, people returned to their homes and a police force was established to keep order. Captain Hall's offer of marines from *Conway* to help was politely declined.[14] The Captain General had sworn that he would only enter Lima as a liberator and not as a conqueror, and six days later the invitation came. On 12 July, San Martin rode into the Peruvian capital to be embarrassed by public rejoicing and obsequious gratitude. A week later, Lord Cochrane visited the capital to join in the festivities where – according to his own account and those of his partisans – he was hailed as the real hero of the hour.

When Cochrane returned to Callao from Arica on 8 July, he had gone immediately on the offensive. Whatever was happening in Lima, Callao still held out. His first act was to countermand an agreement that Commodore Forster had made in his absence that the British merchantmen *Lord Lyndoch* and *Saint Patrick* should be allowed to leave in ballast.[15] His second, was to attack the port three days later, destroying the *Sebastiana*. Then came a setback. On 16 July, while anchored off Chorillos in heavy weather, the only serviceable anchor cable of the *San Martin* parted and the frigate was driven ashore and wrecked. Not even Captain Wilkinson's renowned seamanship, gained as a carpenter and then commander in the East India Company, could save her. She was loaded with corn – which the Captain General had hoped to offer as a gesture of reassurance to the hungry population of Lima – together with British prize goods and money. Of this, only $120,000 in silver was saved. This disaster was, however, followed by a success when, on 24 July, the boats of the squadron under Crosbie successfully penetrated the harbour and, in another spirited action, brought out the corvette *Resolution* and the armed ships *San Fernando* and *Milagro*. Unfortunately, the British merchantmen *Lord Lyndoch* and *Saint Patrick*, whose departure had been vetoed by Cochrane, were badly damaged in the crossfire, the master of the latter being burnt and mortally wounded.[16]

On 28 July, the formal ceremony marking the Independence of Peru took place; and a few days later, San Martin was installed as Protector of the new republic. But the game was not quite over. On 2 September, it was reported that Spanish General José Canterac was advancing from the mountains at the head of a force of 10,000 men. San Martin was taken by surprise but seemed determined to do battle, deploying troops and militia in defence of Lima and summoning reinforcements from Cochrane's ships. Canterac's army marched into sight on 7 September and formed up facing the patriots. The standoff lasted for three days, with neither side making any aggressive move. Cochrane and the General Las Heras could be seen haranguing San Martin and urging him to attack. But the Protector was adamant and did nothing. The two forces were evenly balanced in numbers and San Martin, knowing full well that a single reverse would nullify all the gains he had made so far, was not prepared to gamble. Basil Hall understood his position, writing, 'the slightest military reverse at that moment must at once have turned the tide; the Spaniards would have taken Lima; and the independence of the country might have been indefinitely retarded.'[17] Lord Cochrane on the other hand was filled with contempt at the Protector's caution.

It was Canterac who finally lost his nerve, withdrew his men, and headed for his second objective, the Castles of

Callao. As he marched off, San Martin was delighted, realising that the Spanish force was already short of supplies and was now cut off by land and sea. He predicted that in a fortnight, Canterac would be forced to either retreat or surrender. He was right. In fact, Canterac only lasted nine days before marching out of Callao and heading back the way he had come for the mountains, losing deserters and stragglers as he went. As the royalists approached Lima, participants on the patriot side prepared once more for a bloody and hard fought battle. Many like Paroissien wrote their wills and sent letters of farewell to their friends.[18] But there was no confrontation. San Martin merely stood aside with his army and watched the Spaniards retreat. He was perfectly content for Lima to be saved and for Callao to fall without an unnecessary battle. Indeed, the Governor, General La Mar, surrendered the Castles two days later.

Unfortunately for San Martin, his confidence in the wisdom of his 'wait and see' strategy was not shared by his subordinates. They were dismayed that the Spanish forces had been left undefeated to remain a threat in the mountains. Moreover, the morale of armies depends on victories not on strategic inaction. San Martin's commanders had already become disenchanted. They yearned for a fight and were aghast at his caution during Canterac's advance, then retreat from Callao. It is said that General Las Heras broke his sword across his knee and declared that he would serve no more after such a shameful day. Certainly, the whole affair dealt a blow to San Martin's military reputation from which it never recovered.

Chapter 12
THE ROW WITH SAN MARTIN

For South Americans, 1821 was a momentous year. But for Lord Cochrane, its main feature was not the blockade of Callao, or the surrender of Lima, or even the creation of the Peruvian Republic. It was his blazing row with San Martin. In view of the very different personalities of the two men, a clash of wills was inevitable. Inevitable, that is, taking into account the insubordinate streak in Cochrane's character, his deeply suspicious nature and his inability to keep his opinions to himself. San Martin was a reflective and subtle Latin – a political realist who believed that only authoritarian government would frustrate his countrymen's instinct for anarchy, and a man of strategic vision who saw battles as merely one means to an end. Lord Cochrane, on the other hand, was an impulsive and opinionated Scottish aristocrat who saw the world in simplistic terms – a political romantic who believed in democracy and knew little of the South American temperament, and a man who saw battles and fighting as ends in themselves. Between the two men there was a total lack of understanding.

The first disagreement was over military tactics. San Martin's strategy was to play for time, to politicise the country slowly and avoid action with Spanish forces while internal disputes destroyed their will to fight. He also knew full well that the military forces opposed to him were superior in both numbers and experience and was determined to avoid any risk. Cochrane could not comprehend this reasoning. As a result he watched with incredulity as San Martin avoided one opportunity for action after another, and concluded that the Captain General's behaviour was due either to cowardice or a desire to keep the army intact so that he could keep power after independence. Likewise, he seemed unable to appreciate the difference between liberating a country under occupation and invading an enemy state. His intensely suspicious personality made things worse. San Martin's reluctance to provide him with a military force to create mayhem on the coasts of Peru was put down to 'a violent jealousy which caused him to look at me as a rival'.[1] And it did not take long for Cochrane to convince himself that San Martin was 'employing every effort to lessen my reputation amongst his officers, and endeavouring to the utmost to prevent the squadron from gathering fresh laurels, even sacrificing his own reputation to this insane jealousy'.[2] The notion was absurd.

The next argument was about how Peru was to be run after liberation. In spite of giving assurances that the Peruvians would be free to choose their own form of government, San Martin introduced an authoritarian regime designed to prevent the internal anarchy he feared. His excuse was that until the Spanish were defeated, a democratic system would be divisive and dangerous. Cochrane, who had assumed that the despotism of Spain would be immediately followed by some sort of democracy, was dismayed, and became more so when the politicians around San Martin led by Monteagudo began to feather their nests by persecuting the old Spaniards and acting like despots. Making one of the hasty and misguided assumptions that were a feature of his whole life, Cochrane convinced himself that the unambitious and apolitical San Martin had planned a tyranny from the beginning and had an insatiable thirst for power. As was his wont, on 7 August he subjected him to a lecture on the duties of a ruler, beginning by flattering him as 'the Napoleon of South America' and ending:

> no man had yet arisen, save yourself, capable of soaring aloft with eagle eye embracing the expanse of the political horizon. But if, like Icarus, you trust to waxen wings, your descent may crush the rising liberties of Peru and involve all South America in anarchy, civil war and political despotism. ... Flatterers are more dangerous that the most venomous serpents, and next to them are men of knowledge – if they have not the integrity or courage to oppose bad measures when formally discussed or even when casually spoken of.[3]

But the final clash was not about military tactics or political theory. It was about money. And what brought matters to a head were the methods Cochrane was forced to use in order to keep his squadron at sea. The 1819 campaign against Peru had been uncomplicated in administrative terms. The squadron had operated away from Valparaiso for only short periods before returning for pay and supplies, and had regularly sent enemy prizes and captured property back to Chile for condemnation and sale. The campaign that began in August 1820 was different. This time the squadron remained off the Peruvian coast for 22 months. It was operating far from its base, and Peru was in too much turmoil for money and supplies to be easily available. Three supply ships arrived from Chile in December 1820 and another in February 1821, but after that Cochrane was forced to fend for himself, relying on what he could capture to provide the money, equipment and supplies he needed. The problem he faced in maintaining the squadron's materiel and morale was very real.

San Martin's first complaints were caused by the apparent sloppiness and inconsistency in Cochrane's demands for cash and supplies. But more alarming were the methods Cochrane began to use to get the money he needed. First, Cochrane and his agents charged a huge fee of $71,392 for hiring out the prizes *Potrillo*, *Dolores* and *Aguila* as transports to the Liberating Expedition. Then, early in 1821, instead of arresting blockade runners, Cochrane began to issue 'trading licences', which allowed vessels to trade freely with the Spaniards in Peru on receipt of a payment amounting to 18 per cent of their cargo value, or 3½ per cent if they were carrying specie.[4] Sir Thomas Hardy's protests had already persuaded the Chilean Government to restrict its blockade of Peru to the few hundreds of miles of coast around Callao.[5] Now he was back with another official complaint. O'Higgins was deeply embarrassed by Cochrane's latest actions. Not only was he offending neutrals, but his licensing scheme nullified the whole point of the blockade. Writing to San Martin about the matter, O'Higgins bitterly complained 'I have had to humiliate myself before the British commander-in-chief in order to make up for the stupidities of this man, and have repeatedly written to him about the need for moderation.'[6] In similar vein, when the new Peruvian Government expelled all unmarried Spanish males after confiscating half their property, Cochrane demanded a fee before issuing them with the passport they needed to leave. The amount was said to be between $2500 and $10,000 a head – the sources of the information are divided as to the exact amount.[7] Likewise, during the latter stages of the siege of Callao in August, Cochrane offered surrender terms that would have permitted Governor La Mar to ship out all Spanish property in the port on receipt of a payment of 33 per cent of its value in cash. La Mar refused the offer in one sentence of chilly dignity:

> Most Excellent Sir,
>
>   In all the correspondence which has passed between Don José de San Martin and this Government, there is nothing that refers to the proposal which Your Excellency makes to me in your honourable note of 9th instant.
>
>   God preserve you many years.[8]

Underestimating, or unaware of, Cochrane's real need for cash to keep the squadron paid, fed and supplied, San Martin's entourage, coining the nickname 'el metálico lord', cynically assumed that much of this money was going into his own pocket. Some of it certainly was – but no more than was his due. Paroissien reflected their views when he ruefully commented 'It really is requisite to have more than the patience of an angel when dealing with Lord C. … He appears only to be anxious about making money. Avarice and selfishness do certainly appear to form the groundwork of his character and from his speculative disposition he is often in great want of money to obtain which he is not so scrupulously exact in his word as every man ought to be, particularly a man of his rank and station.'[9]

During the first half of 1821, Cochrane had been able to cope by using equipment, gear and money taken from Spanish and neutral prizes. In March, he had even managed to pay four months salary to his crews. But when, in July, Peru became independent and the war at sea effectively came to an end, this source of supply dried up and the squadron's situation became critical. Things were made worse by the common belief among the sailors that

San Martin had seized a huge treasure in Peru, and that the army was being indulged while they starved. Cochrane now expected San Martin to provide for all the squadron's needs and, at the end of July, he demanded the immediate payment of $420,000 – that is £80,400. This comprised $150,000 in arrears of pay; $110,000 in prize money for the *Esmeralda*; and two promised bonuses – one of $50,000 for capturing the frigate, the other of $110,000 on the fall of Lima.[10] San Martin was unsympathetic. He fully accepted responsibility for the payment of the two bonuses – and, indeed, explained that orders had already been given to collect the $160,000 needed. But as far as he was concerned, the pay of the Chilean sailors was the responsibility of the Chilean Government, and should be distributed in the normal way when the squadron returned to its home port. In regard to *Esmeralda*, he pointed out that the frigate was owned by the Chilean Government, now flew its flag, and that the payment of prize money was therefore its responsibility.[11]

Cochrane and San Martin met on 5 August to sort out these problems. It was a dramatic encounter and was witnessed on the one side by Bernardo Monteagudo and Juan García del Rio and, on the other, by William Bennet Stevenson. Monteagudo was now the Peruvian Minister of Marine and García del Rio was Minister of Foreign Affairs. In the course of the meeting, San Martin and Cochrane both became angry, but there are conflicting accounts about what exactly was said. Cochrane's version – first retailed by Stevenson then repeated by all his other biographers – depicts the Protector as triumphalist, devious and obstructive, while the Vice Admiral is reasonable, honest and positive. Responding to Cochrane's request for money, San Martin is accused of attempting to get the ships under his control by saying that 'he would not pay the Chilean squadron unless it was sold to Peru, and that the payment should be part of the purchase money.' The argument continued until San Martin, turned to Cochrane, rubbing his hands agitatedly, and said 'I am Protector of Peru.' 'Then', replied Cochrane, 'it now becomes me as the senior officer of Chile and consequently the representative of the nation, to request fulfilment of all the promises made to Chile, and the squadron.' San Martin then came forward, snapped his fingers in Cochrane's face and said 'Chile! Chile! I will never pay a single real to Chile! And as to the squadron, you may take it where you please, and go where you choose: a couple of schooners is enough for me.'[12]

It did not take Cochrane's entourage long to ensure that his account of the meeting, and of San Martin's alleged refusal to provide the squadron with funds unless it was handed over to Peru, was being circulated in Chile. San Martin issued an indignant denial. But his version of events never received the same publicity. San Martin's account of the meeting was that he had repeated his position that responsibility for the squadron's pay and prize money lay with Chile and not with him; and had confirmed that a percentage of the customs revenue of Callao had already been earmarked to pay the $160,000 he had promised in gratuities. Regarding the sale of the Chilean squadron, all he had done was to observe that he was on the brink of creating a Peruvian navy, and was prepared to buy some of the ships if it would help to solve Chile's known financial difficulties.[13] He repeated these points in writing on 9 August. Cochrane made no reply except to say that unless he was sent $150,000 immediately, he would be unable to halt 'the tempest' of insubordination by his crews.[14]

The seamen were certainly becoming truculent over the non-appearance of pay, and during September, when the shortage of supplies had became critical, there were disturbing messages from *O'Higgins*, *Galvarino* and *Lautaro* of sailors refusing duty. The morale of the officers was also sagging. And when, on 17 August, San Martin's government began to recruit men for the new Peruvian Navy – sending Paroissien and Spry to lobby them personally – 13 of the squadron's 30 sea officers signed on.[15] Their numbers included five of seven captains and six of 25 lieutenants. Cochrane himself was invited to become its admiral, but indignantly refused. Guise, Spry and Freeman inevitably offered their services – but so did many others who had previously been Cochrane 'followers' like Prunier who was now commanding *Pueyrredon* and had already attracted the Admiral's displeasure. Forster too had fallen from favour, and had resigned his commission after having been excluded from an active role in the capture of the *Esmeralda*.[16] Cochrane claimed that the officers who joined the new navy were bribed to leave the Chilean service with estates and awards. But it is just as likely that they were disturbed by the conduct of the *Valdivia* court martial and by Cochrane's obsession with plots, and decided to leave before they too came under suspicion. In private letters, officers tactfully refrained from revealing their feelings. Captain Henry Hind sidestepped the subject, writing that he was 'no party man',[17] and Miller, on the brink of going off on campaign, told Paroissien darkly that he had much to say but would only do so verbally.[18] It was only later when, describing events at the time, he hinted at his real feelings when he wrote, 'the squadron was divided and agitated by the conflicting parties of Cochrane and Guise. These originated in bickering on some unimportant points of etiquette and were carried to a length which proved highly detrimental to the service. But as these disputes reflect credit on neither party, I will make no further observation.'[19] It was not long after that Miller transferred back to the army.

Then came the final confrontation. At the beginning of September, when General Canterac had marched out of the mountains to threaten Lima and Callao, San Martin not only deployed his troops to defend the capital, but took the precaution of moving the entire contents of the Mint and the State Treasury to the coast. There it was loaded onto the schooner *Sacramento* and taken to the Bay of Ancon, which was being used as the assembly point for prizes. HMS *Superb* was also there, keeping an eye on British interests. On 13 September, Paul Delano, now commanding the frigate *Lautaro*, arrived at the anchorage. He soon became aware of what was on the *Sacramento* and sent immediate word to Cochrane off Callao. The Vice Admiral now had two choices – to seize the schooner and take the money or to wait and rely on San Martin's assurances, for the Captain General had already published orders in the *Gazette* for the bonuses to be paid. Cochrane did not hesitate. Putting to sea with *O'Higgins* and *Valdivia*, he sped to Ancon and, by nightfall on 14 September had seized the *Sacramento* and the money and bullion she carried.[20] It would be difficult to think of any act more insulting to Peru's dignity and prestige. It was also a devastating blow for a country that was financially exhausted and whose monthly government revenue was only $130,659.[21]

The Peruvians estimated that the amount carried on the *Sacramento* was $400,000 – the equivalent of £80,000 – $283,000 of which belonged to the state, $40,000 to private individuals, and the rest to the Army. Cochrane generously agreed to return the latter sums, but was adamant about retaining the $283,000 of state funds. At first the Peruvians demanded the money back. There was little chance of that. The seamen were fully aware that large amounts of money had been seized and transferred to the *O'Higgins*, and demands that it be used to pay them were becoming vocal and violent.[22] Then Tomas Guido arrived with a compromise formula whereby a commissary would come on board, pay the crews, then return to Lima with the balance of the money. Cochrane was on the point of agreeing, but at the last minute changed his mind and decided to keep it all. He distributed $131,618 among his officers and men as one year's pay and an advance of prize money, sent $40,000 back to Valparaiso, and kept the remaining $111,382 for future expenses. He claimed self-righteously that he paid himself nothing. This may be so, but he nevertheless loaded $13,507 – the equivalent of £2700 – in coin and bullion on 14 September onto HMS *Superb* to be shipped back to his bank account in England.[23] Indeed, he had sent another $5000 back to Miers in Chile only a fortnight before.[24] Then he added injury to insult by seizing the schooner *Mercedes* as she was in the act of surrendering to the Peruvian authorities, and hijacking a cargo of rope and supplies from the *Lautaro*, which had been ordered for San Martin's army.

Cochrane may have been secretly satisfied with the way he had cut the Gordian knot, but in the long run it worked to his disadvantage. Zenteno had accepted Cochrane's valuation of *Esmeralda* without question and had already authorised San Martin to pay the squadron $120,000 for the frigate and another $10,000 for the captured schooner *Aranzaza*.[25] Unfortunately for Cochrane, the Peruvians were so affronted by the *Sacramento* incident that they flatly refused to accept the charge, and left him with a worthless letter of credit in his pocket. Likewise, they declined to pay both the $50,000 bonus promised for the capture of the frigate, and the freight costs of the prizes that had been used as transports.[26] San Martin was shocked by Lord Cochrane's behaviour and by his refusal to compromise. He was also amazed by his indiscreet language. San Martin had been surprised to receive official letters from Cochrane publicly blackguarding the Chilean

Government – writing, for example, on 4 August 'to what state has the Senate brought the beautiful and fertile province of Chile. Can confidence be restored? Has not their notorious want of good faith deprived them – notwithstanding the value of their rich mines and their public and confiscated lands, of the resources formerly possessed even by the Spanish Government – of the credit necessary to obtain a single dollar in foreign countries or even in their own.'[27] At the same time, Cochrane was complaining to O'Higgins about San Martin, writing about 'secret plans by the Government of Peru to get the squadron in their power' and the need to avoid letting it fall into the hands of those 'who have made themselves, in my opinion, worse enemies of Chile than the Spaniards'.[28]

At first San Martin confined his complaints against Cochrane to private letters addressed to O'Higgins, in which he enumerated 'the crimes of this noble pirate'. But then he learn that Cochrane's entourage were spreading hostile rumours about his activities in Peru, and were even making public their version of the interview of 5 August and of his alleged plot to get control of the Chilean squadron.[29] By this time San Martin had had enough. On 26 September, he ordered Cochrane back to Chile. Cochrane replied with a long letter of justification and accusation,[30] then led the squadron out of Callao in the opposite direction. San Martin's staff began drafting an official complaint.

The loss of so many officers to the new Peruvian Navy hit Cochrane's squadron hard. The seamen too, now that they had been paid, began to desert in droves and when Lieutenant Wynter of the *O'Higgins* was sent ashore to round them up, he was promptly arrested. Fortunately the crew of the *San Martin* was available for redistribution, and *Lautaro* and *Galvarino* were sent back to Valparaiso to ease the demand for men. Even so, when Cochrane eventually sailed on 6 October 1821 with *O'Higgins, Valdivia, Independencia, Araucano* and the *Mercedes* schooner, the ships were only three-quarters manned, with hardly any foreign seamen, only nine lieutenants and with three newly promoted captains. Where he was bound was unknown, but by not heading for Valparaiso, San Martin's entourage accused Cochrane of disobeying orders. This was not his interpretation. In his view, by becoming Protector of Peru San Martin had relinquished command of the joint expeditionary force and now had no right to tell him what to do. Indeed, Lord Cochrane regarded himself as being the sole representative of the Chilean government. In relation to his destination, however, there was no confusion. After years without a refit, Cochrane's frigates were leaking like baskets, with pumps and other gear worn out. His plan was to take them north to Guayaquil for repairs then to scour the Pacific for the last remnants of the Spanish Navy, the frigates *Venganza* and *Prueba*.

Chapter 13
GUAYAQUIL AND THE SPANISH MAIN

Cochrane's flotilla reached the broad arms of the Bay of Guayaquil on 21 October, skirted the sandy spit that marks the western tip of the Island of Puna and made its way up the 20 miles of river through mangrove swamps and malaria infested mud flats to the port. Guayaquil was a picturesque town, laid out to a grid pattern with churches, convents, and low houses standing white against the greenery of the tropical vegetation around. There was a rapturous welcome from the local inhabitants and an exchange of salutes and congratulations. Cochrane was presented with an illuminated address, to which he responded by treating the inhabitants to a long proclamation spelling out the virtues of constitutional government and liberal trading practices.[1] As a gesture of solidarity with Chile, the head of the local government, José de Olmedo, put the facilities of the dockyard at Cochrane's disposal, though he had to pay the bill.[2] Working flat out in the crushing heat, it took the artificers a month to refit and reprovision the ships. The total cost was $10,428 plus a bonus of $1000, which Cochrane gave as a reward to the dockyard workers.

Cochrane was anxious to concentrate on the work and

resume the task of hunting down the *Prueba* and *Venganza*. But there were two distractions. First, anchored off the town on his arrival he found the brig *San Antonio*, bound for Acapulco from Valparaiso carrying two British-born officers, Brigadier Arthur Wavell and Colonel Philip O'Reilly.[3] The two men carried passports signed by O'Higgins on 3 September 1821, in which the Supreme Director declared that they had been entrusted with a special mission by the Chilean Government and requested the assistance of all in facilitating their journey. Cochrane, unfortunately, tried to do the opposite. Arguing that the presence of the Spanish frigates in Mexican waters made the continuation of *San Antonio*'s voyage too dangerous, he prevented them from sailing. There were weeks of wrangling. Wavell explained that he was charged with a confidential mission to the patriot Government of Mexico – though declined to show his secret orders – and rejected the reason Cochrane put forward for detaining the *San Antonio* by revealing that the latest news was that *Venganza* and *Prueba* had left Acapulco a month before. Cochrane finally relented and gave permission for Wavell and O'Reilly to proceed.[4] When he later recorded these events in his *Narrative of Services*, Cochrane tried to justify his behaviour by discrediting Wavell and O'Reilly and claiming that their credentials were false.[5] As usual, biographers have swallowed and repeated the story even though it has no basis other than Cochrane's desire for self-justification. The second problem was trickier. In the middle of November, one of Bolivar's aides, Colonel Diego Ibarra, had arrived in Guayaquil to make arrangements for the transfer of Columbian troops to the area by sea for a joint assault with San Martin's forces on the royalists in Upper Peru. Finding Cochrane in town, Ibarra immediately requested his assistance. Cochrane, who was now focused on the military necessity – and prize money advantages –

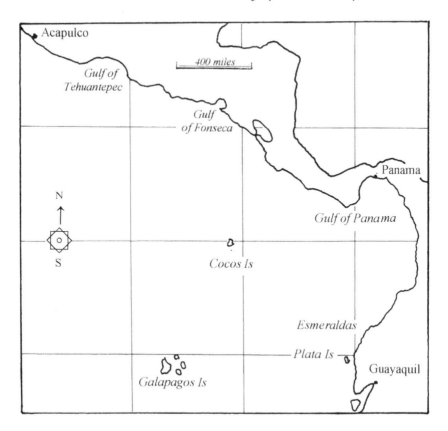

The Spanish Main 1822

of capturing the *Venganza* and *Prueba* was uninterested and evasive. Ibarra returned to Bolivar empty handed, reporting that some intrigue by San Martin lay behind Cochrane's non-cooperation.[6]

At the end of November, work on the Chilean ships had been concluded and Cochrane was ready to go. On 28th, his ships slipped their moorings and after a three-day passage emerged from the brown waters and sultry airs of the Guaya River into the refreshing breezes of the open sea. On 3 December, they rounded the barren flats of the Saint Elena peninsular, found the edge of the southwest trades, and headed northwards up the coast. Two days later, they anchored off the Island of Plata, one degree south of the equator where Sir Francis Drake had allegedly buried treasure two and a half centuries before, to fill their water casks from the fresh streams that cut their way through the thorn covered rocks. That done, Cochrane divided his forces. Captain Robert Simpson in the *Araucano* was ordered to Mexico to investigate the situation in Acapulco, while the handier schooner *Mercedes* was sent north to search the Gulf of Panama under Lieutenant James Shepherd. With his remaining ships, *O'Higgins*, *Valdivia* and *Independencia* – commanded respectively by Thomas Sackville Crosby, Henry Cobbett and William Wilkinson – Cochrane set course for Mexico, 1500 miles to the northwest. Aided by the ocean currents that hook westerly into the Pacific, the flotilla passed quickly through the doldrums and, driven on the starboard tack by north-easterly winds blowing out of the Gulf of Panama, headed northwest for the Island of Cocos. On 11 December, after six days of uneventful blue water sailing, they sighted the jungle covered bluffs that marked their destination. There was immediate excitement when a small pirate ship was spotted hiding in the deep blue waters under the lee of the island. The vessel was taken without difficulty, the crew throwing down their arms when their captain, an Englishman called Blair, was killed. Then, next day, the tiny sail of a felucca rigged boat hove in sight over the horizon, then veered away and frantically tried to escape when it saw the flotilla. A warning shot from *Valdivia*, ordered off in pursuit, soon brought her to a halt. She was manned by British deserters from Peru who, frustrated by having received no pay, had taken over their ship, renamed her *Retribution*, and headed north for freedom. Cochrane heard their story, inevitably sympathised with their plight and, according to the *Narrative of Services*, let them go.[7]

On 12 December 1821, Cochrane's flotilla left the Cocos

Islands and headed northwards for the coast of Central America. After two days, they sighted Costa Rica and turned west to follow the contours of the low green coastline, investigating every inlet for the elusive *Venganza* and *Prueba*. But they were too late. Having spent eight months sheltering in Acapulco while Mexico's almost bloodless struggle for independence reached its successful conclusion, the two Spanish frigates had sailed in October and were now anchored comfortably in Panama.[8] Brigadier Wavell's intelligence had been correct.

Unaware of all this, Cochrane continued to scour the coast for his prey. On 19 December, his ships reached the Bay of Fonseca, passed between the low grey volcanoes that flanked the entrance, and dropped anchor among the green islands and gleaming white beaches within. There, with the fires of half a dozen distant volcanoes sending lazy smoke into the cloudless sky by day and illuminating the darkness by night, Cochrane's men made repairs to the pumps, then hacked their way through the tropical vegetation to the nearest supply of fresh water. A week later they were on the move again, searching the Bay of Tehuantepec, once famous as the haunt of buccaneers and pirates, then heading west for Mexico. They reached Acapulco on 28 January 1822, to find the brig *Araucano* waiting off the port. Simpson was rowed across to the flagship to make his report. His visit to the town had not been a success. Entering the bay cautiously under American colours on 27 December, he had been lured ashore by friendly emissaries and arrested, while *Araucano* had been made to anchor harmlessly under the guns of Fort San Diego. Even with the help of General Wavell and Colonel O'Reilly who had already arrived in the *San Antonio*, it had taken Simpson a week to convince the authorities of his bona fides as a Chilean officer and to secure the release of the brig. The Acapulco authorities claimed that they had mistaken Simpson and his ship for a well-known pirate, but Simpson himself had noticed that he had only been released following the safe departure of two heavily loaded merchant ships from the port – one Spanish, the other American. Perhaps, knowing the enthusiasm of Cochrane's ships for prize-taking, Simpson had been detained to prevent any such incident. On the other hand, he offered an even more sinister explanation – that Wavell and O'Reilly, peeved by the altercation in Guayaquil, had warned the local authorities against Cochrane and denounced his cruise as being unauthorised and piratical.[9]

Acapulco was an unprepossessing town, famous once as the destination of the Manila Galleon: now offering little more than a sheltered bay, a fort, and a small whitewashed town with the usual convents and churches nestling among the tropical greenery. Expecting the worse, Cochrane led his ships cautiously into the port. But he need not have worried. There was no sign of the hostility Simpson had predicted. Indeed, the local governor immediately came on board to offer fulsome compliments, and there were rounds of parties and junketing for the visiting Chileans ashore.[10] As Cochrane reported to Zenteno in the Ministry of Marine,[11] he had established good relations with the authorities and had had an exchange of correspondence with Mexico's strong man, Augustin de Iturbide. But there had been no gun salutes since Mexico, which, although already self governing, was still at that stage technically ruled by the King of Spain, Ferdinand VII. It was only months later when Iturbide became Emperor and Head of State that independence became a reality.

The Chilean flotilla stayed in Acapulco for a week where it was joined by the *Mercedes*. Shepherd's report was inconclusive. He retailed rumours that *Venganza* and *Prueba* were indeed in Panama, but had failed to get near enough to the town to confirm them. Nevertheless, the trail was clear enough and, on 3 February 1822, Cochrane led his ships out of Acapulco and steered east. This time the voyage was less pleasant. Heading against prevailing winds from the northeast, the voyage was a tedious one, alternating between thirsty sun-baked calms, brief torrential rainstorms, and violent gales funnelling through the Isthmus of Tehuantepec and the Gulf of Panama, which tested once more the fabric of their leaky ships. Cochrane ordered *Araucano* away to the coast of California in search of flour and meat, and *Independencia* to conduct a survey in Panamanian waters, then headed southeast once more for the mainland of South America.

On 5 March 1822, Cochrane made his landfall at the palm fringed coast of the *Esmeralda*s to learn that Panama too had declared its independence in January, forcing *Venganza* and *Prueba* to go on their travels once more. Rumour had it that the Spanish frigates were to be found in the south.[12] Cochrane followed and, on 10 March, was once more in sight of the Bay of Guayaquil. Three days later he reached the port to find his quest at an end, for there, moored quietly in the roadstead, was the elusive *Venganza*. But now she flew the red and white flag of Peru. Short of provisions, hunted by Cochrane's squadron, and lacking any base, the captains of the two Spanish frigates had decided to give themselves up. Suitable terms had been negotiated with San Martin's men who now ran Guayaquil, under which the Spanish officers and men were to be paid all the money owing to them; those who wanted it were to be shipped home; and a sum of $100,000 was to be paid to the Spanish Government in compensation.[13] As a result, *Venganza* had been surrendered on the spot while *Prueba* had gone on to Callao.

This time, the change of regime in Guayaquil meant that Cochrane got a frosty reception. But the Vice Admiral was more annoyed at being denied the chance of making a capture. As far as he was concerned, the surrender of the two Spanish frigates was entirely due to his efforts and it was the squadron that should receive both credit and the prize money. Morally, there might have been some truth in the argument; but legally, no prize court would have agreed. All he could do was to send Captain Crosbie to demand that the Chilean flag be raised jointly with the Peruvian, and to obtain an unenforceable agreement that the ship should not be handed over to anyone without Chilean consent.[14]

On 27 March 1822, Cochrane left the Guaya River bound for Callao. But bad luck continued to dog him. No sooner had he reached the entrance to the bay than an open boat filled with men was sighted frantically signalling. On board was Captain Robert Simpson. Off the coast of Mexico, the crew of the *Araucano* had mutinied, put Simpson and a group of loyal hands in the launch, and sailed off into the blue on a piratical cruise! A fortnight later there was another shock. Cochrane put into Gumbacho to repair the *Valdivia*'s pumps and to careen the leaking frigate. To his annoyance, the local governor not only refused to provide supplies but brandished an order from San Martin that prohibited the Peruvian authorities from giving any assistance to the Chilean squadron at all. With his temper even shorter than usual, Cochrane headed for a showdown in Callao.

The situation in Peru had deteriorated in the six months since Cochrane had sailed north. San Martin and his advisers had been busy establishing the principles of the new Peruvian state. On paper at any rate, they had abolished torture and censorship; introduced freedom of the press and habeas corpus; and decreed the abolition of slavery and of the second-class status of the local Indians. On the other hand, the structure of the new state was – to the satisfaction of European observers like Sir Thomas

Hardy – firmly centralised and monarchical.[15] Members of the local aristocracy were permitted to retain their Spanish titles of nobility, and an Order of the Sun was established to reinforce the idea of social hierarchy as much as to symbolise Peru's nationhood. The installation ceremony was attended by Hardy for Britain and Prevost for the United States, and four Englishmen were appointed as grandees of the Order – James Paroissien, Colonel William Miller, Captain Robert Forster and Captain George Guise. But for his estrangement from San Martin, Lord Cochrane would also have been appointed to its most senior ranks.

Discontent, however, was rumbling below the surface. The Protector found himself accused of arrogance and monarchical ambitions. In so far as he was still convinced that a monarchy was the most suitable form of government for the newly independent South American states, the accusation was right. But the self-effacing San Martin had no ambitions for himself. He was convinced that a European Royal should be offered the crown of Peru and indeed, in December 1821, he dispatched a two-man delegation to find one! The men entrusted with this responsibility were James Paroissien and García del Rio. But hostility to San Martin had a deeper basis. The conservative Peruvian aristocracy disliked his social reforms, and indigenous patriots – like the troublesome José de Riva Agüero and the emollient Marquis of Torre Tagle – were jealous and hostile to the fact that the Protector and his closest advisers were foreigners from the Argentine. Likewise, San Martin's military prestige had suffered a severe blow as a result of his reluctance to take on and destroy the Royalist army, which was still lurking in the mountains. It did not take long for the fruits of this policy to turn sour.

In early 1822, General Canterac, the commander of the main Spanish army whose forces were now swollen by unpaid and disillusioned patriot soldiers, advanced in strength from the mountains, put to flight a whole division of San Martin's army near Pisco and threatened the southern coast. Thus, when Cochrane arrived in Callao, he found a deteriorating situation. Led by Blanco Encalada on secondment from Chile, Peru's new navy was busy blockading the affected area, its handful of frigates, brigs and schooners all commanded by officers who had previously served under Cochrane. San Martin's ministers had written a blistering complaint against the Vice Admiral's conduct only months before, but its members were now superficially friendly and congratulatory. Indeed, the situation was so grave that they urged him to take command of the Peruvian Navy, even offering to accommodate him in the house of the Marquis of Torre Tagle – now a member of the government – if he cared to live ashore. But the underlying tension could not be disguised. Blanco Encalada in the flagship *Limeña* scrupulously obeyed his instructions to give Cochrane no official recognition (even though, at the personal level, he was all cordiality) and the prize *Prueba* was packed with guns and 300 men to make sure there was no repetition of the *Esmeralda* incident.[16] Cochrane reciprocated in kind – refusing to go ashore, lying with his guns loaded, and even seizing the *Montezuma*, which suddenly appeared under Peruvian rather than Chilean colours, and turning Lieutenant Robinson and her officers ashore. This caused further annoyance since O'Higgins had given the schooner to San Martin as a personal present. His visit to Callao lasted for two tense weeks. Then Cochrane set sail and headed back to Chile.

Chapter 14
THE FINAL CURTAIN

When the citizens of Valparaiso woke on the morning of 2 June 1822 and looked out to sea, there were two new ships rolling at their anchors in the rain-swept waters of the bay. During the night the *O'Higgins* and *Valdivia* had returned. The news that Cochrane was back spread like wildfire. The town was soon festooned with flags and the streets filled with excited crowds eager to welcome Lord Cochrane and his men after their triumphs in the liberation of Peru. The Chilean Government was no less enthusiastic and wholeheartedly joined in the celebrations. Zenteno had been moved to become Governor of Valparaiso so it was Joaquin de Echeverria, his successor as Minister of Marine, who issued the message of welcome. It began:

> The arrival of Your Excellency in the city of Valparaiso with the squadron under your command has given the greatest of pleasure to the Supreme Director; and in those feelings of gratitude which the glory you have acquired in the late protracted campaign has excited you will find the proof of that high consideration which your heroic services so justly deserve.[1]

A second proclamation announced that:

> His Excellency the Supreme Director, being desirous
> of making a public demonstration of the high services
> that the squadron has rendered to the nation, has
> resolved that a medal be struck for the officers and
> men of the squadron with an inscription expressive of
> the national gratitude towards the worthy supporters
> of its maritime power.[2]

Cochrane and his men deserved no less for their achievements and victories in the war. They had done exactly
what had been required of them: they had seized command
of the sea, driven the Spanish Navy from the Pacific and
ensured the independence of Chile and Peru. Captain Basil
Hall summarised the situation exactly when, in his
memoirs, he praised Cochrane's 'renown, his matchless
intrepidity and his inexhaustible resources in war' and
continued, 'under his hand all things prospered and the
confined naval resources of the country were turned to the
greatest account with a dexterity and professional skill
which astonished everyone.'[3]

One witness to the celebrations that greeted Cochrane's
return to Valparaiso was Mrs Maria Graham, the 37-year-
old widow of the captain of the British frigate *Doris*. Her
husband, Thomas Graham, had died two months before
coming round Cape Horn and Maria had decided to stay
on in Chile to recover her spirits. A star pupil at the
Academy run by the Misses Bright in Drayton, Berkshire,
Maria had emerged with a superior education for a lady
and had mixed freely in literary circles in Edinburgh and
London. She was smaller in stature and slighter in build
than is suggested by the somewhat glamorised picture by
Sir Thomas Lawrence in the National Portrait Gallery, but
her delicate health and recurrent consumption were more

Maria Graham (Lady Callcott), detail from the portrait by Lawrence,
National Portrait Gallery, London

than offset by a determined spirit and an insatiable curiosity.

Indeed, Maria was an inveterate traveller and was already a writer of some note. Based on previous residences abroad with her husband, she had already produced a *Journal of a Residence in India*, and *Three Months*

Quintero, from a sketch by Maria Graham

Passed in the Mountains of Rome during the Year 1819. Now she was keeping a journal of her travels in South America, which was to result in two fascinating and colourful volumes describing the politics, manners and social life of Chile and Brazil. They were also to provide detailed but, alas, prejudiced accounts of Cochrane's adventures in both countries.

Cochrane's first act on arriving in Valparaiso was to go on board the *Rising Star*. The object of considerable curiosity, the steamer had reached the port at last on 27 April, under the command of a Captain Scott and carrying his brother, Major William Cochrane and his long-time secretary, William Jackson. For Cochrane, the successful arrival of the first vessel capable of steam power seen in the Pacific was a historic event and a vindication of his faith in mechanical devices. Also on board were a number of smaller steam engines that Cochrane hoped to sell and see installed in other suitable vessels. On 9 and 10 June, the *Rising Star's* machinery was put through its paces with Chilean officials on board. Cochrane was delighted with its performance and informed Echeverria that the vessel had 'lived up to his most sanguine expectations'.[4]

Cochrane's next task was less agreeable. It was to go ashore and confront his business agent, William Hoseason. It was not a happy meeting. Hoseason had been inefficient in handling his financial affairs and Cochrane soon found that his lack of discretion had made them the talk of the town.[5] The admiral's finances were, as usual, in a sorry state with his total income up to June 1822 standing at $63,324, against outgoings of $95,763 – one-third of which were investments in the Quintero estate and beef business.[6] Fortunately Cochrane was owed $25,000 in pay and prize money – a total of £5000. He also claimed part of the $120,000 (£24,000) prize money for the *Esmeralda*, typically using the system to the full to maximise his share. Under existing practice, he was entitled to receive one-eighth of the $60,000 retained by the government, and another eighth of the $60,000 shared among the captors – a total of $15,000 (£3000). But as an act of generosity to the seamen, it had been agreed to give a double share to anyone wounded in the attack. Cochrane – who had himself been slightly injured – promptly doubled his demand to two-eighths of the captor's half, thus increasing his total personal payment to $22,500 (£4500) and reducing the amount left to be shared among the other officers and men to $45,000 (£9000)![7] Unfortunately, Hoseason seems to have forgotten to tell Cochrane that the Chilean letter of credit issued for the *Esmeralda* prize money had been rejected by the Peruvians and was in his possession. Nevertheless, Cochrane had returned from Peru with $31,595 (£6320) from the local sale of prizes; so was able to lodge $4000 (£800) with Hoseason in cash and gold and to send $16,997

(£3400) back to England – $8500 (£1700) on board HMS *Alacrity* on 8 July, and another $8497 (£1660) on HMS *Doris* on 12 October.[8]

Having sorted that out, Cochrane travelled up the broad carriage road to Santiago to meet Bernardo O'Higgins and his ministers. His first act was to report to the Ministry of Marine and to hand over the squadron's accounts for the Peruvian campaign so that they could be sent to the Tribunal of Accounts for approval.[9] According to Cochrane's calculations, when all the items of income and expenditure had been set against each other, there remained a balance of $67,000, or £13,200, in his favour. He expected speedy repayment. There was, however, an immediate delay and it was not until 8 August that Stevenson was able to provide the original documents and supporting vouchers, which had been kept in a haphazard fashion on the *O'Higgins*.[10] This stimulated a batch of questions about the organisation of the transports that had carried San Martin's army to Peru, how the troops had been fed, and what supplies had been taken. Irritated, Cochrane pointed out that these matters were not his responsibility. On this occasion, Cochrane spent a fortnight in the capital, discussing the squadron's future and lobbying for the repair of his ships and the payment of salaries owed to his men.

In Santiago, Cochrane found much to approve of. O'Higgins was about to introduce a liberal constitution, which created an elected Convention, an executive headed by himself as Director, and an independent judiciary. He was also about to enact commercial regulations designed to promote local manufactures and stimulate trade with the outside world. But on the other side of the coin, the effort of liberating Peru had left Chile impoverished, and the government had so little money that even O'Higgins and his ministers had not been paid for months. They were, however, taking a sensible view of their situation. Other South American governments were rushing to issue loans on an excited London market – Greater Colombia was already trying to raise £2 million, and Peru was about to seek £1.2 million. But the Chileans were more prudent. Aware that the repayments would make the deficit on the state budget even greater, and perhaps realising the costs and risks – for little of the money raised in these loans actually reached the governments involved – O'Higgins explicitly prohibited Antonio Irrisarra, who was now official Chilean Agent in London, from doing the same.[11] Irrisarra unfortunately ignored his orders.

Dogged by these financial problems, it was impossible for the Chilean Government to respond quickly to Cochrane's demands that the squadron be paid and his ships refitted after their long absences. In fact, only six ships remained in service: and of these only *Independencia*, *Galvarino* and the schooner *Montezuma* were fit for use. *Valdivia*, *O'Higgins* and *Lautaro* needed extensive repairs. And of Chile's other vessels, *San Martin*, *Intrepido* and the schooner *Aranzaza* had been wrecked; *Pueyrredon* and *Chacabuco* were worn out; and *Araucano* had been carried off by mutineers on the coast of Mexico.[12] Echeverria and his colleagues were also convinced that the naval war against Spain was effectively over, and knew that Peru now had a navy of its own. Did Chile still need a large naval force any more? Was the enormous cost of repairs justified? The minister intended to make a statement on the subject to the Convention at the end of September, and needed Cochrane's views.

But there was bad news as well. Cochrane learnt that a catalogue of complaint against his actions in Peru had been lodged by San Martin's aides, James Paroissien and García del Rio, who were in Santiago on their way to Europe to find a monarch for independent Peru and to raise a loan. In a closely written document, 12 pages long, the Peruvians had produced a set of detailed accusations against Cochrane for his 'negligence', his 'enormous and inexcusable crimes', his 'predominant passion, avarice' and his attempts to 'slander and speak ill of the administration'.[13] The Chileans were deeply embarrassed – not least because both Echeverria and O'Higgins had replied to the letters in which Cochrane had justified his actions by giving their approval![14] They tried to hush the matter up. But, stunned and furious at any criticism, Cochrane began to compose a bitter list of counter accusations. San Martin's charges were denounced by Cochrane and his supporters for being 'as frivolous as they are base ... hints and innuendos [that] struck at his honour and personal safety and ... atrocious calumnies,' which 'could be disproved from documents in O'Higgins's possession.'[15] But the task of discrediting them was not so easy, for the Peruvian document was filled with detail and direct quotations from his own letters.

When he returned to Valparaiso at the end of June, Cochrane was able to focus his attention on something more agreeable – his steamer, the *Rising Star*. Ordered to conduct sea trials, and anxious to demonstrate the advantages of such advanced technology, on 7 July Cochrane invited friends and local worthies – including Zenteno, Wilkinson, Crosbie, Captain the Honourable Fred Spencer of HMS *Alacrity* and Maria Graham – aboard for a cruise up the coast under steam. At first, all went well and the *Rising Star* forged ahead at a good four miles an hour, her tall double chimneys belching smoke. But as the weather deteriorated and night fell, the machinery broke down. Cochrane, with his usual confidence in mechanical gadgets, had not had the sails bent to the yards before leaving, so there were some uncomfortable and nauseous hours for the passengers amid a blustery wind and an angry sea while that was done. At dawn, with the sky even blacker, the *Rising Star* had to return under sail. This was all very disappointing but Cochrane remained optimistic.

Others were not so sure. In England the engines had given constant trouble and had caused much additional expense. Antonio Irrisarra, the Chilean Agent in London, had found the situation alarming and commented that for the British Admiralty or the King of France to experiment with a steamer might be worth while, but for a poor state like Chile it was a wild and imprudent gamble.[16] Indeed the costs of the *Rising Star* rose so steeply that Edward Ellice, who by then had invested £8000, threatened to pull out and sell the vessel. Alvarez appealed to Major William Cochrane to support his brother and offered an arrangement whereby a contractor would buy the steamship for £6000, iron out the final problems with its engines and then deliver her to Valparaiso. Once there, he guaranteed that the Chilean Government would purchase the vessel for £15,000, and transfer the right to import goods into Chile duty free, which had originally been promised to Edward Ellice. Unwisely, Major Cochrane decided to take on the task himself, and had sold most of his assets, including his commission in the 15th Hussars, to raise the money.[17] Now he had safely delivered the *Rising Star* to Valparaiso. But her arrival put the government in an embarrassing position. It was already desperately short of money. The war at sea was effectively over. And the wonder weapon did not work! Nevertheless, O'Higgins's sense of honour was such that he promised to fulfil the agreement with William Cochrane as soon as his impoverished state could raise the money.[18]

Lord Cochrane was now granted four months' leave and the use of the schooner *Montezuma*, commanded by Lieutenant John Pascoe Grenfell. He spent much of July, August and September in his country estate at Quintero, taking delivery of tools and seeds newly arrived from England, and examining the machinery that engineer John Miers had brought out with him for rolling copper and stamping metal dies. The two had gone into partnership with a view to obtaining contracts for revising the coinage but were running into problems with the Mint. There was more excitement when a state-of-the-art lithographic press arrived – a vital tool for someone with Lord Cochrane's penchant for proclamations. Although he and Jackson were already occupied with a rebuttal of San Martin's charges, Cochrane was able to relax and concentrate on building his new house on the Quintero estate. It was set in a delightful location, amid rolling green pastureland scattered with herds of grazing cattle by the side of a fresh water lake facing the sea against a distant backdrop of the cordillera. These were the animals that were to furnish the raw materials for the business in salted meat and ships' biscuits that Cochrane and Miers hoped to develop. There were also frequent groups of visitors to entertain, which included Miers and his family, William Stevenson and Mrs Maria Graham. Thus present at Quintero at the same time were three people whose published memoirs were to be responsible for publicising the Cochrane story of heroism betrayed. It is hardly surprising that their versions of events were so similar. Another grateful visitor was the erstwhile defender of Valdivia, Colonel Fausto de Hoyos of the Cantabria Regiment. Cochrane had found him imprisoned in Santiago but had managed to persuade the authorities to release him under open arrest under his personal supervision.

Some biographers have tried to add spice to the story by suggesting that a romance developed between Cochrane and Mrs Graham at this time. In the small expatriate community of Valparaiso it was inevitable that they would meet – especially with Scotland, friends and a naval background in common. Maria was a proud – though hard up – member of the ubiquitous Dundas family; her father, George, had been a Rear Admiral; and her husband, Thomas Graham, had been on HMS *Thesis* in 1794 when Cochrane had been midshipman. Maria was certainly overawed by the famous Cochrane but there is no evidence or likelihood that there was any kind of relationship between them. They met seldom and, if not in the company of others, always in the presence of Maria's cousin William Glennie, a midshipman who had been invalided from HMS *Doris* in Chile to recover his health. Likewise, the only references to her in Cochrane's correspondence are cool, expressing only sympathy towards her as a naval widow marooned so far from home.[19] There is every indication that this was true. At a time when the aristocracy were notable for elastic morals and easy liaisons, Cochrane showed little interest in women other than his wife, and conducted himself with strict Scottish propriety in his dealings with the opposite sex. A more likely explanation for the close relationship between Mrs Graham and Cochrane's entourage is that the latter were fully aware of her literary reputation and decided to ensure that her book on Chile would tell the 'correct' story. Certainly, she was fully supplied with copies of Cochrane's official correspondence, and was briefed so successfully by his partisans that the portrayal she gives of San Martin and other of Cochrane's 'enemies' are – for her – unusually severe and inaccurate.

Lord Cochrane's leave was frequently interrupted when urgent matters called him away. There was, for example, the problem of seeing that the squadron was paid. The men were growing increasingly restive, and *Lautaro* was briefly seized by mutineers returning from an attack on the royalist privateer base on the Island of Chiloé. Then, the Chilean Accountant General, Correa de Sa, refused to approve Cochrane's accounts. This created a real problem. During much of the Peruvian campaign Cochrane had been left to fend for himself in finding supplies for the squadron. As a result, he had met his needs from a variety of sources – provisions, in the shape of corn, rice, cordage, naval stores, clothes, hardware and rum from the enemy; and money from seizures, trading 'licenses', and the local sale of prizes ships. The squadron's outgoings were just as complicated, covering the purchase of food, drink, clothing, naval supplies and equipment; and the distribution of pay and prize money to more than 1000 men.[20] All this made the squadron's accounts complex and unusual. An accountant, skilled in the methods of the time, might have been able to keep track of it. But the task was beyond the capabilities of Cochrane's staff – Stevenson and Dean. As a result, the accounts contained irregularities, unauthorised payments, missing receipts and faulty arithmetic. Until these were settled, the Chilean Accountant General, Correa de Sa, would not approve them. On 2 September, he wrote to Cochrane raising 80 queries and asking the Vice Admiral to appoint a representative to go through them in detail.[21] Cochrane was deeply offended. As one of the heroes of independence, he expected his accounts to be nodded through without examination. It was a view that no auditor could accept. Cochrane refused to reply, and the accounts remained unapproved. In retaliation, Cochrane and his partisans depicted the $67,000 balance as a 'debt' that the Chileans were neglecting to repay.

Then, at the end of September Cochrane received letters from Captains Wilkinson and Cobbett reporting a rumour that, while the squadron went unpaid, Cochrane was feathering his own nest by shipping 9000 ounces of gold dust and a similar quantity in gold and silver bars to England on HMS *Doris*.[22] With gold selling at $17 an ounce and silver at $7, this would have amounted to some

$260,000, or £52,200! The letters were accompanied by a petition of support from his remaining junior officers. Cochrane was aghast – especially as he was actually about to put $8497 in cash on the *Doris*! To safeguard his reputation, he hurried to Valparaiso to discover that the story had been spread by a former follower, the unruly Lieutenant Ford Morgell. A letter to O'Higgins quickly put things to rights and ensured the end of Morgell's career.[23] Unfortunately, however, by the time he wrote the *Narrative of Services*, Cochrane's obsession with Zenteno was so great that the unfortunate minister was accused of having been behind the 'plot'.

Then, on 12 October, the Peruvian brig-of-war *Belgrano* dropped anchor in Valparaiso. On board was no less a person than General San Martin. The liberation of Peru had not gone as expected. The royalists had remained undefeated in the mountains, growing stronger and more aggressive, and a meeting in Guayaquil between San Martin and Simon Bolivar, who had recently decisively defeated the Spaniards in Colombia and taken control of Guayaquil itself from San Martin's men, was inconclusive. Ruthless and confident, Bolivar sensed that his rival's cause had lost momentum and was not inclined to throw him a lifeline. The idea of a joint assault on the royalists therefore got nowhere. Politically, too, San Martin was in trouble. In Peru, the situation had deteriorated, with the Protector and his colleagues facing increasing unpopularity and accusations of tyranny and unbridled ambition. Disillusioned, San Martin decided he had had enough. True to his principles, in September 1822, he had handed power to a Sovereign Congress and retired to become a private citizen.

San Martin's arrival in Chile caused a stir, but created no problem. He explained that he was on his way to Europe via his home in the Argentine, and was in Chile to bathe his rheumatic arm in a well-known local Spa. The presence of the General in the country for two months caused some unease, but his stature as a Liberator and his long service to the cause of South American independence ensured that he was received with respect and courtesy. Only Lord Cochrane was out of step. Making one of those misjudgements that studded his career, he wrote to O'Higgins proposing an inquiry into San Martin's conduct with himself as chief prosecutor. He was, he wrote, 'ready to prove his 'usurpation of the Supreme Authority in Peru ...; his attempts to seduce the navy of Chile; his receiving and rewarding deserters from the Chilean service; his unjustifiable placing of the frigates *Prueba* and *Venganza* under the flag of Peru; with other demonstrations and acts of hostility towards the Republic of Chile.'[24] The Chileans tactfully ignored him. Cochrane withdrew once more to his estate to avoid the embarrassment of meeting the former Protector.

But the idyll at Quintero was shattered when, on the night of 19 November, central Chile was struck by the first in a series of tremendous earthquakes. There were tidal waves, violent shifts in the earth and changes in sea level. Valparaiso and others towns were wrecked, and there was wholesale destruction of houses, churches and public buildings. Penitents prayed in the streets to avert what was clearly divine retribution, while the more practical fled inland or took refuge on the ships in the bay. The shocks continued intermittently for a month, and only petered out at the end of December. It was only then that the slow work of repair and reconstruction could begin. But these natural disasters were matched by political turmoil. The honeymoon of Chilean independence was over and, in the south, Cochrane's old collaborator, General Freire, had raised the flag of revolt and had begun the slow march north that would end in the removal of Bernardo

O'Higgins. On Freire's behalf, Captain Casey tried to rally the squadron to join him, but Cochrane declined to become involved.

By this time the Chilean Government had decided on the squadron's future. Inevitably, it was to decommission the bulk of the ships and pay off their crews. In October, stimulated by continuing protests and a petition by their captains, orders were given to collect the necessary money.[25] Within six weeks this had been done and the task of paying the officers and men began.

It was clear to Lord Cochrane that his time in Chile was coming to an end. In four years he had done all that had been expected of him – and more, since by using his own initiative, he had delivered victories that his employers had not thought possible. He was also emotionally drained and depressed by the arguments over pay for the squadron, with San Martin's criticisms, and with his difficulties in getting the money he felt he was owed. Maria Graham noted that he looked far from well. But what of the future? However attractive a rural existence at Quintero may have seemed, it would never have satisfied a man of Cochrane's energetic temperament. He was therefore open to any offer that would enable him to use his military talents and, at the end of November, it arrived in the form of a letter from the Brazilian Agent in Buenos Aires, Antonio Correa da Camera. Brazil was on the brink of a war of independence against Portugal and its Emperor Pedro had given orders that Cochrane, fresh from his triumphs in the Pacific, should be invited to command the Brazilian Navy. Written in French and phrased in irresistible rhetoric, Correa de Camera's letter read:

Come, My Lord, Honour invites you. Glory is calling to you. A Generous Prince and a whole Nation await you. Come, reborn Hercules, and with your honour-

able efforts help to tame the Hundred-Headed Hydra
of a frightful Despotism. The west of America is saved
by virtue of your Arm. ... the Sacred Standard of
Independence is unfurled from the Galapagos as far
as the Cedar Isles of California! Come now and
furnish our Naval Arms with the wonderful order
and incomparable Discipline of Mighty Albion![26]

The Brazilian offer was opportune, and Cochrane
accepted. On 28 November 1822, after another argument
when the Minister of Marine ordered *Independencia* to sea
without his authority, he resigned his commission as Vice
Admiral of Chile.[27] Two days later his reply was on its way
to Correa da Camera. 'I have this day tendered my
resignation to the Government of Chile,' he wrote, 'and am
not aware that any material delay will be necessary
previous to my setting off for Rio de Janeiro ... it being
understood that I hold myself free to decline as well as to
accept the offer made through you by His Imperial
Majesty.'[28] He then began to prepare for the journey.

But Cochrane's Chilean adventures were not quite over.
The Ministry of Marine had made no reply to his letter of
resignation and Cochrane's flag continued to fly. Thus
there was a final clash on 18 December, when *Galvarino*
was ordered to sea without Cochrane being informed. The
Vice Admiral promptly made the brig stay where she was
and told *Lautaro* to fire on her should she attempt to
leave.[29] That seemed to do the trick. Later the same day a
decree was issued, demobilising the Chilean Navy and
placing its officers and men on half pay. The Chileans
wisely exempted Lord Cochrane, Captains Crosbie and
Cobbett and those of their lieutenants who had shown
particular merit during the Peruvian campaign and kept
them on full salary. Finally, a week later, Cochrane's
resignation was tacitly accepted and he was ordered to

hand over control of the ships in commission to the Commandant-General of Marine.[30] His time as commander-in-chief of the Chilean Navy had finally come to an end.

Cochrane's last month was spent at Quintero in the company of friends who – once again – included Miers, Stevenson and Maria Graham. There were occasional dashes to Valparaiso and Santiago as Cochrane tried to wind up his affairs. He had already received $63,500 (£12,700) in prize money, and $25,330 (£5070) in pay and – disenchanted with Hoseason and anxious to end the relationship – had made arrangements for the balance of $15,466 (£3090) owing on the latter to be paid to Kitty through the Chilean Legation in London.[31] But he was still owed money for the captures of *Valdivia* and *Esmeralda*, and for the balance on the squadron's accounts. He was also anxious to get something on his brother's behalf for the *Rising Star*. Alas, none of these problems were settled before he left Chile and Cochrane was forced to leave others to act on his behalf. Paroissien's friend, the Valparaiso merchant J. J. Barnard, was authorised to settle his claims on the *Rising Star* and to sell the extra engines she had carried from England. John Miers was left to develop the coinage initiative, and was left as sole proprietor of the beef and biscuit business in Quintero on a delayed payment to Cochrane of $25,000. Hoseason was paid off with a letter of credit on the government for $17,683 (£3767), which, according to his accounts, was what Cochrane owed him.[32]

By the beginning of 1823 preparations were well advanced for the voyage to Brazil. As a final flourish, on 4 January, Cochrane had three proclamations printed on his new lithographic press. The first was a rhetorical farewell to the Chilean people; the second to the British and foreign merchant community reminding them of the benefits his command had brought; and the third one of thanks to his fellow officers in the Chilean Navy. Two weeks later, the merchant brig *Colonel Allen* arrived in the bay. A succession of boats began to transfer luggage and possessions from the shore. Amongst them were boxes containing $52,000 (£10,400) in gold bullion, which Cochrane was taking with him out of the country.[33] Also accompanying him were five of his followers – Secretary William Jackson, Captain Thomas Sackville Crosbie and Lieutenants John Pascoe Grenfell, James Shepherd and Steven Clewley. Henry Dean also wanted to come but, avoiding the unpleasant duty of dismissing him, Cochrane left him behind in the hope that he would realise his services were no longer required. Cochrane also invited Maria Graham and her invalid cousin William Glennie to join the party. He remembered the relief he had felt when Captain Shirreff of *Andromache* had removed Kitty from a place of danger, and felt that he could do no less for the widow of a fellow naval officer apparently stranded so far from home. On 18 January, all was ready. There was an impromptu piece of ceremonial when Lord Cochrane's flag as Vice Admiral of Chile was lowered for the last time from the main mast of the *Montezuma*. Then, the *Colonel Allen* made sail and slowly slipped out of the Bay bound for Brazil.

Chapter 15

INDEPENDENCE – AT LAST

By the middle of 1823, the three protagonists whose efforts had been so decisive in securing the liberation of Chile and Peru had all left the scene of their triumphs and, alas, tragedies. Lord Cochrane was now First Admiral of Brazil and was about to repeat his performance in the Pacific – securing the independence of the country through a series of astonishing victories against the Portuguese; then leaving under a cloud as a result of a bitter quarrel over money and alleged poor treatment.[1] José de San Martin was back in his native Argentine, but was about to leave for a prolonged exile in London, Paris and Boulogne, where he died a lonely, unhappy and sickly man in 1850. Bernardo O'Higgins, having been under house arrest for months following his overthrow by Ramon Freire, was on his way to Peru to offer his services to Bolivar in the final liberation of the country from the Spanish. Alas, Bolivar saw O'Higgins as San Martin's stooge and gave him a cool reception. O'Higgins was to spend the next 20 years of his life quietly in a ranch south of Lima before the cautious Chileans agreed to allow him to return in 1842. Tragically, O'Higgins died on the journey home and never saw Chile again.

The removal of O'Higgins from the Supreme Director-ship in 1823 did nothing to solve Chile's problems. The country relapsed into chaos, disintegrating in the face of local warring factions. It was only ten years later that the conservative Diego Portales restored order and imposed a centralising constitution that put the new republic on the road to stability and prosperity. The disarray in Chile did Cochrane no favours. As happened in so many South American coups, the incoming governments disavowed or forgot the commitments of their predecessors. The claims Cochrane left behind him therefore got nowhere: the letters of credit given to Hoseason were not honoured; and papers relating to the construction and costs of the *Rising Star* were lost in the upheaval. The new government flatly refused to give anything for the steamship[2] and, with no hope of payment, in May 1824, her agent, J. J. Barnard, sold her lock, stock and barrel for $10,000. Cochrane's own actions did not help his case either. The Auditor General, Correa de Sa, once more wrote to him in Brazil asking for the appointment of a representative to go through the accounts of the Peruvian campaign and to justify the $67,000 he said was owing to him.[3] But Cochrane, who received the letter while blockading the Brazilian port of Salvador de Bahia in June 1823, flatly refused to cooperate and merely replied with a denunciation of the duplicity of the government.[4]

Meanwhile, the commercial ventures that Cochrane had launched with John Miers began to falter. Their plan to produce copper coins was abandoned when the Chilean Mint objected to the supply of currency being put in private hands. The attempt to manufacture salt beef and biscuits in Quintero failed to prosper. Severe drought in the region reduced the numbers of livestock, the price of local beef rose, and the demand for preserved meat was more than amply covered by cheaper imports from Britain and the United States.[5] Then the original landowner initiated a process to reclaim possession of the estate. He eventually succeeded, though only on the payment of compensation. Dean too, who had been left behind when the *Colonel Allen* sailed for Brazil, immediately began to feather his nest at the Admiral's expense, claiming fraudulently that Cochrane had left him in charge of his affairs, and planning a large-scale smuggling operation using his cattle! Fortunately, Miers managed to frustrate Dean's tricks. When, to his relief, Dean left for Brazil with his wife and children, Miers wrote a long and detailed report on his activities, denouncing him as a man who is 'as well known in Brazil as in Buenos Aires and Chile as a complete swindler, … one who since your departure has abused you in violent terms in Valparaiso,' and concluded 'you may rely upon it, he is an extremely dangerous and cunning man.' He urged Cochrane to have nothing more to do with him.[6] Inexplicably, Cochrane re-employed Dean in Brazil, though writing him what can only be described as a letter of warning.[7] It made no impact and Dean proceeded to manipulate the Admiral's prize money and property, ultimately suing him for £14,700![8]

When San Martin led his army across the high passes of the Andes in 1817, the removal of Spanish forces from Peru had been the key to the liberation of South America. Five years later, the challenge was much the same. True, Peru had declared its independence, but San Martin's hope that Spain would accept the inevitable and withdraw its troops had not been realised. Indeed, an army under Viceroy de la Serna remained intact and undefeated in the mountains of Upper Peru and in the fertile valley of the Juaja, only ten days march east of Lima. Without San Martin's firm direction, independent Peru also began to fall apart. The bulk of the population was apathetic, the ruling class ambivalent, the army went unpaid, and the security of the country remained dependent on troops from Chile and Colombia.

In January 1823, a Spanish attack northwards from Arica caused panic in Lima. The determined but unpleasant Riva Agüero seized power, entrusting command of the army to General Andres Santa Cruz and of the navy to Martin Guise, now a Peruvian Vice Admiral. When appeals for foreign assistance fell on deaf ears, Riva Agüero foolishly sent his troops to attack the Spanish forces alone. Outnumbered and outclassed, they were soundly beaten. The royalists seized the initiative to launch a major attempt at reconquest. In Spain, the government sent the 64-gun *Asia* and the brig *Achilles* to the Pacific carrying reinforcements. In Peru, Canterac began to advance on Lima with his Division of 8000 troops, leaving 3000 men under General Valdez to watch Arequipa and another 4000 under General Olañeta to guard Upper Peru. As the Spaniards drew near, the Peruvian Government and army disintegrated before them. While Guise and the navy blockaded the coast, the Marquis of Torre Tagle seized power and fortified the Castles of Callao. Now attacked by land and sea, independent Peru seemed on the brink of extinction. There was only one man who could save the situation – the Liberator, Simon Bolivar.

Answering an appeal from Torre Tagle, Bolivar reached Lima on 1 September, to be greeted with joy, cheering crowds, gala performances at the theatre, and celebratory bull fights. Momentarily he was able to stem the royalist tide. But it was clear to the Liberator that the Spanish forces were formidable and those at his disposal too weak. He therefore withdrew to the northern border with Guayaquil to reorganise his army, leaving Viceroy de la Serna free to reoccupy the country from the east. The high point of the Spanish campaign came in February 1824, when the unpaid black Argentine troops that formed the garrison of Callao mutinied and surrendered the Castles. Lima quickly fell to the royalists, and many of the Peruvian elite hastened to change sides, including Torre Tagle who unleashed a bitter denunciation of Bolivar.

On the verge of victory, the royalist effort suddenly faltered. This was not the result of any action by the patriots, but of splits within the Spanish forces themselves. While de la Serna had been busy occupying Peru during 1823, a French army, acting on behalf of the Holy Alliance of reactionary European monarchs, had been invading Spain with the aim of overthrowing the constitutional government. In October, they succeeded and Ferdinand VII was restored to absolute power. Spain was plunged into a year-long reign of terror in which thousands of officials and liberal sympathisers were purged, imprisoned and exiled. The effects were not confined to Spain. When the news reached South America, one of the Viceroy's divisional Generals, Pedro Antonio Olañeta, promptly seized control of Upper Peru in the name of Ferdinand VII. At a stroke, the Spanish forces were fragmented. Not only was Olañeta's command of 4000 men removed from de la Serna's control, but Valdez's units had to be detached to keep an eye on them.

In the north, Bolivar was now ready to go at the head of some 10,000 men – 3500 Colombians under Antonio de Sucre, 3000 Peruvians under José La Mar – the former American-born Governor of Callao who had now joined the patriot ranks, 500 artillerymen, and 1500 cavalry, including a brigade of lancers commanded by William Miller. Learning of the division within the Spanish forces, Bolivar seized his opportunity. In May 1824, he led his army forward on another epic march across the mountains of Peru. Advancing in three divisions, his men snaked up the high passes, across rocky defiles, through narrow mountain gorges and over rushing torrents, often only able to keep in contact with the units ahead and with the line of march by bugle calls. Without the careful planning that had marked San Martin's crossing of the Andes six years before, there were heavy losses of men and animals from exhaustion, snow blindness and altitude sickness. The army finally emerged from the mountains to unite and recover beneath the Cerro de Pasco, some 100 miles northeast of Lima as the condor flies. On 6 August, Bolivar advanced a few miles south onto the plateau of Junin, surprised Canterac's army, defeated it, and forced it into ignominious retreat towards Cuzco. It was the royalists who were now on the defensive as Bolivar's army surged on.

Meanwhile, further south, *Asia* and *Achilles* were approaching Callao after a three-month stay at Chiloé where Commodore Roque Guruzeta had refitted his ships. On guard outside Callao was Vice Admiral Martin Guise in the frigate *Protector* (the renamed *Prueba*) with two Peruvian ships – the brig *Congresso* and schooner *Macedonian* – and two Colombian brigs. Midshipman James of HMS *Tartar* was thrilled when he met the captains of *Congresso* and *Macedonian* – Young and Robertson – to discover that they were old Royal Navy shipmates. Guise and his men had been on blockade duty for six months, making occasional attacks on Callao, arresting blockade runners and – Cochrane fashion – demanding 25 per cent of the value of cargoes for permission to enter a port. With the Peruvian state in disarray, it was the only way Guise could pay his crews and maintain his ships.[9] Watching him was a flotilla of British, American and French warships, alerted by this renewed threat to their trade. There were HM ships *Cambridge*, *Tartar* and *Fly*, the USS *United States*, and the French ship *Lancier*. The presence of the 80-gun *Cambridge* was an accident. The British Government had announced the previous January that it intended to recognise the independence of the well established states of Mexico, Colombia and Argentina, though it had excluded Chile and Peru from the list in view of the uncertainty of the situation there. Nevertheless, the same month, HMS *Cambridge* had sailed for South America from Portsmouth carrying the full team of diplomats needed to establish official relations with all the new republics on the Atlantic and Pacific coasts – three consul-generals, one consul and five vice-consuls.[10] Unfortunately, by the time the ship reached Peru in May, there was no longer an independent state with which relations could be established.

Nevertheless, Captain Maling made himself useful. Following their defeat at Junin, the royalists had garrisoned Callao but had sent all other available troops to join Canterac's army. As a result, the area around Lima became a lawless no-man's land haunted by bandits and desperadoes, many of them deserters or unpaid soldiers. And when the newly appointed British Consul-General for Lima, Mr Rowcroft, went ashore with his daughter in a private capacity wearing the uniform of the City of London Volunteers, he was promptly shot and killed in an altercation with jumpy security forces. Following a solemn local ceremonial with ships firing minute guns and flags at half mast, Rowcroft's body was sent back to England Nelson-fashion in a barrel of spirits. Following this incident, the Spanish authorities allowed *Cambridge* to send 120 Royal Marines to Lima to safeguard British lives and property. For two months between August and October they were the only agents of law and order in the capital.[11]

The Spanish warships *Asia* and *Achilles* sighted Callao on 12 September 1824, ignored the tacit offer of combat made when Guise's blockading flagship fired a gun and backed his mizzen topsail and – in the words of Commodore Isaac Hull of the *United States* – 'sneaked' into the port. The Governor of the Castles, the ruthless General José Ramon Rodil was unimpressed with his colleague's reluctance to take on the Peruvians in spite of the disparity of force in his favour. In his Journal, Surgeon Cunningham of *Cambridge*, alleges that Rodil coldly greeted the Spanish commander with the words 'Commodore, all the little boys in Lima are saying that Don Roque Guruzeta is a coward!'[12] A month later, on 8 October, Guruzeta finally sailed out to confront Guise with the *Asia*, *Achilles*, a corvette and two locally armed brigs. *Cambridge*, *Tartar* and the *United States* followed them out to watch.[13] Guise and his four smaller consorts immediately dispersed to escape into the intermittent mist, the *Protector* being chased by *Asia* until the frigate's superior speed outdistanced her. But Guruzeta lacked the killer instinct and was too gentlemanly to destroy the smaller patriot warships and left them unmolested. As he wrote loftily in his dispatch, 'these small vessels were so contemptible and so badly handled on that day, that I felt it unseemly to occupy myself with them and concentrated solely on the *Prueba*.'[14] Guruzeta then led his force back to Callao having achieved nothing. After minor repairs, Guise and his blockading ships were soon back in station. Rodil was furious and refused even to speak to Guruzeta.

Bolivar was pleased with his victory at Junin, but believed that there could be no further military operations until the end of the rainy season. So, leaving Sucre in the mountains to block any royalist advance, he withdrew slowly towards Lima. De la Serna, however, was less complacent than Bolivar expected. After Junin, he concentrated his scattered forces on Cuzco, and at the end of November began to move forward with a united army of 10,000 men against Sucre's force which, with fewer than 6000 troops, was heavily outnumbered. The two armies met at Ayacucho on 6 December 1824. The patriots should have lost, but they did not. After a day of brilliant manoeuvring, Sucre defeated the Spanish army in one of the decisive battles of South America. By nightfall, 1900 Spaniards lay dead, while 2500 soldiers, 480 officers, 100 colonels, and eight generals – including Canterac, Valdez and Viceroy de la Serna – had been taken prisoner. The capitulation agreed after the battle was one of total surrender and the withdrawal of the Spanish army. It was the end of all royalist hopes for the reconquest of South America. Only Olañeta's force remained at large, and this was destroyed – and its commander killed – the following March.

When the news of Ayacucho reached Callao, Commodore Guruzeta decided to salvage what naval forces he could for his King. Ordering the corvette and brig to return to Spain via Cape Horn, he sailed with *Asia* and *Achilles* for Manila. Alas, Guruzeta never reached his destination. Open protests from his crews, many of whom were press-ganged South Americans, forced him to hand over the ships to the local patriot authorities. *Asia* was surrendered to the Mexicans in Monterrey, while *Achilles* made for Valparaiso where she was taken into the Chilean Navy.

After Ayacucho, the mainland of Spanish America was firmly in patriot hands. But two tiny Spanish outposts stubbornly continued to resist in the name of King Ferdinand – the Chiloé Archipelago and the Castles of Callao. The Chileans sent two expeditions against Chiloé between 1822 and 1824, but none made any impression. The resourcefulness and courage of the wily Colonel Quintanilla, the poor condition of their ships, and storms and heavy weather, frustrated each attempt. In Callao, Governor Rodil flatly refused to hand over the Castles and conducted a year-long defence of fierce – even manic – intensity, imposing a regime of terror on the 2500 troops he commanded and on the 3000 or so refugees who swelled their ranks. Stores ran out; the inhabitants were reduced to eating rats, cats and mules; unproductive civilians were ruthlessly driven out to die of starvation between the lines; and discipline was maintained with an iron hand. Foreign ships of war were appalled to see those guilty of defeatism or disobedience herded out beyond the walls and shot in daily batches of 30.[15] But no relief or reinforcement arrived. Eventually, Rodil accepted the inevitable and, in January 1826, surrendered the fortress. When the gates were opened, only 444 soldiers had survived the siege – thousands of troops and civilians had perished. Rodil, however, lived on, and returned to Spain as a national hero. Meanwhile, news of the loss of *Asia* and *Achilles*, and the absence of any relief or reinforcement convinced Quintanilla in Chiloé that the end had come and, when Blanco Encalada arrived in command of the last Chilean expedition in 1825, he too capitulated. By the end of January 1826, the Spanish Empire on mainland South America was no more.

Chapter 16
SETTLING ACCOUNTS

In Brazil, Lord Cochrane's contribution to independence was as decisive as that he had made in Chile or Peru. Given command of its navy as First Admiral on a huge salary, Cochrane sailed from Rio de Janeiro to confront the Portuguese forces occupying the eastern seaboard on 1 April 1823. In a brilliant campaign of only six months, he blockaded the enemy's major arsenal in Bahia, expelled an army and a greatly superior naval squadron, and harried it out of Brazilian waters and across the Atlantic. Then, using an audacious trick, he secured the evacuation of the Portuguese garrisons in Maranhão and Pará on the northern coast. Largely as a result of Cochrane's efforts, by December 1823 Brazil had been cleared of enemy troops. It took time for the fact to be accepted diplomatically, but the country was, to all intents and purposes, independent.

A triumphant Lord Cochrane returned to Rio de Janeiro in November to be given all the rewards a grateful nation could bestow. He was made Marquis of Maranhão by the Emperor Pedro, became a Knight Grand Cross of the Order of the Cruzeiro do Sul, received a vote of thanks from the National Assembly, and was made a member of the Privy Council of the Empire. But as happened so often in his career, the renown of his dazzling victories was quickly overshadowed by bitter disputes over prize money and alleged poor treatment. The acrimony was interrupted by an outbreak of rebellion in the turbulent northeast. Now preoccupied with his wrongs, Cochrane applied himself with little energy to the suppression of the outbreak and, in April 1825, effectively absconded to England in a Brazilian frigate ingenuously claiming that the need for urgent repairs had been discovered in mid-Atlantic.

Back in Britain, Cochrane was cheered in the streets and hailed by excited liberals as a conquering hero and the liberator of South America. The Tory Government was less enthusiastic. Many ministers still regarded him as a demagogue and a fraudster. Indeed, a threat to prosecute him under the 1819 Foreign Enlistment Act, which prohibited service in foreign wars in which Britain was neutral, forced Cochrane to go on his travels once more. This time, he accepted command of the Greek Navy in its war for freedom from Turkish oppression, convinced that the squadron of armed paddle steamers he intended to bring with him would sweep the enemy from the seas. But there, Cochrane's career as First Admiral was neither happy nor distinguished. In two years even he could achieve little. The military situation was chaotic, the Greek maritime forces were unreliable and undisciplined, few steamships arrived, and the techniques Cochrane had used so successfully in Chile and Brazil fell embarrassingly flat. When Greek independence did come, it had little to do with Cochrane's activities but was due to allied inter- vention and the destruction of the Turkish Navy at the Battle of Navarino by the combined squadrons of Britain, Russia and France. Depressed by this apparent failure, he retired to Italy to restore his spirits.

Meanwhile, in 1830, Britain experienced a political revolution in which the Tories were ejected after 25 years of power. They were replaced by a Whig government made up of Cochrane's political friends. Seizing his opportunity, Cochrane – who had just inherited his father's title as Earl of Dundonald – returned with Kitty and his family to London determined to clear his name from the Stock Exchange fraud and to secure the restoration of his rank and privileges. His political friends rallied round; the press was favourable; petitions were presented; and strings were pulled. In 1832, Cochrane achieved the first of his objectives by being granted a Royal Pardon for the Stock Exchange conviction and restored to his original position in the Navy List. Indeed, as the list had moved steadily upwards during the intervening 17 years, Cochrane found himself reappointed as a Rear-Admiral of the Blue. Encouraged by this success, he began to lobby for the restoration of the Knighthood of the Bath that had been stripped from him in 1814.

Cochrane's case for rehabilitation was greatly helped by the appearance of a series of books that publicised the heroic aspects of his naval career. First, in 1824, Maria Graham published her *Journal of a Residence in Chile during the Year 1822*. This was followed by William Bennet Stevenson's *Historical and Descriptive Narrative of a 20 year Residence in South America*. Then, in 1826, came John Miers's *Travels in Chile and La Plata*. All of these books included glowing accounts of Cochrane's triumphs in South America; but all three writers had been members of his inner circle and all retailed the admiral's distorted – even paranoid – claim that his victories had been won in spite of plots, obstruction and jealousy. Then Captain Marriott's naval novels began to capture the public imagination. Marryat had been a midshipman on Cochrane's frigates during the Napoleonic Wars and his books were filled with descriptions of actions and of characters drawn from his experiences. Indeed, *Frank Mildmay*, which appeared in 1829, was a fictionalised account of the voyages of the

Imperieuse with the heroic captain easily recognisable as a thinly disguised Lord Cochrane.

Not that Cochrane himself was backward in publicising his own version of events. Aided by a group of friends and hangers-on, who included his secretary William Jackson, in the late 1830s Cochrane began to produce a series of petitions and memorials that related at length his services, feuds and financial claims against the governments of Britain, Chile, Peru and Brazil. The campaign reached its first high point in his 1846 publication, *Observations on Naval Affairs ... including Instances of Injustice experienced by the Author*. The story as he told it, whether it was set in the Napoleonic Wars or in South America, was the same – that of the noble warrior hero achieving miracle victories in spite of disloyalty by his subordinates and persecution by his superiors. Unfortunately, there were few survivors of the wars with France left to contradict his version of events, and information from South America was unobtainable. Cochrane's claims were swallowed whole by the Victorian public. Indeed, the story of the hero being betrayed by lesser men appealed to the sentimental taste of the time. The Queen herself was deeply moved by Cochrane's story of suffering, and took a leading part in ensuring that he achieved his ambition and was restored to the Order of the Bath in 1847.

By this time, Cochrane's rehabilitation in Britain was completed. He was now 72 years old, a Vice Admiral, a Knight Grand Cross of the Bath, the holder of high Chilean, Brazilian and Greek decorations, and the recipient of a special pension for meritorious service. In Britain he was admired as a surviving hero of the Napoleonic Wars, a leading figure in fashionable wars of liberation, and a political radical whose struggles for Parliamentary reform had been vindicated. His opinion was keenly sought by the Admiralty on the technical and tactical challenges posed by steamships, iron and new weapons. In 1848 he was appointed commander-in-chief of the Royal Navy's North America and West Indies Squadron for a three-year term of duty. In 1854 he volunteered his services for the Crimean War, but was refused by a cautious Admiralty, which feared that his impetuosity and habit of disobeying orders might get them into trouble. He may have been 79 years' old at the time, but his reputation lived on!

When Cochrane returned to London in 1831, he had been a rich man. His activities in South America alone had earned him some £42,700 in pay and prize money, and in Greece he had received a handsome advance of salary totalling £37,000. But by 1840, he was in severe financial difficulties. He was unable to control his expenditure at the best of times: now he had real problems. First, the consequences of his South American activities caught up with him. He was sued by his Brazilian prize agents and by Hoseason and Dean who claimed that he owed them £20,000.[1] Then he was taken to law by the owners of French and British merchant ships – such as *Gazelle*, *Admiral Cockburn* and *Edward Ellis* – which he had seized during the Chilean blockades. According to Cochrane, adverse judgements in these actions cost him £14,000.[2] His financial situation was made worse when Kitty demanded a separation in 1839, and moved to France to live in high style on the income from the French bonds that Cochrane had purchased with his Greek pay. Then his eldest children went off the rails, going to moneylenders and running up enormous debts that a despairing Cochrane was forced to settle. And all the while, his fortune was being slowly dissipated by the development costs of his scientific experiments with steamships, new weapons, poison gas, tar and bitumen – all of which seemed to lose money rather than make it. His unsuccessful attempt to turn the armed paddle steamer HMS *Janus* into a viable proposition, for example, soaked up at least £25,000.[3]

With his financial situation deteriorating, Cochrane began to look round for other sources of money. In 1839, he put in a claim for Royal Navy half-pay between 1814 and 1832, ignoring the fact that he had been earning large sums in South America and Greece during this period. Cochrane firmly believed that he had suffered financially and psychologically as a result of the Stock Exchange conviction and, now that he had been given a Royal Pardon, was convinced that he was entitled to compensation for what he had lost. The full extent of what this meant was revealed in *Observations on Naval Affairs*, in which he listed his claims as being £4000 for 18 year's half-pay; £5000 for the fine and costs of the Stock Exchange trial; £40,000 for the loss of a legacy from his rich uncle Basil, who had been turned against him by the 'aspersions and insinuations of those around him'; and £50,000 for the loss of the Culross estate for similar reasons.[4] It was soon made clear to Cochrane that he had no chance of getting the British Government to swallow any of this. He therefore pinned his hopes on South America and on the huge debts that he was convinced were owed to him by Chile and Brazil. Cochrane's initial calculations put these amounts at £126,000 – though the total steadily grew and he thought up more and more claims.

In spite of Cochrane's assertions to the contrary, he had already received all the pay owing to him and a substantial amount of prize money when he left Chile in 1823. But behind him he left two acknowledged debts – the balance owing on his accounts for the Peruvian campaign and his share of the *Esmeralda* prize money. There were two other complaints – that he had received nothing in the way of prize money for the capture of Valdivia; and that after he had left the country the government had taken back the estate he had been granted in Rio Claro. While Chile was in a state of instability, Cochrane could do little to advance his claims. But by 1837, the situation had improved, and he decided to revive them with the help of a local agent called Alexander Caldeclough. First, it had to be decided exactly what Cochrane could legally claim. Caldeclough's view was that this comprised $14,300 for Valdivia and other prize money, a revised figure of $66,100 for the balance on his accounts for the Peruvian Expedition, and $4000 in compensation for the loss of the Rio Clara estate – a total of $80,400, or £16,100.[5] Caldeclough was given the necessary powers to enable him to pursue these claims with the Chilean authorities, and Cochrane produced a powerful *Petition to the President and Congress of Chile,* which described his services during the war of independence and listed his demands. Foreign Secretary Lord Aberdeen was prevailed upon to order the British Consul General in Santiago, Colonel John Walpole, to exert pressure on Cochrane's behalf; and in the early 1840s, his son Arthur, then serving with the Royal Navy's South America squadron, was sent a Power of Attorney and told to add his weight.

In fact they were pushing on a half open door. The Chilean Government had put money aside in anticipation of Cochrane's claims, although nothing had been possible earlier because of his refusal to answer the audit queries on the squadron's accounts.[6] Once he agreed to do so – even though most of the answers he gave were vague and imprecise – the Chileans could not avoid confronting the issue.[7] Walpole and Caldeclough exerted continuous pressure to get a result and, on 6 September 1844, they succeeded. The Chilean Government issued a decree that began with a fulsome tribute to Cochrane's services to independence and ended with an offer of £6000 in settlement.[8] Walpole, who had seen all the figures and arguments, wrote that 'though in amount only a moiety of that claimed, it does not on investigation … appear to me to be unreasonable considering that there were some charges which were not justified by the necessities of his position or by his instructions, and others for which no vouchers have been produced.'[9]

Cochrane, however, was furious. He rejected the offer and in 1845 produced a 14-page closely printed *Memorial to the President and Government of Chile*. He had been busy elaborating his claims, which had now risen to $297,000 (or £60,000)! But this time they had little to do with real debts. Cochrane had managed to convince himself that his pay as Vice Admiral of Chile was only designed to cover his routine duties, and that he was entitled to bonuses for 'extra-official services' – that is, for doing anything else! On the basis of this novel idea, he now demanded more money. Each of his claims covers at least a page of print, but in summary they comprised $66,000 as settlement of the accounts of the Peruvian Expedition; $50,000 for 'planning and executing an attack on Valdivia ... without orders or the knowledge of the government'; $30,000 in prize money for conceiving and personally taking part in the capture of the *Esmeralda*: $20,000, being his share of $200,000 captured in Peru; $15,000 in compensation for losses resulting from law suits by the owners of ships taken during the blockades of Peru; $50,000 for declining the offer to lead the Peruvian Navy and for being 'denied' prize money for *Prueba* and *Venganza*; and $60,000, being Chilean half pay from 1823 to 1844 calculated at $3000 per annum – a matter that had been neither discussed nor agreed during his period of service.[10] The Chileans remained tactfully silent in the face of these shameless demands, and it was not until 1852 that Cochrane saw sense and took the money on offer, accepting it as a token of national gratitude.[11]

The Chilean Government may have had difficulty in accepting Cochrane's financial demands, but they had no doubts that he had played a key role in the liberation of their country. On 28 July 1857, they therefore published a decree that contained a fulsome and admiring tribute to his services and reappointed him as Vice Admiral with the right to receive full salary wherever he lived.[12] When the offer was passed on to him, Cochrane wrote to thank the Chileans for the compliment, but could not refrain from pointing our grumpily that the appointment and the salary meant little to a man who was over 85 years old![13] Among the congratulatory letters that followed was one from Admiral Blanco Encalada writing from Paris,[14] and another from his old subordinate Robert Simpson. In addition to expressing gratitude, admiration and wishing his old chief good health, Simpson, who was now a Vice Admiral and the sole surviving British officer of the wars of independence in the Chilean Navy, may have planted a seed in Cochrane's mind when he added 'I have been requested to procure a biographical sketch of Your Lordship's eventful life in order to secure its publication in this country.'[15]

Meanwhile, Cochrane had set his sights on Brazil, and appointed the local firm of James Moore and Co, to press his claims. The case was more straightforward than in Chile. In response to Cochrane's worries about his terms of service, in 1824, the Imperial Government had issued a decree stating that he could remain First Admiral until he chose to resign; and that thereafter he would be entitled to receive half-pay for life. Likewise, it had solved the political problem caused by the enormous number of seizures made during the war of independence by deciding that the Brazilian Treasury would pay the value of all prizes to the captors whether they were legally condemned or not. Cochrane would have been entitled to one-eighth of all this as commander-in-chief. Unfortunately, neither happened. Cochrane's actions in absconding from Brazil without explanation in 1825, his rejection of orders to return to give an account of his final voyage, and his refusal to resign when the world knew he had been recruited to command the Greek Navy caused the Brazilians to put the whole issue on ice. Eventually it was forgotten. But in October 1847 Cochrane revived it dramatically in a *Petition to the Emperor Pedro II* of Brazil, which described in detail his activities during the War of Independence and enumerated his financial claims.[16] His period of service as commander-in-chief of the Royal Navy's North America and West Indies squadron then intervened; but, in March 1854, he returned to the attack by producing a Description of Services, followed up a year later by a *Memorial to the Legislature of Brazil*.[17]

Cochrane's story had an enormous impact and produced the desired result. After a debate in the Brazilian Legislature on 16 August 1855, the government granted the half-pay pension he had been promised. On 23 February 1857, James Moore and Co triumphantly remitted £34,000 to Lord Cochrane being his pay and his pension backdated to 10 November 1825 calculated at $6000 per annum. But this was not the end of it. Cochrane remained aggrieved about the prize money issue. Unfortunately, the incomplete nature of the records relating to the War of Independence caused endless delays in settling the question. The good news, however, was that new regulations had raised Cochrane's share of prizes taken to one-fifth of the amount available! Alas, he was never to see it. It took years for the Brazilian Government to sort out the matter and its first award of £9459 was not paid until 1865 – five years after his death. The amount was, however, regarded as inadequate, and Cochrane's son, the 11th Earl of Dundonald, returned to the attack, launching a new barrage of demands, most of which were either dubious or imaginary. To prevent the dispute dragging on any longer, the Brazilians went to international arbitration. A lengthy and well-considered judgment was delivered in 1873. It roundly dismissed most of the new demands but concluded that

£34,500 was still owed in prize money. To its credit, the Brazilian Government accepted the findings without demur and promptly paid that sum to Lord Cochrane's heirs.[18]

In 1855, Cochrane reached his eightieth year, and had become one of the monuments of Victorian Britain. He had achieved full rehabilitation and recognition for the astonishing achievements of his life but, alas, the old obsessions with injustice and money still rankled. So, with a mass of documents at his disposal, a team of eager helpers and the outline of his story already available in a mass of petitions and memorials, Cochrane decided to write the story of his life in the way he wanted it remembered. The first two books appeared in 1859 under the title *Narrative of Services in the Liberation of Chile, Peru and Brazil.* They were joined the following year by the *Autobiography of a Seaman*, which recounted, in two further volumes, his adventures and feuds during the Napoleonic Wars. Cochrane never wrote an account of his adventures in Greece, but they were described in 1869, when the 11th Earl of Dundonald produced a two-volume *Life of Lord Cochrane*, which completed the story of his father's life.

Cochrane was 84 years old when these autobiographies were written, deaf, ailing and only able to contributed half-remembered reminiscences. The real author was a professional writer called G. P. Earp, assisted by his former secretary, William Jackson. Although Earp claimed that he had been objective, the declared purpose of these books was to vindicate Cochrane, to prove that he had been right in all his innumerable quarrels, and to justify his financial claims. Indeed, Earp was promised a percentage of any payments the book might stimulate. It is therefore hardly surprising to find that these autobiographies are filled with inaccuracies and present a travesty of the truth. The quality of the various books, however, varies considerably. The *Autobiography of a Seaman* is the best. When Earp wrote it, he had plenty of books, newspaper accounts and memoirs on which to draw, as well as Cochrane's own papers. At the other extreme, the Brazilian volume of the *Narrative of Services* was undoubtedly the worst. The lack of books and background material resulted in an account that not only contained glaring errors of fact, date and geography, but was dominated by Cochrane's vividly misremembered grievances.

The Chilean volume of the *Narrative of Services* fell between these two extremes. On the positive side, Earp was able to draw on the books already published by Maria Graham, Miers and Stevenson. This enabled him to get the chronology of events more or less correct. But in terms of providing a true account of what actually took place, and of the motives and actions of men like San Martin, Zenteno, Guise and Spry, Earp's book is disturbingly distorted. Unfortunately for him, material from South America that might have led him to modify his narrative was unavailable and, although Cochrane's papers included mountains of original documents, most were in Spanish and beyond Earp's comprehension. Likewise, Maria Graham, Miers and Stevenson were blatantly partisan and, rather than help to correct the old Admiral's distorted memories of events, they actually reflected and reinforced them. The result is that as a work of history, the *Narrative of Services* is deeply flawed. It is therefore unfortunate that for more than 150 years, the book has been accepted at its face value and has had a perverse effect on the way the wars of independence in the Pacific has been recorded by British, Spanish and – indeed – Chilean historians.

When his autobiographies were published, Cochrane was a hero and a legend, and his version of his astonishing career in South America was read with respect and total belief. No one seems to have doubted or questioned anything he said. Indeed, the dramatic quality of his story, the nobility of the causes for which he fought and, indeed, the element of betrayal by lesser men – mostly foreigners – confirmed Cochrane in the Victorian imagination as the ideal warrior hero. Inevitably too, the story stimulated a host of supporting legends and myths. Cochrane claimed, for example, that in the Pacific, his fearful enemies had called him 'El Diablo'. There is no evidence for this. Indeed his only known nickname is that recorded by Paroissien – 'el metálico lord', the spirit of which is roughly translated as 'the count of cash' or 'the baron of bullion'! Likewise loose words from Kitty resulted in a story that Cochrane had sent Colonel Charles to rescue Napoleon from St Helena and make him Emperor of South America.[19] This is a complete fable made the more ridiculous by the fact that Charles was killed two months before he is alleged to have set out for the South Atlantic.

Lord Cochrane spent the last years of his life in the home of his son and heir Thomas, at Queen's Gate, Kensington. But he was an old man, and his health and memory were deteriorating rapidly. He underwent two painful operations for kidney stones in 1860 but, alas, did not survive the second and died on 31 October, just short of his eighty-fifth birthday. He was buried on 14 November with all the elaborate ceremonial of a Victorian funeral – an ornate hearse with six plumed black horses, eight carriages of mourners, and silent crowds lining the route as the procession wound its way along Knightsbridge and Piccadilly, through St James Street and Pall Mall and into Parliament Street. The ceremony was attended by a galaxy of naval and political personalities representing the various stages of his career, including Admiral Sir George Seymour of the Royal Navy who had fought with him at the Basque Roads, John Pascoe Grenfell, his old follower in South America who was now a Brazilian Vice Admiral, and the Ministers of Brazil and Chile. As befitted a hero, he was buried in Westminster Abbey.

Chapter 17

EPILOGUE

Lord Cochrane's career as Vice Admiral of Chile was a formative period in his life. Indeed, the war in the Pacific brought out the best and the worst in him. On the positive side, the huge panorama of the naval war and his position as commander-in-chief gave him ample opportunity to exercise his aggression, his ingenuity and his tactical flare. Once again, he was able to demonstrate his astonishing personal courage and leadership in battle and to confirm his reputation as a master of amphibious warfare. The spectacular victories he achieved, notably in the capture of Valdivia and the seizure of the *Esmeralda*, ensured the independence of Chile and Peru and became the corner-stones of his own reputation. They also shattered Spanish morale, forced them onto the defensive and were major contributions to the ultimate victory of the forces of independence.

On the negative side, however, the subordinate role he and the navy were expected to play in the liberation campaign was at odds with Cochrane's temperament and his personal style. Cochrane was never a team player and expected to be given complete operational freedom. Indeed, having no doubts about his own superior abilities, he firmly believed that the best way to ensure victory was for him to be left to operate as he thought fit, unhampered by orders from anyone else. In South America this was not possible. Victory in the liberation struggle could only be gained on the battlefield, and the navy's activities, though important, had to be controlled and coordinated with what took place on land. Cochrane was therefore disconcerted when he was required to operate under tight orders and when, in the invasion of Peru, he was put firmly under San Martin's direction. True, he stretched his orders to the limit, and ignored them when he could – typically achieving a spectacular victory at Valdivia as a result – but the obvious attempts to curb his independence soon triggered the conviction in his mind that he was surrounded by plots and jealousy. He was also disappointed that he was able to exert so little influence on patriot strategy. San Martin and O'Higgins had clear ideas on what was needed to roll back Spanish power in Peru and did not need a newcomer like Cochrane to tell them what to do.

Cochrane's service as Vice Admiral of Chile was his first taste of being responsible for a whole squadron rather than an individual ship. This gave him the opportunity to magnify his impact on the war, but it imposed limitations on his personal activities, which he found irksome. So much so that he often preferred – as at Valdivia – to act with the *O'Higgins* alone. Likewise, while he was perfectly capable of masterminding the squadron's operations, the routine responsibilities of being a commander-in-chief made him bored and careless. Distracted by the search for spectacular opportunities for action, he paid insufficient attention to more humdrum duties like convoying San Martin's army to Peru or rigorously blockading Callao. Likewise, Cochrane found administrative chores uncongenial and left too much to his inexperienced and mistrusted staff. Unfortunately these activities began to occupy more and more of his time. In the Royal Navy – and to a lesser extent

in the navy of Brazil – the infrastructure for pay and
supplies on land, and the traditions of discipline and
obedience at sea were well established, and left Cochrane
to do what he was good at – namely leadership in action.
In the Pacific neither was true. The inability of the Chilean
departments of marine to keep the squadron supplied and
paid placed enormous burdens on him during the invasion
of Peru. Cochrane was left alone to solve these problems,
living off the land and resorting to almost any trick to keep
his ships afloat and his men fed. Unfortunately, neither
Cochrane nor his staff had much understanding of the
bureaucratic traditions and procedures that Chile had
inherited from old Spain, and the pragmatic expedients to
which they resorted were often more than the system could
tolerate. Cochrane suffered the consequences when the
Chilean Auditor General, Correa de Sa, found it impossible
to pass the squadron's accounts for the Peruvian expedition.
The government had of course been aware of this problem
from the beginning and had tried to provide help in the
shape of the experienced Alvares Jonte, who was fully
aware of the legal and financial pitfalls. Unfortunately,
Cochrane seemed oblivious to the problem and, convinced
that there were sinister motives behind the appointment,
quickly got rid of Jonte, leaving no one who really understood how the system worked. All this left Cochrane
stressed and irascible. They also fuelled his deep instinct
that his problems lay not with himself, but in the malice
and deliberate obstruction of others.

Cochrane's record and reputation suggested that he
would have no difficulty in stamping his authority on
Chile's new navy and in establishing himself as its undisputed head. With a heterogeneous collection of officers and
men, recruited in different ways, serving principally for
pay and with no shared traditions of loyalty or obedience,
leadership of this nature was certainly needed. Strangely,

Cochrane seemed unable to provide it. In battle his leadership was spectacular. Out of it, his leadership was poor. There is ample testimony that he was able to exert great personal magnetism on those who were immediately around him on his flagship, but he seemed unable to inspire those who were not. His relationship with these officers was cold and distant, and his naturally suspicious nature and tendency to listen to malicious gossip alienated many with unblemished service records in the Royal Navy and who would have been only too happy to follow his lead. His taciturn nature and his monosyllabic mode of speech did not help. Neither did his favouritism to followers, his brooding suspicions or the self-interest he showed in relation to prize money. He even seems to have gone into denial about the huge sums he was paid, even though he was regularly shipping money back to England.

The problems of keeping the Chilean squadron operational would have tried the patience of a saint. Unfortunately Cochrane was no saint and he had little patience. His instinctive mistrust of anyone in authority quickly asserted itself. The reluctance of Chilean ministers to give him the operational freedom he craved, their failure to solve his problems of supply and pay, and their refusal to accept his strategic recommendations confirmed his deepest suspicions. He rapidly came to the conclusion that ministers were hostile, and so jealous of a foreigner achieving military glory that they deliberately undermined his efforts. He even managed to persuade himself that he was being secretly criticised in high places for his lack of success off Callao and that his superiors were plotting to get rid of him. In fact, nothing was further from the truth. To the Chileans he was indispensable and the authorities amply expressed their gratitude in terms of public praise, high honours and substantial sums of money. Throughout his career Cochrane seems to have had a psychological need for the approval of his superiors. It is strange to see that when it was bestowed in such abundance in Chile and Peru, he could not believe it.

Today in South America, Cochrane remains a hero and a legend. The Chileans venerate him as one of the giants of their country's independence and the creator of their navy, and have generously overlooked the negative side of his troubled and quarrelsome personality. Statues have been erected to his memory, and museums, plazas and streets – even towns – have been named after him. There is always an *Almirante Cochrane* in the Chilean list of warships, two rooms in the Maritime Museum in Valparaiso are devoted to his life and achievements, and dramatic paintings of his victories by Thomas Somerscales fill the walls of the National Congress and the Club Naval of Valparaiso. In terms of his contribution to independence Lord Cochrane deserves this reputation. In his three-year command of the Chilean Navy he had, in typically audacious and spectacular ways, wrested command of the Pacific from the Spaniards and effectively ensured the independence of Chile and Peru. As Maria Graham put it, 'he had taken, destroyed, or forced to surrender every Spanish naval vessel in the Pacific; he had cleared the western coast of America of pirates. He had reduced the most important fortresses of the common enemy, either by storm, or by blockade; and added lustre even to the cause of independence by exploits worthy of his own great name.'

It is Cochrane's tragedy that his uneasy and suspicious personality prevented him from enjoying the fruits of these spectacular triumphs. No sooner had a victory been gained than its effect was squandered in argument and mistrust. Instead of the honours, effusive expressions of thanks and concrete rewards that were visible to everyone else, all Cochrane could see were plots, betrayal and poor treatment. It is the tragedy of succeeding generations that it is this distorted picture of the wars in the Pacific that up to now has been accepted as the truth.

NOTES

Chapter 1: The Andes and the Sea

1. Alvear had been the unwilling witness of a famous naval incident when, in October 1804, a British frigate squadron under Captain Graham Moore comprising *Indefatigable*, *Amphion*, *Lively* and *Medusa* was sent to detain a neutral Spanish force from the River Plate carrying four million dollars – a sum that would have been indispensable to Spain should she join the war on the side of the French as was rumoured. The Spaniards inevitably resisted and, in the subsequent action, the frigate *Mercedes* blew up with the loss of all on board, including the wife, four daughters and three sons of a returning colonial official. The officer and his 13-year-old son only survived because they were travelling on the Spanish flagship, *Medea*. The son spent many years in England as a result, and grew up to become Carlos de Alvear. Ironically, the captured *Medea* was brought into the Royal Navy and was renamed *Imperieuse* – the frigate in which Cochrane consolidated his reputation.
2. Bowles to Croker, 1 March 1817, printed in Graham and Humphries (ed.) *The Navy and South America* (London and Colchester, Navy Records Society, 1962), which comprises transcripts of records from the National Archives, Kew.
3. Bowles to Croker, 9 April 1817 and 14 February 1818, *The Navy and South America*.
4. Hall, Basil, *Extracts from a Journal written on the Coasts of Chile, Peru and Mexico in the Years 1820, 1821 and 1822*, (Edinburgh 1824), vol. 1, p. 56.
5. The Lautaro Lodge had been founded in the Argentine as an alternative to existing freemasonry with the explicit political

purpose of promoting independence. Branches were founded in Chile and Peru following the arrival of San Martin's forces. Members of the Chilean Lodge included San Martin, O'Higgins, Las Heras, Guido, Zenteno, Zañuarte and De la Cruz. See Vicuña MacKenna, *Ostracismo del Jeneral Bernardo O'Higgins*, (Valparaiso 1860).

6. Bowles to Croker, 28 November 1817, *The Navy and South America*.
7. Report annexed in Pilar C Manrubia, *La Marina de Guerra Española en el Primer Tercio del Siglo XIX*, (Madrid, Editoria Naval, 1992), p. 309.

Chapter 2: The Making of the Chilean Navy

1. For details of the profits of carrying 'freight' from South America see, B Vale, *A Frigate of King George: Life and Duty on a British Man-of-War 1807–27*, (London 2001). For details of the *Owen Glendower*, see J. B. Hedderwick, *The Captain's Clerk*, (London 1957), pp. 129–31.
2. Bowles to Croker, 28 November 1817, 10 February 1818, *The Navy and South America*.
3. 'Reglamento Provisional de la Marina', printed in Luiz Uribe Orrego, *Nuestra Marina Militar. Sua Organisacion y Campanha durante la Guerra da la Independencia* (Valparaiso, Tailleres Tipográficos de la Armada, 1910), pp. 25–8.
4. Bowles to Croker, 30 June 1817, *The Navy and South America*. In fact, documents in the Chilean Treasury state that Alvarez was only issued with $33,000 (£6600) when he travelled to London. Archivo Nacional Santiago, Contadura Mayor, quoted in Martel, Alamiro de Avila, *Cochrane y la Independencia del Pacifico*, (Santiago 1976), p. 54.
5. See, for example, the log of HMS *Superb*, NA Kew, Adm 51/3445.
6. For full details of transactions in the USA over these two vessels, see Delano, Jorge Andres, 'The American Influence in the Independence of Latin America: Captain Paul Delano', *Derroteros de la Mar del Sur*, (Lima 1999).
7. Decrees of 3 and 11 August 1818, printed in Orrego, pp. 100–5.
8. Decree of 7 September 1818, printed in Orrego, pp. 114–15.
9. Barros Arana, Diego, *Historia Jeneral de Chile* (Santiago 1884) vol. XI, p. 138.
10. Miller, John (ed.), *Memoirs of General William Miller*, (London 1828) vol. 1, p. 187.
11. Blanco to O'Higgins, 5 and 17 November 1818, Printed in Orrego, pp. 159–62.

12. Guise to Zañuarte, 24, 27 July 1818. Orrego, 164. *Hecate* (actually renamed *Lucy* at this stage) arrived at Valparaiso on 14 October and was sent south as *Galvarino* on 29 October.
13. *Especulación, San Fernando, Atocha* and *Santa Maria.*
14. Quoted in Orrego, p. 67.
15. Barros Arana, vol. XI, p. 194.

Chapter 3: The Coming of Lord Cochrane

1. Alvarez to Zenteno, 12 January 1818 (1), printed in Orrego, p. 179.
2. Alvarez to Zenteno, 12 January 1818 (2), printed in Orrego, pp. 117–19.
3. Bulnes, Gonzago, *Historia de la Expedicion Libertadora del Peru*, (Santiago 1887-8) vol. 1, pp. 288–9.
4. See *Naval Chronical* XXXIX, 1818.
5. 8 July 1818, quoted in Turrado, Gaspar Pérez, *Las Marinas Realista y Patriota en la Independencia de Chile y Peru*, (Madrid 1996), p. 127.
6. Cochrane to Alvarez, 1 August 1818, printed in Orrego, p. 123.
7. Historians, including de Avila Martel and Cubitt, have conjectured that a number of Cochrane's followers accompanied him on the *Rose*, notably Thomas Sackville Crosbie, Henry Cobbett, John Pascoe Grenfell and Robert Simpson. There is, alas, no evidence for this. Indeed, the names of Simpson and Grenfell do not appear in Chilean records before 1820 and the latter is said to have been employed as 5th Mate on an East Indiaman at this time.
8. Miller, J. (ed.), *Memoirs of General William Miller*, vol. 1, p. 207.
9. Decree of 10 December 1818, printed in Orrego, p. 177.
10. Cochrane, Lord, *Narrative of Services in the Liberation of Chile and Peru*, (Ridgeway, London, 1859), vol. 1, p. 5.
11. The *Reglamento* laid down that the annual pay and allowances of a Vice Admiral were $6000. This is what Cochrane received and was the basis of the claim for half pay contained in his *Memorandum* of 1845 (National Archive of Scotland (NAS) GD 233/31/238). The decree appointing Blanco as his successor specifically states the same amount.
12. Stevenson, William Bennet, *Historical and Descriptive Narrative of 20 years Residence in South America*, (London, 1825), vol. 3, p. 148.
13. Spry Court Martial Proceedings, 3 and 5 March 1821, NAS GD 233/38/258.
14. Lieutenants Passing Certificates, NA Kew, Adm 107/25: Steel's *Navy Lists* 1809–15. It is difficult to reconstruct Guise's career between 1803 and 1809 as the *Navy Lists* for these years do not

show the ships in which officers were serving, and his page in Officer's Records in Adm 9/5 (no 1522) has been torn out.

15. Officer's Records, NA, Kew, Adm 9/5 (1533), O'Byrne, William, *Biographical Dictionary*, (London, John Murray, 1848), vol. 1.
16. Bowles to Croker, 21 December 1818, *The Navy in South America*.
17. Bowles to Croker, 15 March 1819, *The Navy in South America*.
18. Pezuela accepted the position of the United States on blockades by agreeing that in future alleged American blockade runners would not be immediately seized but would be warned off by the blockading squadron and have their logs endorsed. Only if they tried to run the blockade a second time would vessels be arrested. This concession only applied to American ships.
19. Cochrane's correspondence with Biddle was published in the *Gazeta Ministerial de Chile* on 16 January 1819, printed in *Archivo de D Bernardo O'Higgins*, (Santiago, Academia de Historia, 1946-68), vol. XII. Also NAS GD 233/39/262.

Chapter 4: The Callao Campaign

1. *Gazeta Ministerial de Chile* of 2 January 1819, ibid.
2. O'Higgins letters to San Martin, January to June 1819, printed in *Archivo de D Bernardo O'Higgins*, vol. VIII.
3. Zenteno to Cochrane, 7 January 1819, printed in Orrego, pp. 186–90. NAS GD 233/35/258.
4. Blanco Encalada to Zenteno, 15 January 1819, printed in Orrego, pp. 193–4.
5. Report of Lima Merchants to Shirreff, 19 January 1819, National Maritime Museum (NMM), SHI/2.
6. Hickey to Bowles, 24 May 1819, *The Navy and South America*.
7. Shirreff to Supercargoes of British ships, Callao,13 February 1819, NMM, SHI/2.
8. Cochrane–Pezuela correspondence, printed in full in *Gazeta Ministerial de Chile*, 10, 17 and 22 July 1819, *Archivo de D Bernardo O'Higgins*, vol. XIII.
9. In both Cochrane's memoirs and other biographies there has been uncertainty about the dates and nature of his operations of the coast of Peru in April and May. The whole story is clearly told in the run of dispatches from Cochrane and Blanco Encalada to the Minister of Marine printed in Orrego, pp. 213–49.
10. Antonio Vacaro (Naval Commander at Callao) to Secretary of the Navy, Madrid, 6 July 1819, quoted Turrado, p. 138.
11. *Gazeta Ministerial de Chile*, 16 May, 10 and 22 July 1819, ibid.

12. Quoted in Worcester, Donald E., *Sea Power and Chilean Independence*, (Gainesville, University of Florida Monographs), No 15, Summer 1962, p. 45.
13. Cochrane to Zenteno, 21 June 1819, NAS GD 233/39/261.
14. Cochrane to William Cochrane, 9 August 1819, NAS GD 233/26/186.
15. Cochrane to William Cochrane, 7 August 1819, ibid.
16. Journal of Charles J. Deblois quoted in Billingstay, Edward B., *In Defense of Neutral Rights: the US Navy and the Wars of Independence in Chile and Peru*, (University of N Carolina, 1967), p. 83.
17. Cochrane to O'Higgins, 9 Aug 1819, NAS GD 233/31/239 Zenteno to the Senate, 14 August 1820, printed in Zenteno J. I., *Documentos justificativas sobre la Expedicion Libertadora del Peru: Refutacion de las memorias de Lord Cochrane*, (Santiago, 1861), p. 7.
18. Cochrane to O'Higgins, 9 August 1819, ibid.
19. Zenteno to the Senate, 27 August 1820, printed in Zenteno J. I., *Documentos justificativas*, 12. Decree of 1 September 1819, NAS GD 233/32/240.
20. O'Higgins to San Martin, 20 September 1819, printed in *Archivo de D Bernardo O'Higgins*, vol. VIII.
21. Cochrane's Orders, 9 September 1819, NAS GD 233/39/261, printed in Orrego, pp. 259–62.
22. Correspondence between Cochrane and Pezuela printed in Cesáreo Fernández Duro, *La Armada Española (desde la union de los reinos de Castilla y Leon)*, vol. 9, (Madrid, 1973), pp. 210–11; and Cochrane's (English) Letter Book, NAS GD 233/39/262.
23. Cochrane to Zenteno, 2 October 1819, *Gazeta Ministerial de Chile*, 12 October 1819, *Archivo de D Bernardo O'Higgins*, vol. XIII.
24. *Narrative of Services*, vol. 1, p. 26.
25. Cochrane to O'Higgins, 8 October 1819, *Gazeta Ministerial de Chile*, 12 November 1819, *Archivo de D Bernardo O'Higgins*, vol. XII; NAS GD 233/37/255.
26. Zenteno to Cochrane, 4 May 1820, printed in Zenteno J. I., *Documentos justificativas*, pp. 38–40; NAS GD 233/37/256.
27. Cochrane to Zenteno, 7 October 1819, printed in Orrego, p. 275.
28. Cochrane to O'Higgins, 8 October 1819, NAS GD 233/35/252.
29. O'Higgins to Cochrane, 28 November 1819, NAS GD 233/35/252.
30. Graham, Maria, *Journal of a Residence in Chile during the Year 1822*, London, Longman, 1824 (reprint New York, Praeger, 1969), p. 54.
31. O'Higgins to Cochrane, 29 November 1819 (passing the news to Cochrane off the coast of Chile), NAS GD 233/35/252.

Notes

Chapter 5: The Capture of Valdivia

1. O'Higgins to Cochrane, 29 November 1819, NAS GD 233/35/252.
2. *Gazeta Ministerial de Chile*, 12 October 1819 to 26 February 1820, *Archivo de D Bernardo O'Higgins*, vol. XIII.
3. Zenteno to Cochrane, (Private), 26 Nov 1819, NAS, GD 233/37/258.
4. Cochrane to Zenteno, 21 January 1820, printed in the *Gazeta Ministerial de Chile*, 29 January,1820 and in Orrego, p. 301.
5. See, John Miers, *Travels in Chile and La Plata*, (London 1826) vol. 1, 490; Miller, vol. 1, p. 245.
6. *Narrative of Services*, vol. 1, p. 5.
7. Stevenson, vol. 3, p. 212.
8. Stevenson, vol. 3, p. 216.
9. Miller to Cochrane, 4 February 1820, printed in Orrego, p. 302.
10. Beauchef to Cochrane, 4 February 1820, printed in Orrego, p. 304.
11. Cochrane to Zenteno, 5, 6 and 19 February, printed in Maria Graham, pp. 58-61. All the dispatches regarding his capture of Valdivia are in Cochrane's (Spanish) Letter Book, NAS GD 233/39/262.
12. Proceeds of the Sale of *Dolores* etc 30 May 1820; and Cochrane to Zenteno, 8 March 1820, quoted in David J Cubitt, *Lord Cochrane and the Chilean Navy 1818–23* (University of Edinburgh Ph.D. Thesis 1974), p. 158.

Chapter 6: 'Heartfelt Gratitude at that Signal Achievement'

1. *Gazeta Ministerial*, 19 February 1820, *Archivo de D Bernardo O'Higgins*, vol. XIII.
2. Decree of 1 March 1820.
3. Zenteno to Cochrane, 22 February 1820. The first part of the letter is printed in Grimble, Ian, *The Sea Wolf*, (London, 1978), p. 209; the whole in NAS GD 233/39/262 and Zenteno J. I., *Documentos justificativas*, p. 21.
4. Cochrane to O'Higgins, 10 February 1820, quoted in Cubitt, pp. 163–4.
5. *Narrative of Services*, vol. 1, p. 53; Maria Graham, p. 59; Miers, vol. 1, p. 492.
6. *Narrative of Services*, vol. 1, p. 71.
7. Chisholm, Stuart M, *The Independence of Chile*, (London, T. Warner Laurie, 1959).
8. Zenteno's' letters NAS 233/37/256-257-258
9. *Narrative of Services*, vol. 1, p. 74.
10. *Narrative of Services*, vol. 1, p. 47. The accusation is not mentioned in

Miers or Maria Graham but by 1859 had become part of Cochrane's complaints.

11. Miers, vol. 1, p. 432.
12. *Narrative of Services*, vol. 1, p. 129; San Martin, *Manifiesto de las acusaciones que a nombre del General San Martin hicieron sus legados ante el Govierno de Chile contra el Vice-Admiral Lord Cochrane y vindicaciones de este dirigida al mismo San Martin*, (Lima, 1823).
13. O'Higgins to the Senate, 22 March 1820, printed in Zenteno J. I., *Documentos justificativas*, p. 24.
14. Cochrane to O'Higgins, 14 May 1820, printed in Stevenson, vol. 3, p. 243.
15. Cochrane to Paroissien, 14 May 1820, Essex Record Office (ERO), A/1895A.
16. Hoseason's Summary Accounts 1819–21, NAS GD 233/39/260.
17. Ibid. The purchase of Quintero cost Cochrane $50,000 plus the cost of the livestock, NAS GD 233/37/256.
18. Spry and Forster's reports on Herradura, NAS GD 233/34/246.
19. Cochrane to O'Higgins, 24 April 1820, printed in Stevenson, vol. 3, pp. 231–2. Unfortunately the date is wrongly given as 14 May.
20. Zenteno to Cochrane, 4 May 1820, printed in Zenteno J. I., *Documentos justificativas*, p. 30.
21. Guise to Cochrane with Annexes, 9 May 1820, NAS GD 233/31/237.

Chapter 7: Plots and Paranoia

1. Prevost to Adams, 13 September 1819, quoted in Cubitt, p. 231.
2. Maria Graham, p. 39.
3. Thomas, John, *Historical Sketch of the Chilean Navy*, Archivo Nacional de Chile (Archivo Vicuña MacKenna – AVM) vol. 104, quoted in Cubitt, p. 204.
4. See, for example, Guise to Cochrane, 11 August 1820, (over the exclusion of *Lautaro* from a prize money distribution), NAS GD 233/36/253; Miller to Paroissien, 15 February 1821, (concerning Bennet's offering to sell prize bullion from Valdivia to the Chilean Merchant J. J. Barnard), ERO A/1895A; Miller to Cochrane, 6 October 1821, (over non-payment of troops), NAS GD 233/35/252; Cobbett to Cochrane, 25 September 1822, (about dilatory payments by Bennet), NAS GD 233/31/239; Wilkinson to Cochrane, 25 September 1822, (about money shipped out on *Doris*), ibid.
5. Thomas, *Historical Sketches*, AVM, vol. 104, quoted in Cubitt, p. 52.
6. Wilkinson to Cochrane, 27 June 1819; Ramsey to Cochrane, 14 April

Notes

1820, Charles to Cochrane, 16 April 1820; Delano to Cochrane, 11 October 1820; Carter to Cochrane, 8 September 1819, Cobbett to Cochrane, 4 May 1920, Crosbie to Cochrane, 18 April 1821 – all in NAS GD 233/36/253.

7. Thomas, *Historical Sketches*, AVM, vol. 104, quoted in Cubitt, p. 248.
8. Cochrane to San Martin, 10 July 1821, quoted in Cubitt, p. 26.
9. Miers to Cochrane, 16 March 1823, NAS GD 233/36/255.
10. Cochrane to Guise, 19 Dec 1819, NAS, GD 233/36/255.
11. Cochrane to Guise, 1 April 1821, NAS GD 233/38/258.
12. Hoseason's Summary Accounts 1819–21, NAS GD 233/39/260.
13. Guise-Cochrane correspondence, 19 Dec 1819, NAS, GD 233/36/255.
14. Thomas, *Historical Sketches*, AVM vol. 104, quoted in Cubitt, p. 56.
15. Maria Graham, p. 138.
16. Lieutenants Passing Certificates, NA, Kew, Adm 9/12.
17. Maria Graham, p. 80.
18. *Gazeta Ministerial*, 26 February 1820, *Archivo de D Bernardo O'Higgins*, vol. XII.
19. Charges against Guise, NAS GD 233/36/255. By the time he wrote his memoirs, Cochrane had come to the absurd notion that Zenteno and San Martin were somehow behind Guise's 'insubordination.' *Narrative of Services*, vol. 1, p. 104.
20. Zenteno to Cochrane, printed in Grimble, p. 213.
21. Guise to Zenteno, 25 July 1820; Guise to Cochrane, 11 August 1820, NAS GD 233/36/253.
22. Petition from Officers, GD 233/31/237, and *Narrative of Services*, vol. 1, pp. 66–7.
23. *Narrative of Services*, vol. 1, p. 65.
24. Minutes of Spry Court Martial, NAS 233/36/253.
25. Cubitt, David J., 'Manning the Chilean Navy', *Mariner's Mirror*, May 1877, pp. 115–27.

Chapter 8: Invasion and Blockade

1. Paroissien's journal, ERO, A/1895A.
2. Grimble, p. 220.
3. Zenteno to Cochrane, no 293, 19 August 1820, NAS GD 233/31/239.
4. Ibid.
5. See Avila Martel, p. 196.
6. Orders to *Venganza* and *Esmeralda*, 9 February 1820, Archivo General da la Marinha, Madrid (AGM), Expediciones a Indias, legajo 68.

7. *Memorias de Pezuela*, p. 769, quoted in Cubitt, p. 298.
8. Paroissien's Journal, 29 August 1820, ERO, A/1895A.
9. Paroissien's Journal, 31 August 1820, ERO, A/1895A.
10. Hall, vol. 1, p. 71.
11. *Narrative of Services*, vol. 1, p. 79.
12. Cochrane to Paroissien, 3 March 1821, ERO, A/1895A.
13. Hall, vol. 1, pp. 73–4.
14. Paroissien's Journal, 26, 27 October 1820, ERO, A/1895A.
15. British merchants to Shirreff, 24 August 1820, NAS GD 233/38/253. In fact the merchants had probably misunderstood Cochrane's orders. The Chilean declaration of blockade promulgated on 20 April 1819 and reissued on 20 August 1820, laid down that all neutral ships carrying contraband or enemy property, or which attempted to enter Peruvian ports, or which carried duplicate papers obscuring the origins of their cargoes were liable to seizure. The only amelioration was that six months grace was given before the arrest of ships proceeding from Europe and the United States, and 3 months to those coming from the Plate. Alberto Cruchage, *Jurisprudencia de la Cancilleno Chileno*, (Santiago 1835), quoted in Avila Martel, pp. 189–90.
16. Hardy to Croker, 30 September 1820 with enclosures, printed in *The Navy and South America*.
17. Croker to Hardy with enclosures, 12 December 1820, printed in *The Navy in South America*.
18. Hardy to Croker, 28 July 1820 and Searle to Hardy, 2 June 1820, printed in *The Navy and South America*.
19. Hetherwick, p. 117.
20. Hardy to Croker, 30 September 1820, printed in *The Navy and South America*; Shirreff to Walker, 23 February 1821, National Maritime Museum (NMM), Shirreff Letter Books, SHI/2.
21. Hardy to Croker, 2 April 1821, printed in *The Navy and South America*.
22. Hall to Hardy, 17 June 1821, with letters from Cochrane dated 17 June 1821, printed in *The Navy and South America*.
23. Hall, vol. 1, pp. 94–5.
24. Correspondence between Shirreff and Lima Merchants, January to March 1821, NMM SHI/3.
25. Hall, vol. 1, pp. 121–9.

Chapter 9: The Capture of the *Esmeralda*

1. Minutes of Council of War on *Prueba*, 22 November 1820, AGM, Expediciones a Indias, legajo 68.

2. Orders printed in *Narrative of Services*, vol. 1, pp. 88–9.
3. Hall, vol. 1, p. 79.
4. Grenfell's description of the action, University of Liverpool Special Collections, (ULSC), Grenfell 1–2.
5. Turrado, p. 167.
6. Searle to Hardy, 8 November 1820, NA Kew, printed in *The Navy and South America*.
7. Paroissien's Journal, 7 November 1821, ERO A/1895A.
8. San Martin to O'Higgins, 9 November 1820, *Gazeta Ministerial*, 4 December 1820, *Archivo de D Bernardo O'Higgins*, vol. XIV, also in Grimble, p. 225.
9. San Martin to Cochrane, 26 January 1821, NAS GD 233/38/252.

Chapter 10: The *Valdivia* Court Martial

1. Court Martial Proceedings, 2 March 1821, NAS GD 233/38/258.
2. *Narrative of Services*, vol. 1, pp. 101–2.
3. Officers to Guise, letter of 2 February 1821, NAS GD 233/38/258; sent on with Guise to Cochrane, 11 February 1821, NAS GD 233/37/256.
4. Court Martial Proceedings, 2 March 1821, ibid.
5. Cochrane to O'Higgins, nd, NAS, GD 233/36/255. By the time he wrote his memoirs, Cochrane had absurdly come to the conclusion that the 'plotters' were acting under instructions from San Martin. *Narrative of Services*, vol. 1, p. 104.
6. Cochrane–Guise correspondence, 20, 21 February 1821, NAS GD 233/38/258.
7. Ibid.
8. Court Martial Proceedings, 2 March 1821, ibid.
9. Spry Court Martial Proceedings, 3 and 5 March 1821, NAS GD 233/38/258.
10. Cochrane–Spry correspondence, 22/23 Feb 1821, ibid.
11. *Narrative of Services*, vol. 1, p. 103.
12. Spry Court Martial Proceedings, 3 and 5 March 1821, ibid.
13. Thomas, AVM vol. 104, quoted in Cubitt, p. 204.
14. Spry Court Martial Proceedings, ibid.
15. Cochrane to Guise, 12 March 1821, ibid.
16. Guise to Cochrane, 19 March 1821, ibid.
17. Correspondence, Cochrane–Guise and the officers, 22–24 March 1821, NAS GD 233/37/256.
18. Cochrane to Guise, 1 April 1821, NAS GD 233/38/258.
19. Report by Miller, 26 March 1821, NAS GD 233/37/256.

20. Cochrane to San Martin, 30 March and 14 April 1821; San Martin to Cochrane, 6 April 1821, NAS, GD 233/31/239; Cochrane's Letter Book, NAS, GD 233/32/240.
21. Barnard to Paroissien, 24 March 1821, ERO, A/1859A.
22. Shirreff to Forster, 7 January 1821; Searle to Cochrane, 30 November 1820, NAS GD 233/36/253.
23. Correspondence between Shirreff to the captains of *Edward Ellis*, *Lord Suffield*, *Indian* and *Speculator*, 5 January 1821, NMM SHI/3; J. J. Barnard to Paroissien, 24. March 1821, ERO A/1895A.
24. Quoted in Grimble, p. 228.
25. Log of *Andromache*, NA Adm 51/3012.
26. Miller, vol. 1, p. 298.
27. Log of *Andromache*, NA Adm 51/3012.
28. Cochrane to O'Higgins, 10 March 1821, NAS GD 233/31/239.
29. Hetherwick, pp. 117–19.
30. Ibid, p. 125.

Chapter 11: The Liberation of Peru

1. De la Serna to Spencer, 11 May 1821, NA Adm 1/26. Hardy to Croker, 28 July 1821, printed in *The Navy in South America*. Intent on neutrality and doubting the effectiveness of any agreement, the request was refused by the British.
2. Timothy Anna, *Spain and the Loss of America*, (London and Lincoln 1983), pp. 238–9.
3. Paroissien's Journal, 26 February 1821, ERO A/1859A.
4. Cochrane's Orders to Miller, 1 May 1821, NAS GD 233/37/256.
5. *Narrative of Services*, vol. 1, pp. 107–11. Typically ignorant of the wider political picture, Cochrane concluded that the armistice had been arranged so as to prevent further victories by himself. *Narrative of Services*, vol. 1, p. 111.
6. Hall, vol. 1, p. 190.
7. Hardy to Croker, 26 June 1821, printed in *The Navy in South America*.
8. Hall to Hardy, 14 June 1821, printed in *The Navy in South America*.
9. Hardy to Croker, 28 July 1821, printed in *The Navy in South America*.
10. Ironically enough, the British strategy of protest and reliance on the prize courts seems to have worked. Of the 19 ships arrested by the Chilean Squadron (the list include in Hardy's dispatch to Croker of 12 November 1821, omits the Mary), only *Indian* and the cargoes of *Rebecca* and *Colonel Allen* were condemned and confiscated. The remaining ships were released, three – *Joseph*, *Robert Fuge* and

Notes

Admiral Cockburn – having ransomed themselves by paying Cochrane's 'license' fee.

11. Hardy to Croker, 26 June 1821, printed in *The Navy in South America*.

12. Hall, vol. 1, pp. 212–13.

13. Ibid.

14. A mistake perpetuated in many books on this subject (including one written by this author) is to state that *Conway*'s marines did actually keep order in the streets of Lima before San Martin entered the city. A careful check with *Conway*'s papers and the journals of its officers makes it clear this is not true. The common source for this error lies in a statement in Cochrane's *Narrative of Services*, vol. 1, p. 120 that they did – yet another example of the unwisdom of accepting any of Cochrane's claims without corroboration.

15. Hardy to Croker, 19 August 1821, printed in *The Navy in South America*.

16. Ibid.

17. Hall, vol. 1, p. 72.

18. See R A Humphries, *Liberation in South America 1806–1827: The Career of James Paroissien*, (London 1952), p. 96.

Chapter 12: The Row with San Martin

1. *Narrative of Services*, vol. 1, p. 106.

2. Ibid.

3. Cochrane to San Martin, 7 August 1821, *Narrative of Services*, vol. 1, pp. 129–132.

4. Hall to Hardy, 14 June 1821, printed in *The Navy and South America*.

5. Zenteno to Cochrane, 2 July 1821 (enclosing the revised blockade decree of 22 June 1821), NAS GD 233/37/257.

6. O'Higgins to San Martin, 6 August 1821, printed in *Archivo de D Bernardo O'Higgins*, vol. VIII.

7. Anna, Timothy E, *The Fall of Royal Government in Peru*, Lincoln and London, University of Nebraska Press, 1979.

8. La Mar to Cochrane, 9 August 1821, printed in *Manifiesto de las acusaciones*; NAS GD 233/37/255.

9. Paroissien's Journal, 27 October 1820, ERO A/1859A.

10. Cochrane to San Martin, 30 June 1821, quoted in San Martin, *Manifiesto de las acusaciones*.

11. San Martin to Cochrane, 9 August 1821, printed in *Narrative of Services*, vol. 1, pp. 132–4.

12. Stevenson, vol. 3, pp. 352–5.

13. San Martin, *Manifiesto de las acusaciones*.
14. Cochrane to Monteagudo, 12 September 1822, quoted in San Martin, *Manifiesto de las acusaciones*.
15. List of officers joining Peru, annexed to Cochrane to O'Higgins, 12 June 1822, printed in Orrego, 388–9; NAS GD 233/37/255.
16. Cochrane to Grenfell, 21 December 1854, ULSC, Grenfell/3–155. Cochrane claims that Forster lacked courage and that he refused to take part in the cutting out of the *Esmeralda*. This allegation is contradicted by both Forster's service record and his own letter to Cochrane dated 31 October 1820, in which he volunteers his services in the attack. NAS GD 233/36/253.
17. Hind to Paroissien, 29 March 1821, ERO A/1859A.
18. Miller to Paroissien, 13 March 1821, ERO A/1859A.
19. Miller, vol. 1, p. 275.
20. The only clues which survive as to the exact timing of these events lies in papers in Cochrane's possession originating in the Mint in Lima, which give details of the $135,977 worth of silver and gold bullion carried on *Sacramento* (NAS GD 233/31/239), and the log of HMS *Superb* (NA Adm 51/3445). These sources indicate that the money was loaded onto the schooner on 3 September; that Delano arrived at Ancon in *Lautaro* on 13 September, and that Cochrane seized the money late the following day. Unfortunately the officers of *Superb* were so busy dealing with the day to day administration of the big two-decker – opening barrels of beef, repairing rigging, punishing defaulters etc. – that they neither realised nor recorded exactly what was going on.
21. Anna, Timothy E, *The Fall of Royal Government in Peru*, p. 189.
22. Crosbie to Cochrane, 13 September 1821, NAS GD 233/31/240.
23. The receipt can be seen in NAS GD 233/31/239.
24. Miers to Cochrane, 8 September 1821, NAS GD 233/39/262.
25. Zenteno to San Martin, 8 May, 1821, NAS GD 233/31/239.
26. On return to Valparaiso in 1822, Cochrane had to urge the Chileans to obtain the bonus and the freight changes on his behalf. The total demanded was $110,632, one-eighth of which would have belonged to Cochrane. Cochrane to Echeverria, 20 June 1822, NAS GD 233/31/240.
27. Cochrane to San Martin, 4 August 1821, quoted in San Martin, *Manifiesto de las acusaciones*.
28. Cochrane to O'Higgins, 24 September 1821, printed in Orrego, pp. 365–7.

Notes

29. San Martin to O'Higgins, 29 October 1821, printed in *Archivo de D Bernardo O' Higgins*, vol. VIII.

30. Cochrane to Monteagudo, 28 September 1821, printed in *Narrative of Services*, vol. 1, pp. 164–5.

Chapter 13: Guayaquil and the Spanish Main

1. Printed in Maria Graham, pp. 100–3.
2. Olmeda to Cochrane correspondence, NAS GD 233/36/254.
3. Wavell to Cochrane, 15 October to 15 November 1821, NAS GD 233/36/254.
4. Wavell to Cochrane, nd, ibid.
5. In *Narrative of Services*, vol. 1, 170–2, Cochrane claims that the credentials Of Wavell and O'Reilly must have been false because the passport was issued before Mexican independence was achieved. This is no truth in this. The achievement of Mexican independence was an extended process comprising three of four significant events in 1821, during the course of which the Mexican patriots regularly asked their colleagues in the south for assistance. The accusation that the two officers carried false credentials is pure imagination and self-justification on Cochrane's part.
6. Urrutia, Carlos Lopes, 'Lord Cochrane y la Expedicion a Mexico, 1822', *Derroteros de la Mar del Sur*, Lima. 1998, p. 116.
7. *Narrative of Services*, vol. 1, p. 176.
8. Turrado, p. 176.
9. Simpson to Cochrane, 28 January 1822, NAS GD 233/36/254.
10. Urrutia, p. 127. Simpson's story of a poor reception following false information laid by Wavell and O'Reilly is the version given by Cochrane in the *Narrative of Services*. As usual with Cochrane, once Wavell and O'Reilly have been identified as 'enemies', they can only do wrong.
11. Cochrane to Zenteno, 2 February 1822, printed in Urrutia, p. 126, and Orrego, pp. 378–9.
12. Cochrane to Zenteno, 7 March 1822, printed in Orrego, p. 379.
13. Terms of the Capitulation printed in Turrado, p. 177.
14. Terms of Agreement of 14 March 1822 printed in Orrego, pp. 380–1.
15. Hardy to Croker, 23 December 1821, printed in *the Navy and South America*.
16. Miller to Paroissien, 10 May 1822, ERO, A/1859A.

Chapter 14: The Final Curtain

1. Echeverria to Cochrane, 4 June 1822, NAS GD 233/34/246, printed in Maria Graham, p. 110.
2. Echeverria to Cochrane, 19 June 1822, ibid.
3. Hall, vol. 1, p. 60 and p. 64.
4. Cochrane to Echeverria, 18 June 1822, printed in Orrego, pp. 130–1.
5. Cochrane to Hoseason, no date (but July 1823), NAS GD 233/39/260.
6. 'Lord Cochrane in Account with William Hoseason', October 1822, NAS GD 233/39/262.
7. Cochrane to O'Higgins, Annex, NAS GD 233/39/259. Hoseason's Summary Account (in his law case against Cochrane), NAS GD 233/39/260; Cochrane to O'Higgins, 25 June 1822, NAS GD 233/31/239.
8. 'Lord Cochrane in Account with William Hoseason', October 1822, NAS GD 233/39/262; Hoseason's Summary Account (in his law case against Cochrane), NAS GD 233/39/260; Receipts for *Doris* and *Alacrity* in NAS GD 233/39/261.
9. Acknowledgement in NAS GD 233/34/246. Detailed receipt dated 8 August 1822, NAS GD 233/36/252.
10. José Santago de Campiño to Cochrane, 8 August 1822, NAS GD 233/39/252.
11. Fodor, Giorgio, 'The Boom that Never Was? Latin American Loans in London 1822–5', Universita'Degli Studi di Trento, 2002.
12. Message to the Convention, 20 September 1822, printed in Orrego, pp. 413–16.
13. San Martin, *Manifiesto de las acusaciones*.
14. O'Higgins to Cochrane, 12 November 1821, Echeverria to Cochrane, 13 November 1821,NAS GD 233/35/252; NAS GD 233/36/257.
15. Maria Graham, p. 332.
16. Irrisarra to the Chilean Minister of Foreign Affairs, 21 July 1819, printed in Orrego, pp. 124-8.
17. Petition by Major W Cochrane to the Chilean Government, nd, NAS GD 233/34/245.
18. Echeverria to Cochrane, 19 June 1822, printed in Orrego, p. 131.
19. Cochrane to Chamberlain; Cochrane to Dr Dickson, both 31 March 1825, NAS GD 233/35/450.
20. The squadron's outgoings were considerable. Between September 1821 and April 1822, its supplies and maintenance cost $430,552 – this included $67,840 at Arica, $26,178 on the first visit to Guayaquil, $10,111 at Acapulco, $8790 at the second visit to

Notes

Guayaquil and $6567 at Callao. During the same period, $159,000 was distributed in pay and $71,630 in prize money. Stevenson's summary accounts for the cruise NAS GD 233/39/260.

21. Correa de Sa-Cochrane correspondence, 2 September 1822, NAS GD 233/39/260, 233/31/239 and 233/34/247.
22. Wilkinson to Cochrane, 25 September 1822, NAS GD 233/31/239; Cobbett to Cochrane, 25 September, 1822, NAS GD 233/39/262.
23. Echeverria to Cochrane, 1 October 1822, NAS GD 233/36/256 O'Higgins to Cochrane, 3 October 1822, NAS GD 233/39/262.
24. Cochrane to O'Higgins, 12 October 1822, NAS GD 233/39/262, printed in *Narrative of Services*, vol. 1, p. 229.
25. O'Higgins to Cochrane, 3 October 1822, NAS GD 233/39/262.
26. Correa da Camera to Cochrane, 4 November 1822, printed in *Narrative of Services*, vol. 2, p. 7.
27. Cochrane to Echeverria, 28 November, NAS GD 233/36/256.
28. Cochrane to Correa da Camera, 29 November 1822, printed in *Narrative of Services*, vol. 2, p. 7.
29. Exchange of correspondence between Cochrane and Zenteno, 18 December 1822, printed in Orrego, pp. 420-1.
30. Echeverria to Cochrane, 23 December 1822, NAS GD 233/36/257 printed in Orrego, p. 423.
31. The face value of Cochrane's total pay was $40,785 (£8160), but some was received in letters of credit which Hoseason had to exchange at a discount of $1900, NAS GD 233/39/260. The final payment was made in London in March 1823. 'Abstract of Account between the Earl of Dundonald and the State of Chile', NAS GD 233/39/262, and NAS GD 233/39/260.
32. Unfortunately, the Chilean Government refused to honour Cochrane's letter of credit; see nd (but July 1823), NAS GD 233/39/260. Cochrane was unmoved by the news and wrote sharply to tell Hoseason to sort out the problem himself. Hoseason eventually took Cochrane to law, claiming the debit of £3767 plus a percentage on all his prize and salary dealings.
33. Note showing calculation of the profits of service in Chile and Brazil, NAS GD 233/20/450.

Chapter 15: Independence – At Last

1. Vale, Brian, *Independence or Death! British Sailors and Brazilian Independence, 1822–25*, (London, 1996).
2. O'Higgins to Cochrane, 29 March 1823; J. J. Barnard to Cochrane, 15 July 1824, Orrego, pp. 131-3.

3. Note by Correa de Sa, 28 June, 1838, NAS GD 233/31/239 and 233/34/48.
4. Cochrane to Correa de Sa, off Bahia June 1823, NAS GD 233/39/260.
5. MacFarlane to Cochrane, 23 March 1823, Miers to Cochrane, 25 March 1823, NAS GD 233/39/262.
6. Miers to Cochrane, 16 March 1823, ibid.
7. Cochrane to Dean, 10 November 1823, NAS GD 233/31/239.
8. Papers relating to Dean's case against Lord Cochrane, NAS GD 233/34/246 and 233/51–4/109.
9. Guise remained commander-in-chief of the Peruvian Navy until 1828 when he was killed during a brief war between Peru and Colombia over control of Guayaquil. In fact neither state was strong enough to impose its will, and Guayaquil and the adjacent provinces declared their own independence as the Republic of Ecuador.
10. Cunningham, John (Surgeon of HMS *Cambridge*), *Remarks During a Voyage to the Pacific 1823–5*, (unpublished Manuscript), NMM JOL/21.
11. Ibid.
12. Ibid.
13. James E, *Life of Commander Henry James RN*, (London 1899), p. 86.
14. Guruzeta to Rodil, 8 October 1824, quoted in Turrado, p. 221.
15. James, p. 76.

Chapter 16: Settling Accounts

1. NAS GD 233/51–4/109 (Dean's Case), NAS GD 233/59-60/113 (Hoseason's case).
2. *Narrative of Services*, vol. 1, pp. 271–85
3. Letter from Kitty to Arthur Cochrane, quoted in Grimble, pp. 364–5.
4. See *Observations on Naval Affairs*.
5. Green and Nelson to Cochrane, 18 Nov 1837; Caldeclough to Cochrane, 11 Dec 1837 and 20 Aug 1842, NAS GD 233/39/262.
6. Memo by Correa de Sa, 28 June 1838, NAS GD 233/34/248.
7. Cochrane's answers to the Audit Enquiries 1838, ibid; Caldeclough to Cochrane, 14 Aug 1843, NAS GD 233/340/262.
8. Decree of 6 September, 1844. NAS GD 233/31/237.
9. Walpole to Bidwell, no 52, 2 Dec 1844, NAS GD 233/31/237.
10. *Memorial to the President and Government of Chile*, 3 Feb 1845, NAS GD 233/31/237 and 233/34/248.
11. Decree of 20 Feb 1852, NAS GD 233/31/237.

Notes

12. Decree of 28 July 1857; Haines to Clarendon, no 45, 29 Aug 1857, Shelborne to Cochrane, 2 October 1857, NAS GD 233/34/246.
13. Cochrane to the President of Chile, nd NAS GD 233/34/246.
14. Blanco Encalada to Cochrane, 4 October 1857, ibid.
15. Simpson to Cochrane, 15 October 1857, ibid.
16. *Petition to Pedro II*, no date, NAS GD 233/24/264.
17. *Memorial to the Legislature of Brazil*, ibid.
18. For a detailed account of the Brazilian negotiations and claims see, Vale, *Independence or Death!*, pp. 179–86.
19. See for example, Thomas, Donald, *Cochrane* (London, *Star*, 1978), p. 248, p. 263.

BIBLIOGRAPHY

Anna, Timothy E, *The Fall of the Royal Government of Peru*, (Lincoln and London 1980)

Anna, Timothy E, *Spain and the Loss of America*, (Lincoln and London 1983)

Archivo Histórico Naval, *Vicealmirante Lord Thomas Alexander Cochrane*, Papers in six volumes (Armada de Chile 1993–9)

Archivo de D Bernardo O'Higgins, (Santiago, Archivo Nacional, Imprensa Universitaria 1953), 28 vols

Barros Arana, Diego, *Historia Jeneral de Chile* (Santiago 1884–1902) 16 vols

Billingsley, Edward B, *In Defense of Neutral Rights: the US Navy and the Wars of Independence in Chile and Peru*, (Chapel Hill 1967).

Bulnes, Gonzago, *Historia de la Expedicion Libertadora del Peru*, (Santiago 1887-8), 2 vols

Chisholm, M, *The Independence of Chile*, (London 1912)

Clissold, S, *Bernardo O'Higgins and the Independence of Chile*, (London, 1968)

Cochrane, Lord, *Narrative of Services in the Liberation of Chile, Peru and Brazil*, (Ridgeway, London 1859), 2 vols

Cochrane, Lord, *Observations on Naval Affairs … including Instances of Injustice experienced by the Author*, (London 1847)

Cubitt, Donald J., *Lord Cochrane and the Chilean Navy, with an Inventory of the Dundonald Papers relating to his Service in Chile*, (University of Edinburgh Ph D Thesis 1974)

Cubitt, Donald J., 'The Manning of the Chilean Navy in the War of Independence 1818–1823', *Mariner's Mirror* (May 1977)

Cunningham, John (Surgeon of HMS *Cambridge*), *Remarks During a Voyage to the Pacific 1823-5*, (unpublished Manuscript), NMM, JOL/21

Bibliography

Deblois, Charles J., *Journal of* ... (US National Archives Microfilm Collection), M 876

De Kay, James T, *Chronicles of the Frigate 'Macedonian'*, (New York 1995)

Delano, Jorge Andres, 'The American Influence in the Independence of Latin America: Captain Paul Delano', *Derroteros de la Mar del Sur*, (Lima 1999)

Dundonald, 11th Earl, *Life of Lord Cochrane*, (London 1869), 2 vols

Duro, Cesáreo Fernández, *La Armada Española desde la union de los reinos de Castilla y Leon*, (Madrid, 1973), 9 vols

Ellis, James H, *Mad Jack Perceval: A Legend of the Old Navy*, (Naval Institute Press Annapolis 2002)

Fodor, Giorgio, 'The Boom that Never Was? Latin American Loans in London 1822-5', Universita'Degli Studi di Trento, 2002

Gazeta Ministerial de Chile, 1819-22, printed in *Archivo de D Bernardo O'Higgins*, vols XII, XIII and XIV, (Santiago, Archivo Nacional, Imprensa Universitaria, 1953)

Gotch, Rosamond B, *Maria, Lady Callcott, the Creator of 'Little Arthur'*, (John Murray, London, 1937)

Gough, Barry M, 'Specie conveyance from the West Coast of Mexico in British warships, 1820-70, *Mariner's Mirror*, (vol. 69, 1983) pp. 419-33

Graham G S and Humphries R A (ed.), *The Navy and South America*, (London and Colchester, Navy Records Society 1962)

Graham, Maria, *Journal of a Residence in Chile during the Year 1822*, London, 1824 (Reprint Praeger, New York 1969)

Grimble, Ian, *The Sea Wolf*, (London 1978)

Hall, Basil, *Extracts from a Journal written on the Coasts of Chile, Peru and Mexico in the Years 1820, 1821 and 1822*, (Edinburgh, 1824), 2 vols

Hedderwick, J B, *The Captain's Clerk – Biography of Thomas Collings, Clerk of the Owen Glendower*, (London 1957)

Harvey, Robert, *Liberators, South America's Savage Wars of Freedom 1810-30*, (London 2000)

Hill, Richard, *The Prizes of War, the Naval Prize System in the Napoleonic Wars 1793-1815* (Sutton 1998)

Hudson, Thomas, *The Life and Times of General William Miller*, Royal Artillery Historical Association, 17 September 2003

Humphries, R A, *Liberation in South America 1806-1827: the Career of JamesParoissien*, (London 1952)

James E, *Life of Commander Henry James RN*, (London 1899)

Lynch, John, *San Martin: Argentine Patriot, American Liberator*, University of London Occasional Papers, No 25

Manning, William (ed.), *Diplomatic Correspondence of the United States concerning the Independence of the Latin American Nations*, (New York 1825), 3 vols

Manrubia, Pilar C. *La Marina de Guerra Española en el Primer Tercio del Siglo XIX*, (Madrid Editoria Naval 1992)

Martel, Alamiro de Avila, *Cochrane y la Independencia del Pacifico*, (Santiago 1976)

Miers, John, *Travels in Chile and La Plata*, (1826), 2 vols

Miller, John (ed.), *Memoirs of General William Miller*, (London 1828), 2 vols

Naval Chronical, vols XXI, XXXIX

O'Byrne, William, *Biographical Dictionary*, (London, John Murray 1848)

Orrego, Luis Uribe, *Nuestra Marina Militar. Sua Organisacion y Campaña durante la Guerra de la Independencia*, (Valparaiso 1910)

San Martin, General José de, *Manifesto de las acusaciones que a nombre del General San Martin hicieron sus Legados ante el Gobierno de Chile contra el Vice Almiral Lord Cochrane y vindicaciones de este dirigido al mismo San Martin*, (Lima 1823)

Stevenson, William Bennet, *Historical and Descriptive Narrative of 20 Years Residence in South America*, (London 1825), 3 vols

Thomas, John, *Historical Sketches of the Chilean Navy*, Archivo Vicuña MacKenna (Archivo Nacional de Chile)

Turrado, G P, *Las Marinhas Realista y Patriota en la Independencia de Chile y Peru*, (Madrid 1996)

Urrutia, Carlos Lopez, 'Lord Cochrane y la Expedicion a Mexico 1822', *Derroteros de la Mar del Sur*, (Lima 1999)

Vale, Brian, *A Frigate of King George 1808–12: Life and Duty on a British Man-of-War 1807–27*, – the story of HMS *Doris*, principally on the South America station – (London 2001)

Vale, Brian, *Independence or Death! British Sailors and Brazilian Independence 1822–25*, (London 1996)

Webster, C K, *Britain and the Independence of Latin America 1812-30* (OUP/British Council 1944), 2 vols

Whitaker, A P, *The United States and the Independence of Latin America 1800–30*, (Baltimore 1941)

Worster, Donald E, *Sea Power and Chilean Independence*, (Gainsville, University of Florida Monographs 1962)

Zenteno, José Ignacio (junior), *Documentos justificativas sobre la expedicion libertadora del Peru: Refutacion de las memorias de Lord Cochrane*, (Santiago 1861)

INDEX

Index

Index

Index